A Short Course in Structured BASIC Programming on IBM Personal Computers

(to accompany Robert H. Blissmer's **Introducing Computers**)

John E. Castek
University of Wisconsin, La Crosse

WILEY

JOHN WILEY & SONS
New York, Chichester, Brisbane, Toronto, Singapore

Castek, John E.

  A short course in structured BASIC programming on
IBM personal computers.

ISBN 0-471-60171-3

Printed in the United States of America

10 9 8 7 6 5 4 3 2 1

Brief Contents

Contents

2: Designing Problem Solutions

3: Introduction to BASIC

Contents

4: Input/Output—Numeric Expressions

5: Selection Statements

6: Repetition Statements

7: Data Types

Preface

This book has a twofold purpose: (1) to present a method of designing solutions to problems that provides a powerful problem-solving tool applicable to any subject field, and (2) to introduce structured BASIC programming.

The design of algorithms using top-down design and stepwise refinement is emphasized throughout the book. This approach to designing solutions to problems seems to make intuitive sense to most students and typically results in solutions that are efficient, correct, and structured. Flowcharts are introduced only as a means of documenting programs and to illustrate basic control structures, not as a tool for design.

The term "structured BASIC" is considered by many experts in computer science to be almost contradictory, as BASIC is a language that does not lend itself well to structured programming. This text illustrates an approach, however, that permits structured BASIC programs to be designed and written. The Microsoft version of BASIC found on the IBM families of microcomputers was selected for use in this text for two reasons: (1) it has become nearly a de facto standard for personal computers since it is furnished with most IBM and IBM-compatible microcomputers, and (2) it has the special features needed to implement a truly structured form of BASIC programming.

Some of the special features of this book, which distinguish it from other BASIC programming texts are:

1. Emphasis on top-down design and stepwise refinement as a problem-solving technique. These techniques are first introduced in Chapter 2 and then used consistently throughout the remainder of the text.
2. The use of pseudolanguage to design structured algorithms.
3. The conversion of these structured pseudolanguage solutions to problems into equivalent structured BASIC language programs on a line-to-line basis.
4. Emphasis is placed on writing "good programs"—programs that are:
   a. Structured
   b. Easy to read, understand, and modify because of:
      1. Use of indentation to show control structure logic
      2. Use of meaningful variable names
      3. Modular programming
      4. Documentation
      5. Severely restricted use of the GO TO statement
   c. Efficient
   d. Correct — the need for testing is emphasized
   e. User-friendly
5. All program examples are written in structured BASIC.

Each chapter begins with a list of objectives for the chapter. The material needed to attain these objectives is presented next, along with appropriate top-down design and program examples. Each chapter concludes with a summary of the major concepts presented, a table listing the BASIC statements introduced, and a selection of exercises and programming problems designed to reinforce the concepts discussed in the chapter.

The first chapter in the book introduces basic concepts of computer hardware and software, as well as providing specific information on using the IBM personal computers.

Chapter 2 is devoted entirely to problem definition and algorithm design. Formal problem definition, top-down design, stepwise refinement, and pseudolanguage are explained and illustrated in this chapter.

Chapters 3 through 6 present the essentials of structured programming in BASIC. The three basic control structures—sequence, selection, and repetition—are discussed, and their implementation in BASIC is demonstrated in numerous program examples.

Chapter 3 describes the general form of all BASIC statements, use of the BASIC editor, and system commands.

Chapter 3 describes the general form of all BASIC statements, use of the BASIC editor, and system commands.

Input/output statements, and the writing and evaluation of numeric expressions, are explained in Chapter 4.

Chapter 5 discusses selection statements (the IF-THEN and the IF-THEN-ELSE) and how their pseudocode form may be converted to BASIC while retaining their structure.

The two forms of the repetition control structure in BASIC the FOR-NEXT and WHILE-WEND statements — are explained in Chapter 6 and illustrated with several example programs.

Data types are discussed in Chapter 7. Character string and numeric data types are explained, and formatted output is illustrated.

The major emphasis of this entire text is on the designing and writing of efficient, structured programs in BASIC. A primary advantage of learning to design and program in the manner taught in this text is that these design and programming techniques may be directly applied when learning to program in languages such as Pascal, Modula-2, dBASE III, and other structured languages. It is much easier to learn correct programming habits initially, rather than to first learn an unstructured form of BASIC and then have to unlearn these bad habits when learning a structured language.

My thanks to those who contributed to making this a better book. The following people read part or all of the manuscript and made valuable comments and suggestions: John W. Davenport, Georgia Southern College; John P. Grillo, Bentley College; David A. Kay, Moorepark College; Rose Laird, Northern Virginia Community College; John Lloyd, St. John Fisher College; and R. Waldo Roth, Taylor University.

John E. Castek

CHAPTER 1

Introduction

When someone uses a computer for the first time, it may seem as though it is a magic box; lights blink, displays appear and disappear on the screen, a printer suddenly begins clattering. This introductory chapter attempts to explain how some of these "magic tricks" occur, and to dispel some of the mystery that often surrounds the operation of these useful machines.

A computer is basically a device that stores and manipulates information. This is true of the multimillion dollar supercomputer as well as the relatively inexpensive personal computer. They all contain the same fundamental parts. Since the user of a personal computer has considerable control over the operation of these individual components, it is important that you as a user have some understanding of what each of these parts is, and how they function together.

A computer's hardware, its mechanical and electronic components, is of little practical use without software, the programs that instruct the hardware to perform a particular task. The different types of software, and what kinds of tasks they perform, are discussed in this chapter. A brief explanation of how programming languages are used to communicate with the computer is provided next. The chapter concludes with a discussion of the operation and use of the IBM family of personal computers.

1.0 OBJECTIVES

After reading this chapter, the student should be able to:

1. Define the terms "computer" and "microcomputer."

2. List and briefly describe each of the major components of a computer system.

3. Explain the function of each of these major hardware components.

4. Differentiate between systems programs and applications programs.

5. List and briefly describe some of the major programming languages.

6. List the steps involved in turning on the computer, loading the operating system, and loading and executing a program.

1.1 WHAT IS A MICROCOMPUTER?

Computers come in all shapes and sizes. They range from a tiny microprocessor embedded in a digital watch to a large supercomputer that fills an entire room. They range in price from a few dollars to several million dollars. Even though computers vary immensely in size and cost, they all basically operate in the same manner. They all perform a particular task or solve a specific problem by unquestioningly following the instructions provided to them by a human operator.

With such a large diversity in size and cost, how is it possible to define the term "computer" in such a way that it applies to all computers? An operational definition might be:

> A computer is an electronic device that manipulates symbols according to a series of instructions, called a program, which are stored in the device itself.

The idea that the program is contained inside the computer is a major concept that is referred to as the "stored program" concept. This is one of the main features that differentiates between a calculator and a computer. For example, if several sets of three numbers are to be added together using a calculator, the user must press the appropriate calculator keys in the correct order each time in order to sum each set of three numbers. If the same task is to be performed with a computer, however, the sequence of steps to be performed, the program, is stored within the computer, and the sets of three numbers will be added together correctly each time the program is executed without the user's needing to instruct the computer as to what to do next.

As was mentioned before, computers vary considerably in size and cost. The largest, most expensive computers are called *supercomputers*. They are used for such tasks as weather forecasting, oil exploration, and weapons research. *Mainframe computers*, which are somewhat smaller and less expensive, perform typical business functions for large companies, such as payroll, inventory control, and other common accounting procedures. They may also be found doing computations involved in scientific and medical research. *Minicomputers* are smaller and less expensive yet, and are typically used to perform many of the same kinds of tasks as mainframe computers, but on a smaller scale. A *microcomputer*, which is lowest on this scale of cost and size, is typically used to perform tasks like computation and office work for a single user, or to direct the control of a complex piece of equipment. Since we will be concerned primarily with microcomputers in this book, we will restrict the rest of our discussion to this type of computer, even though the same concepts apply to all computers.

Even though nearly everyone "knows" what a microcomputer is, it is very difficult to precisely define the term "microcomputer." For example, on the scale discussed above, where do microcomputers end and minicomputers begin? Even computer experts have difficulty defining exactly what a microcomputer is.

There are several ways in which to describe a microcomputer. One way is physical size. The prefix "micro" would seem to indicate that a microcomputer is a small computer, which is certainly correct. However, what is meant by small? In the last ten years, all electronic devices, and in particular computers, have become smaller and smaller. A modern mainframe computer is as small as if not smaller than a minicomputer of ten years ago. It is generally agreed that a microcomputer is normally no larger than a size that can be easily placed on a desktop.

Another way in which to describe a microcomputer is in regard to cost. Microcomputers are generally considered to be relatively inexpensive. They range in price from a few hundred dollars to several thousand dollars. Again, it is difficult to draw the line on price between the most expensive microcomputer and the least expensive minicomputer. There may very well be overlap.

A third way in which a microcomputer might be described is in terms of its internal components. Microcomputers are typically defined to be those computers whose central processing units are contained on a single silicon chip. This characteristic of a microcomputer is becoming less definitive also, however, as many modern minicomputers also use a central processor contained on a single chip.

As you can see, it is very difficult to clearly define exactly what is meant by the term "microcomputer." For our purposes, however, the following definition will suffice:

A microcomputer is a relatively small, inexpensive computer whose central processing unit is contained on a single chip.

Let's examine the components of a microcomputer, or any computer for that matter, in more detail.

1.2 HARDWARE CONCEPTS

The electronic and mechanical components of a computer are referred to as the computer's *hardware*. All digital computers are composed of the following major components:

The *central processing unit*, or *CPU*, is the "brain" of the computer. This device controls the other parts of the computer, and also performs the calculations on and comparisons of data used in solving a particular program. *Main memory* is the part of the computer in which program instructions and data are stored. Some experts consider main memory to be part of the CPU, but we will discuss it as a separate unit.

Peripheral devices are connected to the CPU to perform a variety of functions. A typical computer system usually includes some type of input device to permit the user to enter data and instructions into the computer, and some type of output device to display the output produced by the computer. These input and output devices are examples of peripherals.

The *bus* connects the CPU to main memory and to various peripheral devices. A bus is simply the set of wires over which information travels between the CPU, main memory, and the various peripheral devices connected to the computer.

A diagram of these components may be examined in Figure 1.1. Let's examine each of these major components in more detail.

The CPU

The CPU, or *central processing unit*, consists of two major parts: the *control unit*, which directs the operation of the various hardware components of the computer, and the *arithmetic and logic unit (ALU)*, which performs the arithmetic operations of addition, subtraction, multiplication, and division, and also performs logical comparisons on data such as greater than, less than, and equal to. In today's modern microcomputer, this entire CPU resides on a single silicon chip smaller than the size of your thumbnail.

Figure 1.1 The major hardware components of a computer.

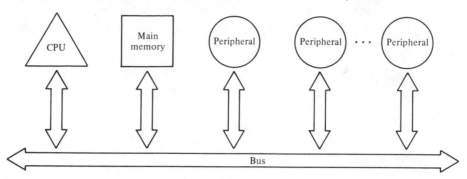

Main Memory

The current program being executed by a microcomputer resides in main memory. This is a temporary storage area in which the instructions that comprise the current program are stored, as well as data arriving from the input device that is needed in the calculations to be performed by the arithmetic and logic unit. Main memory may also be used to temporarily store the results of these calculations until they are sent to the user by the output device.

Main memory can be thought of as an area containing a number of boxes, or storage locations, each of which can contain a single computer instruction, or a single data value. Each location is assigned a unique number, called an *address*, which allows the computer to reference a particular memory location when necessary. A memory address may be thought of as being similar to a street address. It identifies where a particular storage location in memory is to be found, just as a street address identifies where a particular house is to be found on a street.

The number of locations contained in main memory is normally expressed in terms of *bytes*. A *byte* is the amount of memory needed to store a single character, such as a single letter of the alphabet. A term that is often used when describing the size of a computer's main memory is the symbol K. A computer with 16K bytes of main memory means that there are approximately 16,000 addressable memory locations in the computer's main memory. A K of memory is slightly more than 1000 locations—1024 locations, to be exact.

Main memory is composed of silicon chips, the number of which determines the amount of main memory contained in the particular computer being used. Typical microcomputer configurations contain 64K, 256K, or even more, of main memory. The amount of memory a computer contains determines the maximum size of programs that can be executed by it, and also, to some extent, how fast these programs will execute.

As a program is executed, instructions are fetched, one at a time, from main memory and sent to the CPU. The control unit interprets each instruction that has been fetched and directs the appropriate hardware component to perform the operation indicated by the instruction. Modern microcomputers can fetch and execute several hundred thousand instructions per second.

I/O Devices

With the CPU and main memory we have a way in which to perform calculations and to store programs and data, but a way is also needed to enter data and programs into the computer and receive answers from it. I/O (input/output) devices perform these functions. These devices may be in one of several forms.

The most common input device used with a microcomputer is the *keyboard*. It usually contains the normal typewriter keys, as well as certain special keys that allow special commands to be sent to the microcomputer to indicate that certain functions are to be performed. A typical keyboard is shown in Figure 1.2.

Figure 1.2   The IBM-PC and IBM-XT keyboard. (Courtesy of John H. Leisgang.)

Output from the computer may be displayed in one of several ways. Most microcomputer systems use a television type of display screen to communicate with the user. This is referred to as a *CRT* (cathode ray tube), and may display either monochrome or color output.

IBM enhanced color display. (Courtesy of International Business Machines Corporation.)

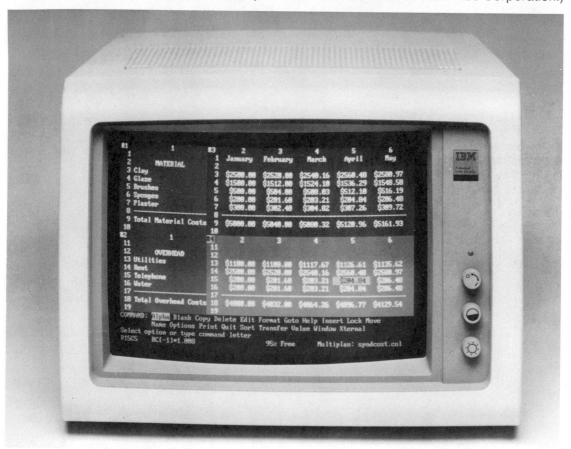

If a more permanent display of output than that obtained from a CRT is desired, various types of *printers* may be interfaced with the computer to provide printed results on paper. Output produced by a printer is referred to as *hardcopy output*, and may be obtained in either black on white or color. A typical microcomputer printer is shown in Figure 1.3.

Figure 1.3 IBM graphics printer. (Courtesy of International Business Machines Corporation.)

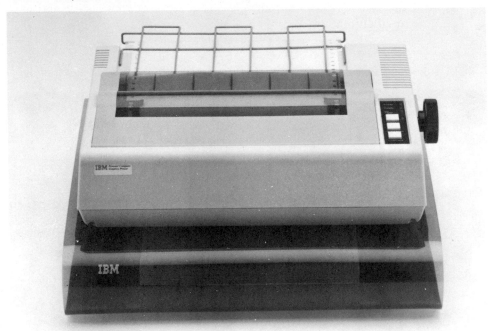

Numerous other types of input/output devices are also used with microcomputers. A joystick, a bar code reader, a mouse, and a graphics tablet are all examples of input devices that may be interfaced with the computer for particular applications. Plotters, speech synthesizers, and computer output microfilm recorders are examples of output devices that may be useful for certain applications.

All these input/output devices are connected to the CPU and main memory by the *bus,* a set of wires over which information may be sent. Transfer of data over the bus is directed by the control unit of the CPU. If we think of the control unit as the brain of the computer, the bus is the network of "nerves" that allows the "brain" to communicate with the different components of the entire computer system.

Secondary Storage

Main memory, as was discussed earlier, is used to store the current program being executed, as well as data received from an input device, or data waiting to be sent to an output device. Information may be transferred in and out of main memory very rapidly, which is of vital importance if the computer is to operate at all efficiently. Main memory is *random-access* storage, which means that instructions or data stored in main memory may be accessed in any order. It is not necessary to first access the item in the first storage location, then the item in the second storage location, etc. Any location in main memory may be accessed just as rapidly as any other location.

There are two major shortcomings of main memory, however. First of all, main memory is *volatile* storage. By this is meant that information stored in main memory is retained only as long as electrical power is maintained to the computer. When the computer is switched off, or if a power failure occurs, all data and programs stored in main memory are lost. Second, main memory is limited as to the amount of storage it contains. If there are a large number of programs or a large amount of data to be stored, main memory may not be large enough to hold all this information. For these reasons, an additional larger storage area that is nonvolatile is needed.

Two major types of auxiliary, or secondary, storage are typically used with microcomputers. These are *magnetic tape* and *magnetic disk.* Programs and data may be recorded on magnetic tape just as are music or television programs. A normal audiocassette tape recorder may be used to store and retrieve information from cassette tape. Magnetic tape was used extensively as a secondary storage medium on early microcomputers since it provides a relatively inexpensive type of storage. The major problem with magnetic tape is that it provides *sequential* storage. If a particular program stored on tape is being sought, all the information on the tape must be searched in a sequential manner until the desired program is found, even if it is known that the program desired is the last one on the tape. This is the principal reason that magnetic-disk storage has become the predominant type of secondary storage used with microcomputers.

Magnetic-disk storage also provides a way of storing large amounts of information. A prime advantage of magnetic disk over magnetic tape is that magnetic disk provides random access to the data stored on the disk. It is not necessary to sequentially search for information stored on a magnetic disk, as is the case with magnetic tape; rather, each item of information stored on a magnetic disk can be accessed directly. This type of storage is typically implemented on microcomputers with a "floppy-diskette" or a "hard-disk" unit.

A *floppy-disk drive* permits information to be both written to and read from a removable floppy disk that has been inserted into the disk drive. The diskette itself is made of a flexible material, hence the name "floppy disk" or "floppy diskette." Information stored on a floppy disk is recorded on a series of concentric circles of magnetic material. Each of these circular paths is referred to as a *track.* Information may be read from any track on the disk by a *read-write head* that moves across the diskette surface as the diskette is rotated at a rapid rate of speed. This allows information to be retrieved from diskette storage much more rapidly than it can be from magnetic tape. A floppy disk will typically store anywhere from 300,000 to over a million characters of information.

The floppy diskette drive in the IBM personal computer is seen in this illustration. The diskette is inserted in the slot shown and the drive door closed to engage the diskette in the drive. (Courtesy of John H. Leisgang.)

Hard-disk units use a disk constructed from a rigid storage medium rather than the flexible material used for floppy disks, hence the name hard disk. Hard disks are normally not removable, and therefore the hard-disk drives may be manufactured with much closer tolerances than are possible with the floppy-disk units. This permits the tracks on a hard disk to be placed much closer together, and therefore much more information can be stored on a hard disk than can be stored on a floppy. Hard disks typically store 10, 20, 40, or even 80 million characters of information, depending upon the size of the unit. Since the hard disk is built as a sealed unit with much closer tolerances than a floppy-disk unit, the disk in a hard-disk storage unit may be rotated much more rapidly than a floppy disk can be. This permits much more rapid access of information stored on a hard disk.

The hard-disk unit in the IBM personal computer XT is the dark unit on the right side of the systems unit in the illustration. A floppy-diskette drive is the left half of the dark area. (Courtesy of International Business Machines Corporation.)

Regardless of the type of secondary storage used by a particular computer system, the purpose of this secondary storage is the same: to provide a large amount of nonvolatile, relatively long term storage for data and programs.

The hardware of a computer system is useless, however, without the programs to make it operate and perform useful tasks. Let's examine next what types of programs are necessary in order for the computer to be a useful problem-solving tool.

1.3 SOFTWARE

When most people think of a computer, they think of the CRT display, the keyboard, and the printer. It is the *software* (or programs) of the computer, however, that brings the hardware to life. Without the software, a microcomputer is little more than an expensive paperweight.

During the early years of computing, the majority of research in computer science dealt with designing faster, more powerful, and more reliable hardware. The continually decreasing cost and increasing computing power of computer hardware is evidence that this research has been most productive. For example, it has been said that if automotive technology had progressed at the same rate as the advances made in computer technology, a new Rolls Royce today would cost about $4.95.

Unfortunately, even as rapid advances have been made in computer hardware, parallel advances in the design of computer software have not occurred. More than half of the total cost of a typical computing system today is software costs. This situation can be graphically represented as shown in Figure 1.4. As software costs have become a larger and larger portion of the total cost of a system, more research interest has begun to be placed on software. Only in the last decade have there been major advances in software design. The goal of producing efficient, reliable programs at a reasonable cost, however, has still not been fully realized. Much more work remains to be done.

Programming Languages

Programming languages allow computer instructions to be written in a language mutually understandable to both people and computers. Many different programming languages have been developed, each with its own unique vocabulary, grammar, and uses. Even though several hundred programming languages are in common use today, they may all be classified as one of three types: a machine language, an assembly language, or a high-level language.

Machine language is the lowest, most elementary level of programming language, and was the first type of programming language to be developed. In machine language programming, program instructions are written in the internal binary code of the computer. Each model of computer has its own unique set of

Figure 1.4   Total cost of a computer system.

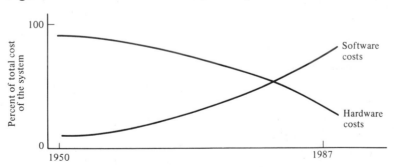

machine language instructions. Machine language programming is slow, tedious, and error-prone.

Assembly languages were the next level of languages developed. Assembly languages use alphabetic codes called *mnemonics* to represent the operations to be performed rather than the pure binary codes used in machine languages. Assembly language programming is still somewhat cryptic from the beginning programmer's point of view, but it is a big improvement over machine language programming. Programs written in assembly language require the use of language translator programs called *assemblers* to translate the assembly language instructions into machine language instructions directly understandable by the computer.

High-level languages were developed to make the programmer's job easier yet. Programs written using a high-level language consist of instructions called statements that resemble human language or standard mathematical expressions. When a high-level language statement is translated into machine language, it usually results in several machine language statements. This translation process is performed by a high-level language translator program called a *compiler* or an *interpreter*.

High-level languages are relatively *machine-independent*. This means that a program written in a high-level language will execute correctly with only minor changes, if any, on computers built by different manufacturers. Some of the more popular high-level languages are:

BASIC: <u>B</u>eginners <u>A</u>ll-purpose <u>S</u>ymbolic <u>I</u>nstruction <u>C</u>ode. This language was developed at Dartmouth College as a simple user-oriented language for interactive time-sharing computer systems. It has become a popular language on microcomputers, and is used for general problem solving and other personal computing tasks.

COBAL: <u>CO</u>mmon <u>B</u>usiness <u>O</u>riented <u>L</u>anguage. COBOL is widely used for business data-processing tasks, that is, accounts receivable, inventory control, payroll, etc. COBOL is typically used when large amounts of data need to be processed and only simple arithmetic calculations need to be performed.

FORTRAN: <u>FOR</u>mula <u>TRAN</u>slation. This was the first high-level language developed, and is typically used to solve mathematical and scientific problems that involve complicated mathematical calculations.

LOGO: This is an interactive graphics language that is designed to be used to teach children the concepts of geometry as well as how to operate and program a computer.

PASCAL: Pascal is a general-purpose language named for the famous French mathematician, Blaise Pascal. Developed by Niklaus Wirth, Pascal is a modern structured language used extensively in computer science education to teach programming concepts.

These are but a few of the high-level languages available. New languages are continually being invented. By the time you read the descriptions of the languages listed above, there may very well be several new languages that have replaced one or more of the above languages in general use.

Applications Programs

Computer programs are classified as one of two general types—applications programs and systems programs. Applications programs are programs written to solve a specific problem for a user. Examples of applications programs would be a program to compute a company's payroll, a program to solve a mathematics problem, or a program to record student grades.

Applications programs are typically written in a high-level language such as one of the languages described above. These are the type of programs we will be learning to design and write in the succeeding chapters in this book.

Systems Programs

Systems programs are the programs that direct the operation of a computer's hardware. When you press the key on the keyboard that has the letter A on it, a systems program is what causes the same letter A to appear on the CRT screen. When you request that a file of information or a program be retrieved from a floppy disk, it is a systems program that causes the disk drive to begin rotating the disk, and the desired information or program to be read from the disk.

Systems programs also manage the resources of the computer. They determine where in main memory program instructions and data are to be stored, as well as where information is to be stored in secondary storage. Systems programs are designed to operate the computer efficiently, with as little need for human intervention as possible.

Another type of systems programs is the compiler and interpreter programs that perform the translation of high-level language statements into machine language instructions. Other systems programs perform such tasks for the user as sorting data into order and permitting the easy updating of information contained in files.

The collection of all the systems programs used with a particular computer system is referred to as the *operating system* for that computer. Some of the more popular operating systems for microcomputers are PC-DOS, MS-DOS, CP/M, and UNIX-like operating systems such as XENIX.

Most systems programs in the past were written in assembly language. More recently, however, special high-level languages such as C have been developed for the specific purpose of writing systems programs.

1.4 USING THE IBM-PC AND IBM PS/2 MICROCOMPUTERS

There are two major families of IBM microcomputers: the original IBM-PC family, which consists of the IBM-PC, the IBM-XT, the IBM-AT, and the IBM-PC Jr; and the IBM Personal System 2 (PS/2) family, introduced in the spring of 1987, which consists of the Models 30, 50, 60 and 80. Models 30 and 50 are similar to the original PC family in that they are desktop units (see Figure 1.5). With models 60

Figure 1.5   The IBM-PS/2 Model 30 computer system. (Courtesy of John H. Leisgang.)

Figure 1.6   The IBM-PS/2 Model 60 computer system. (Courtesy of John H. Leisgang.)

and 80, however, the system unit sits in a vertical position on the floor under a desk as shown in Figure 1.6 and only the keyboard and display monitor are on the desktop.

There are obviously many differences between the new PS/2 family and the original PC family other than appearance. The new units are faster, typically contain more main memory, and all use a three and one-half inch diskette for auxilliary storage rather than the five and a quarter inch diskette used with the original PC's. Figure 1.7 shows the diskettes used with the two different systems. An optional five and a quarter inch external diskette drive is available for the PS/2 machines which allows them to utilize programs and data stored on the older type of diskette.

The operating system most commonly used on both the IBM-PC and IBM PS/2 families of microcomputers is PC-DOS, which is a version of the MS-DOS operating system developed by Microsoft Corporation and licensed by IBM Corporation for use on their personal computer systems. This operating system is referred to interchangeably as either DOS or PC-DOS. A number of revisions and improvements have been made to this operating system since it was first released by IBM in 1981. As each new revision was released, it was assigned a version number. The versions are upward-compatible, which means that programs written under control of an earlier version will execute under a later version. The version of the DOS operating system you are using will be found on the DOS diskette label, and also on the Disk Operating System manual furnished with your machine. The

Figure 1.7 Floppy diskettes. *Left*: 5¼ inch diskette used on IBM-PC systems. *Right*: 3½ inch diskette used on IBM-PS/2 systems. (Courtesy of John H. Leisgang.)

program examples in this book have all been prepared using version 2.1 of PC-DOS.

Operation of the IBM-PC and IBM-PS/2 is similar, but there are enough differences that they will be discussed separately in the sections that follow. Carefully read the discussion that applies to the particular model of computer you are using.

Using the IBM-PC Keyboard

The IBM-PC uses a keyboard similar to a typewriter keyboard, although there are some special keys not found on a typical typewriter keyboard. In order to communicate effectively with the computer, it is necessary to become familiar with the keyboard, since it is usually the principal device used to enter instructions and data into the computer. A diagram of the keyboard used with the IBM-PC and IBM-XT models is shown in Figure 1.8. The IBM-AT has a similar keyboard, with only a few of the keys shown above relocated. The IBM-PC Jr keyboard is also somewhat different from the keyboard shown above, but all the functions that may be performed with the larger keyboards may also be accomplished with the Jr's keyboard.

The keys on all these keyboards are *typematic*. This means that if a key is held down, the key will repeat. If you want the code represented by the key sent to the computer only once, press the key quickly and release it immediately.

The keys on the keyboard are grouped into three major sections: the function keys, the typewriter keys, and the numeric keypad. Let's first look at the 10 keys on the left side of the keyboard, the Function keys. This section of the keyboard is shown in Figure 1.9. Many of the programs that are designed to run on the IBM personal computers make use of these function keys to indicate a particular operation is to be performed by the program when one of these keys is pressed. For

Figure 1.8 Diagram of the IBM-PC keyboard. (Courtesy of International Business Machines Corporation.)

Figure 1.9 Function keys on the IBM-PC keyboard. (Courtesy of John H. Leisgang.)

example, many programs use function key 1 (F1) for a 'Help' key. When this key is pressed, information about the particular operation the user is performing is displayed on the screen. Whenever you see the notation of a capital letter F followed by a number from 1 to 10 in this book (i.e., F4), or in the IBM manuals furnished with your computer, reference is being made to one of the function keys.

The middle portion of the keyboard is similar to a typewriter keyboard. The letters of the alphabet are found on these keys, along with several special symbols. Notice that the numbers from 1 through 0 are on the top row of keys of this section of the keyboard. Be sure to use the zero key (0) on the top row of keys for typing a number, and not the 'Oh' key (O), which is on the row of keys below. Likewise, use the one key (1) for the number one, and not the lowercase L key. Even though these keys produce similar symbols on the screen, they send different codes to the computer.

When keys contain two symbols on them, such as the symbols ';' and ':', the upper symbol is obtained by holding down the *Shift key* while the key with the desired symbol is pressed. Capital letters also are obtained by using the Shift keys, which are the two keys located one row above and to either side of the space bar and are imprinted with the large upper arrows (⇧).

When you type a letter or a digit on the keyboard, the letter or digit appears on the screen immediately after you press the key. The position on the screen where the letter or digit will appear is indicated by the *cursor,* which is a blinking underline or small rectangle on the screen. Normally the cursor will appear as an underline character. When you are in insert mode, however, the cursor becomes a blinking rectangle. As you type characters, the cursor continues to move across the screen, always indicating where the next character typed will appear.

The *Caps Lock key,* located immediately below the right shift key, is used to lock the keyboard into uppercase. It functions somewhat differently than the Caps Lock key on a standard typewriter in that it affects only the letter keys on the keyboard. The upper symbols on keys that contain two symbols must still be accessed by holding down one of the Shift keys while the key is pressed. If a letter key is pressed while Caps Lock is on and a Shift key is being held down, a lowercase letter is obtained. Caps Lock is disabled by pressing the Caps Lock key again. The AT keyboard has a light that indicates when Caps Lock is on. With the other PC keyboards, the only way to determine if Caps Lock is on is to press a letter key and observe what is displayed on the screen.

The *Backspace key* is located on the top row of keys on the extreme right of the typewriter portion of the keyboard. It is an arrow pointing to the left ($\leftarrow$), and operates in a manner similar to the backspace key on a typewriter—every time it is pressed, the symbol to the immediate left of the cursor is erased. Remember, this key is typematic, so don't hold it down unless you wish to erase several characters.

The *Enter,* or *Return, key* is located immediately below the Backspace key, and has a bent arrow symbol on it ($\hookleftarrow$). This key is used to send a command or instruction to the CPU to be executed. Once an instruction has been typed on the keyboard, pressing the Enter key indicates the end of the instruction. The cursor also automatically returns to the left side of the screen and moves down one line when this key is pressed.

The *Ctrl* and *Alt keys* are located on the left side of the typewriter portion of the keyboard, above and below the left Shift key, respectively. These keys are used in conjunction with other keys on the keyboard to send special commands to the computer. The *Esc key,* located in the upper left corner of the typewriter portion of the keyboard, is also used in this fashion. The use of these keys will be described in more detail later.

The *Tab key* is located just above the Ctrl key, and may be used to move the cursor to preset horizontal positions on the screen. Notice that the symbol on this key is two arrows, the lower one pointing to the right and the upper one to the left. When this key is pressed, the cursor will move to the first tab setting to the right of its present position. If the Shift key is held down while the Tab key is pressed, the cursor will move over one tab setting to the left.

If the computer you are using has a printer attached, a copy of all the information currently on the screen may be sent to the printer by holding down the

Shift key and pressing the key directly below the Enter key, the *PrtSc* (Print-Screen) *key*. This operation may be thought of as being similar to taking a snapshot of the screen with a camera.

A running copy of the information appearing on the screen may be sent to the printer by holding down the Ctrl (Control) key and pressing the PrtSc key. Pressing Ctrl—PrtSc again will disable this feature.

The third portion of the keyboard is the numeric keypad. It is illustrated in Figure 1.10. This rightmost section of the keyboard consists of keys that contain the digits 0 through 9, as well as several special keys. Notice that all the numeric keys other than the 5 key also contain other symbols on them. If it is desired to use the number keys on this section of the keyboard to enter numbers, the *Num Lock key*, located above the numeric keys, must be pressed once. This enables the numeric values on the keys.

Normal mode of operation for the numeric keypad is not numeric entry. When the keypad is not locked in numeric mode, the *arrows* located on the 2, 4, 6, and 8 keys are used to move the cursor about the screen. The *Ins key* (the numeric key 0) is used to insert characters within a string of characters on the screen. The *Del key* located next to this key may be used to delete characters from a string of characters on the screen. *PgUp* (page up), *PgDn* (page down), *Home,* and *End* are used in several applications programs to change the material displayed on the screen.

The *Scroll Lock (Break) key,* located in the upper right corner of the keypad, is used in conjunction with other keys. If the Ctrl key is held down when this key is

Figure 1.10 Numeric keypad on the IBM-PC keyboard. (Courtesy of John H. Leisgang.)

pressed, current operations on the computer are halted; that is, listing or executing a program will be terminated. *Ctrl—Num Lock* will also suspend operations, but when these two keys are pressed, pressing any other key will cause operations to resume at the point at which they were suspended.

Using the IBM-PS/2 Keyboard

All models in the PS/2 family of IBM microcomputers use the keyboard shown in Figure 1.11. The very top row of keys contains the *Function keys,* as well as some special purpose keys. Below this row, on the left side of the keyboard, are a large group of keys similar to a *typewriter keyboard.* To the immediate right of the typewriter portion of the keyboard are two groups of keys, one above the other. The upper group of six keys are special purpose keys often used in various applications programs. Below this group of keys is a set of four *cursor control keys,* used to position the cursor on the screen. On the far right side of the keyboard is a *numeric keypad.* Let's examine each group of keys in more detail.

As illustrated in Figure 1.12, the leftmost key in the top row of keys is the *Esc* (Escape) *key.* This key is used in conjunction with other keys on the keyboard to send special commands to the computer. Immediately to the right of the Esc key are the *Function keys,* numbered F1 through F12. Many applications programs designed to run on IBM personal computers use these function keys to indicate that a particular operation is to be performed by the program when one of these keys is pressed. For example, Function key 1 (F1) is used in many programs as a 'Help' key.

Figure 1.11   The IBM-PS/2 keyboard. (Courtesy of John H. Leisgang.)

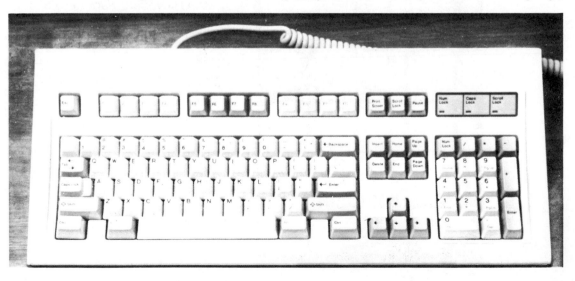

Figure 1.12 The top row of keys. (Courtesy of John H. Leisgang.)

When this key is pressed, information concerning the particular operation the user is performing is displayed on the screen.

To the right of the 12 function keys is the *Print Screen key*. If the computer you are using has a printer attached, a copy of all the information currently on the screen may be sent to the printer by pressing this key. This operation may be thought of as being similar to taking a snapshot of the screen with a camera.

The *Scroll Lock key* is the next key in the top row of keys. Pressing this key during program execution stops information from scrolling off the screen. This key "freezes" the screen and permits the cursor control keys to be used to view information before or after the information currently displayed on the screen. An indicator light at the far right of the top row of keys indicates when the Scroll Lock key has been pressed. When lit, scroll lock is enabled and no scrolling occurs; pressing any other key on the keyboard causes the indicator light to go off and screen scrolling resumes.

The last key in the top row of keys is the *Pause/Break key*. Pressing this key causes current operations on the computer to be suspended—pressing any other key will cause operations to resume at the point at which they were suspended. If the Control key is held down when this key is pressed, program execution is terminated, not suspended.

The second major grouping of keys on the PS/2 keyboard is the *typewriter portion* of the keyboard, shown in Figure 1.13. The letters of the alphabet, the numbers from 1 through 0, and numerous special symbols, are located on these keys. When typing the number 0, be sure to use the zero key (0) on the top row of keys, and not the "Oh" key (O), which is on the row of keys below the number keys.

Figure 1.13 The typewriter keys. (Courtesy of John H. Leisgang.)

Likewise, use the one key (1) for the number one, and not the lowercase L key. Even though these keys produce similar symbols on the screen, they send very different codes to the computer when they are pressed.

When you press a letter or digit key on the keyboard, the letter or digit appears on the screen immediately after you press the key. The position on the screen where this symbol will appear is indicated by the *cursor*—a blinking underline or small rectangle on the screen. Normally the cursor appears as an underline character, but when the computer is placed in insert mode the cursor takes the form of a blinking rectangle. In either form, however, the cursor moves across the screen as you type characters, always indicating where the next character typed will appear.

When keys contain two symbols on them, such as the symbols "?" and "/", the upper symbol is obtained by holding down the *Shift key* while the key containing the desired symbol is pressed. Capital letters are also obtained by using the Shift keys, which are the two keys located one row above and to either side of the space bar. The Shift keys have both the word "Shift" on them and a large upper arrow (⇧) symbol.

The *Caps Lock key*, located immediately above the left shift key, is used to lock the keyboard into uppercase mode. It functions somewhat differently than the Caps Lock on a standard typewriter in that it affects only the letter keys on the keyboard. The upper symbols on keys containing two symbols must still be accessed by holding down one of the Shift keys while the key is pressed. If a letter key is pressed, while Caps Lock is on and a Shift key is being held down, a lowercase letter is obtained. Caps Lock is removed by pressing the Caps Lock key again. A signal light located above the numeric keypad indicates when Caps Lock is on. When the light is on, Caps Lock is on; when the light is off, Caps Lock is off.

The *Tab key* is located just above the Caps Lock key and may be used to rapidly move the cursor to preset horizontal positions on the screen. Notice that along with the word Tab on this key are two arrows, the lower one pointing to the right and the upper one to the left. When this key is pressed, the cursor will move to the first tab setting to the right of its present position. If the Shift key is held down when the Tab key is pressed, the cursor will move one tab setting to the left.

At the extreme right of the top row of keys on the typewriter portion of the keyboard is the *Backspace key*. Both the word Backspace and an arrow pointing to the left (←) are on this key. The Backspace key operates in the same manner as the backspace key on a typewriter; every time it is pressed, the symbol to the immediate left of the cursor is erased. Be careful not to hold down this key since it is typematic, like most keys on the keyboard, and several characters may be erased before you release the key.

The *Enter key* is located immediately above the right Shift key. This key, with both the word Enter and a bent arrow symbol (↵) on it, performs a function similar to the Return key on a typewriter; it returns the cursor to the left side of the screen and moves it down one line. The Enter key performs an additional function,

Figure 1.14 Special and cursor control keys. (Courtesy of John H. Leisgang.)

however. When a command or instruction is typed on the keyboard, pressing the Enter key indicates the end of the instruction and sends the command to the CPU to be executed.

A pair of *Ctrl* and *Alt keys* are located on both the left and right side of the space bar. These keys are used in conjunction with other keys on the keyboard to send special commands to the computer. For example, pressing the Print Screen key while holding down the Ctrl key turns on "screen echoing". Once these keys have been pressed, whatever appears on the screen is also displayed on the printer. This feature may be turned off by pressing Ctrl - Print Screen again.

Two groupings of keys, illustrated in Figure 1.14, are located to the right of the typewriter portion of the keyboard. The top group of six keys contains special keys that are used in many applications programs. Some programs, for example, use the *Home key* to move the cursor to the upper left corner of the screen. The *Insert key* is frequently used to place the computer in insert mode. In this mode, corrections may be inserted into information already appearing on the screen.

The bottom four keys on this portion of the keyboard, the *cursor control keys,* are used to move the cursor about the screen. The cursor is moved in the direction indicated by the arrows on these keys.

The rightmost portion of the keyboard, the *numeric keypad,* is illustrated in Figure 1.15. This section of the keyboard consists of keys that contain the digits 0

Figure 1.15 The numeric keypad. (Courtesy of John H. Leisgang.)

through 9, as well as several special keys. Notice that all the numeric keys other than the 5 key also contain other symbols on them. If the number keys on this section of the keyboard are to be used to enter numbers, the *Num Lock key*, located in the upper left corner of the numeric keypad, must be pressed once. This enables the numeric values on the keys, as is indicated by the signal light to the right of the top-most row of keys. Pressing Num Lock again will extinguish the Num Lock indicator light, and place the keypad in nonnumeric mode.

When the numeric keypad is in nonnumeric mode, as indicated by the Num Lock signal light being off, the special symbols on the numeric keys are enabled. This means, for example, that the 2, 4, 6, and 8 keys may be used for cursor control, the *Ins* (Insert) *key* may be used to change to insert mode, etc.

Loading the Operating System

In order for the computer to make use of the operating system programs, they must be loaded into main memory. This is accomplished by inserting the DOS diskette into diskette drive A: (the left drive if your machine has more than one drive, or the upper drive if your computer uses half-height drives), and then turning on the power to the machine. If the computer you are using has a hard-disk drive, DOS is normally loaded from the hard disk. To load DOS from the hard disk, make sure that floppy disks are not in any of the floppy disk drives and then turn on the power switch. DOS will then be loaded from the hard disk. Once the computer has completed a self-diagnostic check of its electronic components, the operating system is read into main memory from the DOS diskette or the hard disk.

If your computer has already been turned on, the operating system may be loaded by inserting the DOS diskette into drive A:, holding down the keys on the left side of the typewriter portion of the keyboard marked 'Ctrl' and 'Alt', and then pressing the 'Del' key, which is below the numeric keypad on the bottom right of the keyboard. Release all three keys, and DOS will be read into main memory from the diskette in drive A:. Again, if your computer contains a hard-disk drive, make sure that none of the floppy disk drives contain diskettes before pressing the Ctrl, Alt, and Del keys.

Once DOS is loaded, you will be requested to enter today's date in the form of mm-dd-yy (two digits for the month, dash, followed by two digits for the day, dash, two digits for the year). The current time will be requested next, which is to be entered in the form of HH:MM:SS (hours, colon, minutes, colon, seconds). The value for hours is to be between 0 and 23, with morning hours entered as usual, and hours in the p.m. increased by 12 (3 p.m. would be entered as 15). If you do not wish to enter the date and time, either or both of these prompts may be responded to by simply pressing the Enter key. In this case, the date will be left at the default value of 01-01-80 and the time at 00:00:00.

The next display on the screen will be the DOS prompt, A>. This prompt indicates two things: (1) DOS is awaiting a command, and (2) the default diskette drive is drive A:. The default drive being A: means that if you issue a command without specifying which diskette drive is to be accessed, drive A: will be chosen. If you have loaded DOS from the hard disk, the DOS prompt will be C>, which means that the default drive is C:. DOS commands are entered by typing in the command and then pressing the Enter key.

A table listing some of the more frequently used DOS commands follows:

DOS Commands

Command	Function
CHKDSK	CHKDSK examines the specified diskette's files and directory to ensure that they match. It also gives you a status report on the diskette and main memory.
COMP	This command compares the contents of two files and indicates their differences, if any.
COPY	COPY copies one or more files specified to the same or another diskette.
DATE	Permits entry of a date into the computer.
DIR	Displays a list of the names of all the files contained on the specified drive.
DISKCOMP	DISKCOMP compares two diskettes and determines whether or not their contents match.
DISKCOPY	Copies the entire contents of one diskette to another.
ERASE	Remove(s) the file(s) specified from the diskette.
FORMAT	Prepares a new diskette for use on the system.
MODE	Permits changing the amount of information displayed on the screen or printer. It also permits the screen display to be shifted to the right, if necessary.
RENAME	Allows the name of a file stored on a diskette to be changed.
SYS	Transfers a copy of DOS to a diskette.
TIME	Permits the computer's internal clock to be set to a time entered.
TYPE	Displays the contents of a file on the screen.

The Disk Operating System manual provides further details regarding these commands, as well as the remaining DOS commands.

Executing Programs

Some programs can be executed directly from DOS. Programs having the filename extension EXE or COM may be executed by simply typing the name of the program in response to the DOS prompt, A>, or C>, and pressing the Enter key. A *filename extension* is the set of three characters following a period in a filename, and indicates the type of file. Normally filenames with extensions of COM or EXE specify files that contain machine language programs. As you may recall from an earlier discussion, machine language programs may be executed directly by the computer without the need for interpreters or compilers to translate them into machine language.

1.5 SUMMARY

This chapter has provided a brief overview of several major concepts important in understanding computers. The wide range in size and cost of computers was briefly discussed, and a working definition of the term "microcomputer" was given.

Computer hardware is the electronic and mechanical components of a computer system. All digital computers are composed of a central processor, main memory, a bus, and numerous peripheral devices. The central processing unit (CPU) is the "brain" of the computer which controls all the other components. Main memory stores current program instructions and data needed in the solution of a problem. Peripheral devices allow instructions and data to be entered into the computer and output to be obtained from it. The bus is a set of wires that connects the various components together and allows information to be sent from one component to another.

Additional storage for programs and data aside from the storage available in main memory is provided by several types of secondary storage devices. Magnetic tape provides inexpensive storage, but it is somewhat cumbersome to use. Magnetic disk storage is becoming more and more popular because of its random-access capability. Both floppy-diskette and hard-disk storage devices are discussed.

To communicate with a computer, instructions to the computer must be written in a particular language that is understandable to both the computer and the human user, a programming language. Programming languages can be classified as being of one of three types: a machine language, an assembly language, or a high-level language. Many different programming languages are in common use today, and new languages are being developed continually.

Software, the programs that direct the hardware components, is of two major types, applications programs and systems programs. Applications programs are programs written to solve user-specific problems. Systems programs are the programs that direct the operation of the computer's hardware. The collection of systems programs furnished to operate a particular computer is referred to as an operating system.

Since most data and instructions are entered into a microcomputer from a keyboard, the keyboards of both the IBM-PC and the IBM-PS/2 families of microcomputers are discussed in some detail. The purpose of those keys which are not typically found on typewriter keyboards is explained.

PC-DOS, the operating system most frequently used on IBM microcomputers, is briefly introduced in this chapter. How to load it into main memory, and some of the more important DOS commands are explained.

The chapter concludes with a short explanation of how programs may be executed from DOS, and how such programs may be identified.

EXERCISES

1. The major feature that differentiates between a calculator and a computer is:
   a. The relative sizes.
   b. The relative costs.
   c. The stored program concept.
   d. A computer has a printer.
   e. A computer uses floppy diskettes.

2. Which of the following lists is arranged in the correct order as to size from largest to smallest?
   a. Mainframe, supercomputer, minicomputer, microcomputer.
   b. Supercomputer, minicomputer, mainframe, microcomputer.
   c. Minicomputer, supercomputer, mainframe, microcomputer.
   d. Supercomputer, mainframe, minicomputer, microcomputer.
   e. Supercomputer, mainframe, microcomputer, minicomputer.

3. The major *hardware* components that all digital computers contain are the:
   a. CPU, main memory, operating system, and the bus.
   b. Main memory, peripheral devices, the bus, and the CPU.
   c. CPU, peripheral devices, operating system, and main memory.
   d. Operating system, floppy-diskette drive, keyboard, and CRT.
   e. Control unit, ALU, CPU, and main memory.

4. The central processing unit (CPU) contains two main parts, the:
   a. Control unit and the arithmetic and logic unit (ALU).
   b. Bus and main memory.
   c. Control unit and main memory.
   d. Operating system and main memory.
   e. Arithmetic and logic unit (ALU) and main memory.

5. One K of main memory consists of approximately ____ addressable storage locations.
   a. 10.
   b. 100.
   c. 1000.
   d. 10,000.
   e. 1 million.

6. Which of the following is a shortcoming of main memory?
   a. Main memory is volatile storage.
   b. Main memory is a random-access type of storage.
   c. Transfer of information in and out of main memory is very fast.
   d. Each storage location in main memory is directly addressable.
   e. Both data and instructions may be stored in main memory.

7. Which of the following is a sequential type of secondary storage medium?

  a. Floppy diskette.
  b. Hard disk.
  c. Magnetic tape.
  d. Main memory.
  e. CRT.

8. Which of the following is *not* an I/O device?

  a. CRT.
  b. Keyboard.
  c. Printer.
  d. Joystick.
  e. Bus.

9. Computer software refers to:

  a. Programs.
  b. Magnetic tape.
  c. Floppy diskettes.
  d. Data.
  e. Storage locations.

10. Which of the following statements regarding computer hardware and software is *true*?

  a. Hardware is becoming more expensive while software is becoming less expensive.
  b. Hardware is becoming less expensive while software is becoming more expensive.
  c. Both hardware and software are becoming more expensive.
  d. Hardware costs are the major portion of the cost of a computer system; software is a relatively small part of the cost.
  e. None of the above are true.

11. In which of the following programming languages are instructions written in the internal binary code of the machine?

  a. Assembly language.
  b. BASIC.
  c. FORTRAN.
  d. Pascal.
  e. Machine language.

12. Which of the following is *not* a high-level programming language?

  a. Pascal.
  b. Assembly language.
  c. COBOL.
  d. BASIC.
  e. LOGO.

13. Which of the following programming languages is most widely used for business data processing?

  a. BASIC.
  b. COBOL.

    c. FORTRAN.

    d. LOGO.

    e. Machine language.

14. Computer programs are classified as being one of two different types. These two types are:

    a. Systems programs and machine language programs.

    b. Assembly language programs and applications programs.

    c. Assembly language programs and high-level programs.

    d. Systems programs and applications programs.

    e. Machine language programs and high-level programs.

15. An operating system is:

    a. The collection of applications programs needed in a particular business.

    b. The collection of systems programs used on a particular computer.

    c. The hardware components needed for a complete, usable computer system.

    d. Both the hardware and software needed to comprise a complete, usable system.

    e. Another name for the control unit of the CPU that directs the operation of all hardware components.

16. Which two keys on the IBM-PC keyboard may be used to erase incorrect characters from the screen?

    a. The Ins key and the Backspace key.

    b. The Esc key and the Break key.

    c. The Backspace key and the Esc key.

    d. The Backspace key and the Del key.

    e. The Backspace key and the Erase key.

17. The Caps Lock key affects:

    a. All the keys on the typewriter portion of the keyboard.

    b. Only the letter keys on the keyboard.

    c. Both the letter and number keys on the typewriter portion of the keyboard.

    d. The letter and number keys on the typewriter portion of the keyboard, as well as the number keys on the keypad portion of the keyboard.

    e. Only the function keys.

18. PC-DOS may be loaded into the computer by:

    a. Inserting the DOS diskette into drive A: and turning on the power to the computer.

    b. Inserting the DOS diskette into drive A: and typing the command, "PC-DOS."

    c. Inserting the DOS diskette into drive A: while the power is on, and pressing the Ctrl, Alt, and Del keys simultaneously.

    d. Inserting the DOS diskette into drive A: and typing the command, "LOAD DOS."

    e. Two of the above will work.

19. Which of the following is *not* one of the DOS commands listed in the chapter?

    a. COPY.

    b. LOAD.

    c. DIR.

    d. FORMAT.

    e. TYPE.

20. Programs that can be executed directly from DOS normally have the filename extension of either:

    a. RUN or EXE.

    b. BAS or EXE.

    c. COM or RUN.

    d. COM or RUN.

    e. EXE or COM.

CHAPTER 2

Designing Problem Solutions

One of the most difficult tasks for the beginning programmer is trying to decide how to begin when attempting to write a problem solution. This chapter deals with design—how and where to start, how to proceed, and how to know when you are done.

Techniques for writing "good programs"—programs that are easy to read, understand, and modify—are explained and illustrated. The control structures of structured programming are used to develop problem solutions by applying the methods of top-down design and stepwise refinement.

2.0 OBJECTIVES

Upon completion of this chapter, you should be able to:

1. State the rationale for first designing a solution to a problem rather than immediately beginning to write code.
2. List and briefly describe the parts of a formal problem definition.

3. Write a formal problem definition from a general problem description.

4. List the three basic control structures needed for problem solution.

5. List the pseudocode statements needed to develop pseudocode solutions to problems.

6. Perform a complete top-down design of a problem given a general problem description.

2.1 THE IMPORTANCE OF DESIGN

When a problem is to be solved or a task carried out, several approaches might be taken to solve the problem or proceed with the task. One method is to begin immediately with the first idea thought of and begin carrying out the task without thinking it all the way through first. A major problem with this approach, however, is that many times it soon becomes evident that this first idea is not going to work, and it will be necessary to start all over again. This trial-and-error approach to problem solving is not a very efficient way to try to solve a problem or perform a task, particularly if it results in the waste of materials or time.

Another approach is to first design a complete, carefully thought out plan before beginning work. A carpenter building a house works from a set of blueprints—a detailed description in graphic form of how the finished house is to look. This results in a structure that makes efficient use of materials and eliminates waste of building materials and the carpenter's time. It is unlikely that carpenters would find many people willing to employ them if they simply started out sawing boards and nailing them together without first having a detailed plan of how the finished building is to appear and how it is to be constructed. The chances of ending up with a well-built house are greatly improved if time is first spent on design.

The same concepts hold true for computer programs. Programs that are carefully designed before any actual program language statements are written are more apt to be "good programs." Good programs are programs that:

1. Are shorter in length.
2. Are more efficient.
3. Are easier to read, understand, and modify.
4. Contain fewer logic errors that need to be identified and corrected during program testing.

Time spent on design of a problem solution is recovered many times over during the actual programming phase. It is very true in computer programming, unfortunately, that "Typing is no substitute for thinking."

The steps we will follow in developing programs to solve problems are as follows:

1. Define the problem.
2. Design a solution to the problem, using pseudocode and top-down design.
3. Translate the pseudocode solution into an actual programming language.
4. Test the program to see that it executes correctly.

2.2 FORMAL PROBLEM DEFINITION

Developing a *formal problem definition* first is a technique used to ensure that the programmer has clearly defined the problem that is to be solved before attempting to design and write a solution to this problem. Frequently the person writing the program is not the person who will be operating the program or the person who will be using the resulting information produced by the program. In such a situation it is vital that the program operate in the manner expected, and produce the output desired by the user—in the format the user wishes. Otherwise, it may be necessary for the programmer to modify the program several times before it finally is acceptable to the user. Extensive modifications are kept to a minimum if a formal problem definition is prepared and agreed to by both user and programmer before any design or coding begins.

How Can You Solve a Problem Unless You Know What the Problem Is?

If you were asked to design a solution to the following problem, what are some of the questions you would need answered before you could try to solve the problem?

Write a program to convert the lengths of several boards to centimeters.

One of the first questions that needs to be answered is "What units are the boards measured in originally?" Another question is "How many boards are there?" We also need to know what conversion factor to use. That is, if the lengths of the boards are given in inches, "How many centimeters are there in one inch?" Also, "How does the user wish the results displayed?" "Is the output to be on the screen, or is it to be printed?" As you can see, much more information about the problem is needed before an attempt can be made to design a solution to it.

The Parts of a Formal Problem Definition

A formal problem definition consists of five parts:

1. General description
2. Input specifications
3. Output specifications
4. Normal example
5. Unusual or error conditions

Using the problem given in the preceding section, let's see what a complete formal problem definition of this problem might look like:

General Description

A program is to be written to convert the lengths of four boards measured in feet and inches to centimeters. Output is to consist of a table listing the lengths of the boards in feet and inches, and their corresponding lengths in centimeters. Output is to be appropriately labeled.

The *general description* provides an overall description of the problem to be solved. It gives a general, overall "feel" of what the problem is all about. It still, however, lacks specific answers to all the questions that need to be answered if an acceptable solution is to be designed. For example, although the general description indicates that the lengths of four boards are to be converted from feet and inches to centimeters, the form in which this input will be provided is still not specified. Will all input be on a single line? Are prompts requesting input to be displayed to the user? Will the number of inches be a whole number, a decimal, or a fraction? Enough specific information about the problem has still not been provided to permit a solution to be written.

The second part of the formal problem definition, which is the *input specifications*, might be written as follows:

Input Specifications

Input to the program is to consist of the lengths of four boards in feet and inches. The length of each board is to be entered on a separate line. The length in feet is to be separated from the length in inches by a comma. "Prompt" the user for each line of input with the message:

```
Enter the length of the board in feet, inches
```

The length in feet is to be a whole number, and the length in inches is to be either a whole number, or a decimal value.

Much of the additional information contained in this section is not specifically given in the general description part of the definition but is decided upon by the programmer and user jointly as the complete specifications for the program are developed. This is the time to make decisions about how the program is to operate—not after the program has been written and tested.

The form in which the output is to be displayed is described in the third part of the formal problem definition, the *output specifications* section:

Output Specifications

Output from the program is to appear on the screen in tabular form. The table is to have the following column headings:

```
        Length in                                              Length in
     Feet and Inches                                          Centimeters
```

Following these headings, print a blank line, followed by the body of the table, which is to be single-spaced. The input values are to be printed under the first heading, with the length in feet separated from the length in inches by three spaces. The lengths in centimeters, calculated by multiplying the lengths of the boards in inches by 2.54, are to be centered under the second column heading. The length of each board in centimeters is to be printed correct to two decimal places.

A *normal example,* the fourth part of a formal problem definition, is developed using the information provided in the second and third parts. If any questions occur during the writing of the normal example that cannot be answered by referring back to the input and output specifications sections, these parts may need to be rewritten. What occurs in the normal example section is that the specifications given in the preceding two parts are followed to indicate, by means of an example, how the program will operate once it has been written.

Normal Example

Input:

```
Enter the length of the board in feet, inches
?8,10
Enter the length of the board in feet, inches
?6,4
Enter the length of the board in feet, inches
?5,0
Enter the length of the board in feet, inches
?9,3.25
```

Output:

Length in Feet and Inches		Length in Centimeters
8	10	269.24
6	4	193.04
5	0	152.40
9	3.25	282.58

The last part of a formal problem definition is a list of *unusual or error conditions*. This section describes how the program will behave when unusual or incorrect data is encountered. Obviously, not all possible errors that might be made can be discussed. Normally, four or five of the more typical kinds of errors that may occur during data entry or program operation are listed, and the behavior of the program in response to these errors is described. Some of these error-handling responses will need to be designed into the program by the programmer—others are handled automatically by the system.

The unusual or error conditions section for this problem might look like this:

Unusual or Error Conditions

1. If more than two values are entered on a line, only the first two values will be used.
2. If the two input values are not separated by a comma, they will be interpreted by the program as a single input value. Reentry of the entire input line will be requested by the system prompt "?Redo from start".
3. If character data, such as "feet" or "inches," is entered as part of the input data, the system prompt, "?Redo from start", will be displayed. The entire line of input must then be reentered.
4. If a negative length in feet and/or inches is entered, the program will continue and give a negative length in centimeters for this entry.

As was indicated earlier, these are certainly not the only errors that might be made during program operation, but they are errors that could easily occur. The first error condition listed would be handled automatically by the computer system in the manner described and would not necessitate any extra coding on the part of the programmer. The errors listed in 2 and 3 above would also be handled by the system automatically and would not need to be of concern to the programmer. Error 4 simply indicates that the program will not identify or correct unreasonable data values but will merely perform the calculations using the data provided.

Writing Formal Problem Definitions

The only way in which proficiency in writing formal problem definitions can be gained is through practice. Therefore, it would seem worthwhile to try writing a couple more. There is certainly more than one correct formal problem definition for any given problem, since many of the details in the formal problem definition come about as the result of the discussions between the programmer and the user. If the solutions to the following examples are different from what you might construct, it doesn't necessarily mean that I'm right and you're wrong; it may just mean that you would supply different details than I.

□ **Example 1**

Given the following problem description, write an appropriate formal problem definition. Supply any necessary additional information, but be careful not to change the general sense of the problem.

Identify the character from a set of three input characters that would appear first in an alphabetical list.

As this problem description is read, a general idea of what the program is to do is obtained, but several unanswered questions remain. "How will the characters be entered—one per line, or all on one line?" "What is meant by 'Identify the character'?" "How will the program behave if less than three or more than three characters are entered?" Obviously, some decisions with regard to these and other questions are going to have to be made as the formal problem definition is developed. Some of these points can be clarified as a general description is written:

General Description

A program is to be written that will accept any three capital letters, all entered on a single line. Output from the program is to be a list of the three input characters, followed by the character, appropriately labeled, that would appear first in an alphabetical list.

This general description answers some of the questions, but the problem requirements can be specified even more clearly in the remaining sections of the formal problem definition.

Input Specifications

Input consists of any three uppercase alphabetic characters, all on a single line, separated by commas. The input is to be prompted by the message:

```
Enter any three capital letters
```

Output Specifications

Each of the three input characters is to be displayed, one per line in the order in which they were entered. Following this echoing of the input, a blank line is to be output, followed by the line below:

```
The first character from above is <char>
```

where <char> is replaced by the input character that would appear first alphabetically.

Remember that the normal example, which comes next, must exactly follow the format indicated by the input and output specifications.

Normal Example

Input:

```
Enter any three capital letters
?X,B,T
```

Output:

```
X
B
T

The first character from above is B
```

The last section, unusual or error conditions, contains information as to how the program will behave if incorrect or unexpected data is entered.

Unusual or Error Conditions

1. If fewer than three characters are entered, no output will occur.
2. If more than three characters are entered, only the first three are processed—the rest are ignored.
3. If no commas are placed between the characters, they will be treated as a single input value, and no output will be produced.
4. If any of the input characters are not uppercase alphabetic characters, the following message is printed after all characters are echoed:

```
Invalid character encountered—Warning!
```

The invalid character will not be considered in determining the lowest character.
5. If any two, or all three, of the input characters are the same, and they are first alphabetically, then that character is displayed as usual.

Once the formal problem definition has been completed, as it has been above, the intended behavior of the program has been clearly described. Design of a solution to this problem could now be attempted. But first, let's work through one more example.

☐ **Example 2**

Write a formal problem definition for the following problem:

Calculate the average of a set of input values.

This problem statement, while quite short, definitely presents a clear-cut problem to solve. There are many unanswered questions, however. Perhaps the exact scope of the problem can be more specifically stated in the general description:

General Description

Design and write a program to calculate the average of a set of input values. The number of values to be averaged will be entered first, followed by the actual values themselves. Output is to consist of the number of values to be averaged and their average, both output values appropriately labeled.

As can be seen, it was necessary to supply additional information so that an acceptable general description could be written. The information added did not alter the problem; it merely clarified it. If you were writing the formal problem definition, you might choose to add different information. This would be fine, as long as the problem was not materially changed.

Input Specifications

The first line of input is to be prompted by the message:

```
How many values are to be averaged?
```

The value entered in response to this prompt is to be a single whole number. Following this line will be as many lines of input as the initial whole number indicates. Each of these succeeding values will be on a separate line, each prompted by the message:

```
Enter value
```

Output Specifications

Three lines of output will be produced. The first line will be:

```
The number of values to be averaged is: <n>
```

where <n> is the number entered in response to the prompt, "How many values are to be averaged?" This line is followed by a blank line, followed by the third and last line of output:

```
The average is: <a>
```

where <a> is the average of the values entered in response to the prompts, "Enter value." The average is calculated by adding these input values together and dividing that sum by the number of values (the first value entered).

Normal Example

Input:

```
How many values are to be averaged?
?4
Enter value
?2
Enter value
?2.5
Enter value
?−1
Enter value
?10.5
```

Output:

```
The number of values to be averaged is: 4
The average is: 3.5
```

Unusual or Error Conditions

1. If any nonnumeric values are entered, the system will respond with the message, "?Redo from start."
2. If the first input value is not a whole number, the noninteger portion of the value will be truncated.
3. If the first input value is less than one, the following message will be output:

```
Impossible to average fewer than one number!!
```

4. If fewer values are entered to be averaged than the first value entered specified, no output will occur.
5. If more values are entered to be averaged than the first value entered specified, the additional values will be ignored.

2.3 CONTROL STRUCTURES

Now that a method to define problems in a clear, concise manner has been developed, how to design "good" solutions to these problems needs to be considered. Remember, a "good program" is one that is efficient, easy to read and understand, and needs little time spent in identifying and correcting errors. Fortunately, designing and writing such programs has become much easier recently since the discovery that only a relatively few constructs are needed to design solutions to any problems amenable to computer solution.

Flowcharts

Before continuing with the discussion of the control structures needed for problem solution, it might be a good idea to briefly discuss the use of flowcharts to graphically illustrate program logic. A flowchart is a diagram of the logical sequence of operations performed in a program or program segment. The order in which operations are carried out is indicated by arrows connecting the symbols that represent the operations to be performed in the program. The specific operation to be performed by a given flowchart symbol is written inside the symbol. Common flowcharting symbols used are illustrated in Figure 2.1.

The *Terminal* symbol is used to indicate a starting or stopping point in a flowchart. To indicate a starting point, the word START or BEGIN might be placed inside the terminal symbol. An ending point in a flowchart would be indicated with the terminal symbol enclosing the word STOP, END, or HALT.

The *Input/Output* symbol is used in a flowchart to show where input is to be interjected into a process, or where the program is to produce output data on the screen or printer. If the symbol is to indicate an input operation, the word READ or INPUT will be placed inside it. An output operation is indicated by the words WRITE or PRINT appearing inside the symbol.

The *Processing* symbol in a flowchart normally indicates that calculations are to be performed at this point in a program, or values are to be assigned to variables. The actual calculation to be performed, or process to be carried out, is written inside the symbol.

The use of a *Decision* symbol in a flowchart indicates that alternate paths exist for the program to take based upon some condition that is to be evaluated. This

Figure 2.1 Flowcharting symbols.

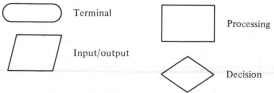

condition may be thought of as a question to which there is a yes or no answer. If the answer to the question is "yes," one particular path will be taken; if the answer is "no," an alternate path will be taken.

Figure 2.2 is an example of a simple flowchart of the following problem:

Enter two numbers, A and B. If the first number entered, A, is larger than the second number, B, display the first number, A. If not, display the sum of A and B.

This flowchart of a solution to the problem makes use of all the flowcharting symbols given. Program execution would begin at the point indicated by the terminal symbol containing the word BEGIN, and proceed along the path indicated by the arrows. Two numbers would be entered next, as indicated by the Input/Output symbol. The Decision symbol, which occurs next, asks the question, "Is the first number entered, A, larger than the second number entered, B?" If the answer to this question is "yes," program execution continues down the pathway to the left, which causes the value of A to be displayed, and then the program halts. If the answer to the question in the Decision symbol is "no", however, program execution proceeds along the pathway on the right—the sum of A and B is calculated, and then displayed.

Flowcharts are useful tools for graphically showing the flow of logic in a program, once the program has been written. They are a useful documentation tool

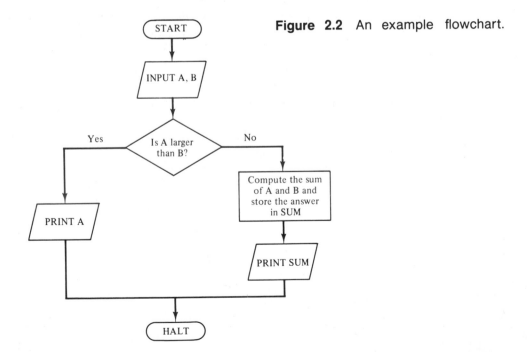

Figure 2.2 An example flowchart.

in that they help a programmer understand how a program operates. They are not a very useful tool, however, in designing solutions to problems. We will learn a different technique—top-down design—to help us design solutions to problems.

The Three Control Structures Needed for Problem Solution

Much of the credit for the modern structured approach to program design is owed to two Italian mathematicians, Bohm and Jacopini, who in 1966 published a scientific paper in the *Communications of the ACM* in which they mathematically proved that even the most complex program logic could be expressed through the use of only three control structures: *sequence, selection,* and *repetition.*

A second important event that helped to further the interest in writing "good programs" was the publication of a letter in the same journal in 1968 by Edsger Dijkstra under the heading, "Go To Statements Considered Harmful." In this letter Dijkstra argued the case that programs containing a large number of GO TO statements tended to be poorer programs than those programs which use this statement sparingly, if at all. Programs containing a large number of GO TO statements are sometimes referred to as "spaghetti code," as tracing through the flow of logic in these programs becomes similar to attempting to straighten out a bowl of spaghetti.

Fortunately, programs written making use of only the three control structures described by Bohm and Jacopini do not need to make extensive use of the GO TO statement and therefore are more apt to be good programs. Programs written in this manner are referred to as *structured programs.* Let's briefly examine the three control structures needed for structured programs.

Sequential operations are those steps in a problem solution which always occur one after the other in order, that is, in sequence. This type of control structure can be diagramed as shown in Figure 2.3.

Figure 2.3 Sequential control structure.

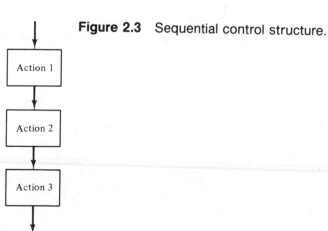

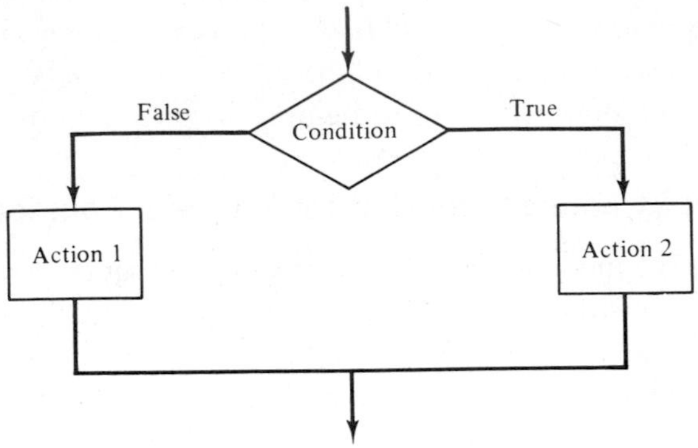

Figure 2.4 Selection control structure.

```
                    │
                    ▼
      False    ◇ Condition ◇    True
   ┌──────────                ──────────┐
   ▼                                    ▼
┌─────────┐                       ┌─────────┐
│ Action 1 │                       │ Action 2 │
└─────────┘                       └─────────┘
   │                                    │
   └──────────────┬───────────────────┘
                  ▼
```

The *selection* control structure is used when the action to be taken is dependent upon whether some condition is true or false. If the condition is true, one set of operations is performed; if false, another set of operations is performed. This structure may be diagramed as shown in Figure 2.4.

The *repetition*, or looping, control structure is needed if one or more operations or actions are to be repeated as long as some condition remains true. A diagram of this structure would appear as shown in Figure 2.5.

Now that a brief introduction has been given to the three fundamental control structures needed for problem solution, a more detailed look at how they might be used in some specific problem situations might be helpful.

Sequence

As mentioned above, the first and simplest control structure needed is that of sequence. There may be certain operations in a solution to a problem that are always performed one after another—in sequence. An example of a sequential operation is: suppose that the purchase of a soft drink is to be made from a vending machine. There is a definite set of actions that must be performed to carry out this task—in a definite order. First, money must be inserted in the coin slot, then the button pressed to indicate the choice of drink, and then finally, the drink must be

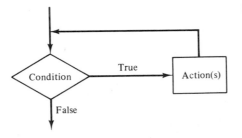

Figure 2.5 Repetition control structure.

Figure 2.6 Purchasing a soft drink from a vending machine.

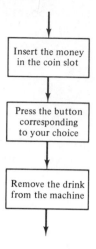

removed from the machine. These actions must be performed in this order, one after the other, or sequentially.

A flowchart of the actions that must be performed to carry out this task would be as illustrated in Figure 2.6. As the flowchart indicates, each operation follows one after the other—in a sequential order.

In the first formal problem definition developed—the problem of converting a length in feet and inches to a length in centimeters, a series of sequential operations is necessary to solve the problem: Enter the length of the first board in feet and inches, convert this length to all inches, convert the length in inches to centimeters, and then display both the original length in feet and inches and the equivalent length in centimeters. Each of the above operations occurs one after the other, that is, in sequence. A flowchart of this series of operations appears in Figure 2.7.

Selection

The selection control structure indicates that a certain operation or group of operations is to be performed only if a certain condition is true. For example, it might be wished to modify the above example so that the second set of calculations is performed and a line of output produced only if the length of the board is positive (greater than zero). (If this change were to be made, the formal problem definition would need to be modified appropriately.) This structure could be diagramed as shown in Figure 2.8. Once the length of the board has been converted to all inches, the question is asked, "Is the length greater than zero?" If the answer to this question is "yes," the two steps indicated under the "yes" branch are performed. If the answer to the question is "no," these two operations are skipped and program execution continues with the next statement in the program.

Figure 2.7   A series of sequential operations.

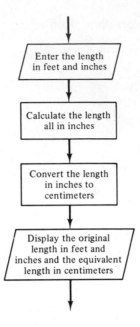

Figure 2.8   A selection structure.

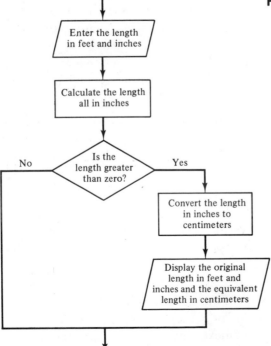

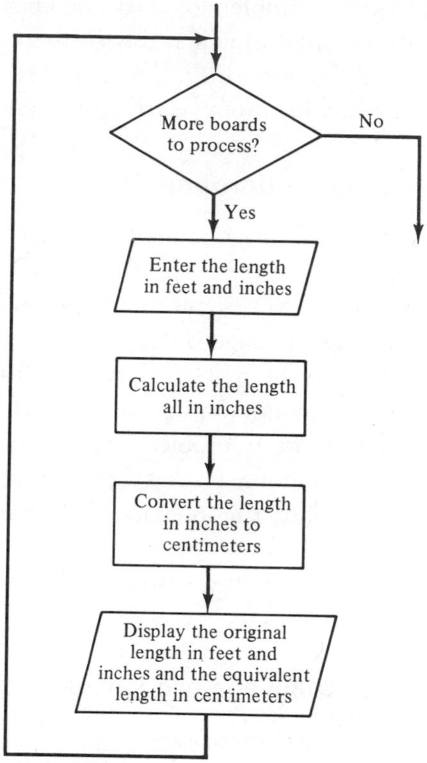

Figure 2.9 A repetitive control structure.

Repetition

The repetition structure is used when a series of actions or operations is to be performed more than once. For example, in the board problem previously discussed, the lengths of four boards are to be processed. The same series of steps needs to be performed on each board. Rather than designing the solution as a series of sequential operations, in which the same steps are performed four times by listing each of these steps four times, the steps could be listed just once and then placed inside a repetitive control structure as shown in Figure 2.9. As long as the answer to the question "More boards to process?" remains "yes," the sequence of operations converting the length of the board in feet and inches to centimeters continues. When the answer to the question becomes "no," the flow of logic passes to the "no" branch and the processing of board lengths ceases.

2.4 PSEUDOLANGUAGE—A TOOL FOR DESIGN

Pseudolanguage, or *pseudocode* (the two terms may be used interchangeably), is a set of English-like commands used during the design process to state the set of instructions that must be followed to solve a problem or carry out a task. When this group of instructions is performed in the order in which the instructions are listed, the problem will be solved, the task will be performed. This set of pseudolanguage instructions that will solve a given problem is often referred to as an *algorithm.*

A Generic Language for Developing Algorithms

Pseudolanguage is a *design language, not* a programming language like BASIC, FORTRAN, or COBOL. Algorithms written in pseudocode will *not* directly execute on a computer. The main advantage to designing a solution to a problem in pseudocode rather than in a programming language is that emphasis can be placed on the design of the solution rather than on the syntax of a particular programming language or on a particular version of that programming language, which runs on a particular computer. Once the solution to a problem has been designed in pseudocode, the hard part of the programming process has been completed. It becomes an almost trivial task to translate the pseudocode solution into the programming language desired.

The following table lists some of the important differences between a programming language and a pseudolanguage:

Differences between a Programming Language and Pseudolanguage

Programming language	Pseudolanguage
Programs can be executed by some computer	Programs cannot be executed by a computer
Difficult language in which to design a problem solution	Provides best method known for design of a problem solution
Syntax and format of statements is of major concern	Prime concern is design of an efficient, correct solution
Flow of logic and control structures may be masked by language syntax requirements	Typically easier to read than a solution written in a programming language

Although the final goal is, of course, to create a computer program that will execute on a computer, the program will be more apt to work correctly and be more efficient if it is first designed in pseudocode. Once a pseudocode solution to a problem has been written, it can easily be translated into whatever programming language is desired.

The Pseudocode Statements

In order to design solutions to problems in pseudocode, the form of the particular pseudocode statements to be used needs to be defined. Since it will be necessary to indicate in solutions to problems where output is to be produced by a program, a pseudocode *output statement* will be needed. Similarly, a statement to indicate where input is to occur is essential, so a pseudocode *input statement* will be necessary. Calculations may need to be performed in a given problem, or a value assigned to a variable, so a statement that performs this operation must be defined (this type of statement is commonly referred to as an *assignment statement*). All the statements mentioned thus far are sequential statements since the operations they perform always occur one after another.

Other pseudocode statements that will be needed are statements to implement the other two control structures discussed earlier in this chapter—*selection* and *repetition*. Statements will be needed to implement each of these structures.

A last statement type that may be useful is the *comment statement*. This statement allows inclusion of comments or remarks in a program to help clarify and document the program. Comments are especially helpful when programmers need to modify someone else's program or a program that they themselves wrote some time ago. Comments documenting how the program operates help the programmer to read and understand the program more easily so that needed modifications can be made.

The general form of each of the pseudocode statements that is to be used in designing problem solutions is given below.

General Form of Pseudolanguage Statements

Comment statement:

> {*All remarks or comments are placed inside curly brackets*}

Input statement:

> *READ (list of variables, or a single variable)*

Output statement:

> *WRITE (variables and/or constants)*

Assignment statement:

> *variable ← expression or constant*

Selection statements:

> *IF   condition*
> *THEN*
> > *statement(s)*
> *ENDIF*

or

IF   *condition*
THEN
       statement(s)
ELSE
       statement(s)
ENDIF

Repetition statements:

WHILE *condition*
       statement(s)
ENDWHILE

        or

FOR *variable* = *expression* TO *expression*
       statement(s)
NEXT *variable*

The *comment statement* is used to add explanatory remarks to a pseudocode problem solution. Any remark or comment the programmer wishes to include in the pseudocode solution is placed inside a set of curly brackets ({ }):

{*This is an example of a comment statement*}

These comments do not cause any program action to be taken; they merely clarify and document the program. They will be translated into remark or comment statements in the programming language translation of the pseudocode solution when this translation is performed.

The *READ statement* is the form of the input statement to be used in pseudocode. Its use in a pseudocode program indicates that the user is to type in the value of a variable or variables at that particular point in a program. If the user responds to the question mark produced by a READ statement by typing in a value(s), that value, or those values, are assigned to the location(s) in the computer's memory named by the variable name(s) listed in the parentheses following the word READ. For example, if the following statement were used in a pseudocode program:

READ (SCORE)

and the user was to type the number 87 in response to the question mark generated by this READ statement, the value 87 would be assigned to the memory location named SCORE:

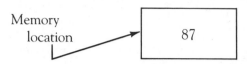

SCORE (programmer's symbolic name)

Memory location → 87

Address NNN (computer determines location)

A READ statement can contain more than one variable. For example, if the READ statement:

READ (NUMBER, PRICE)

were executed, and in response to the question mark generated by this statement the values 20 and 3.25 were typed, separated by a comma, the variable NUMBER would be assigned the value 20 and the value 3.25 would be assigned to the variable PRICE:

NUMBER

20

PRICE

3.25

The *WRITE statement* in a pseudocode program is used to indicate that output is to be produced. Both the value of variables and/or messages can be displayed using a WRITE statement. If a message is to be printed by a WRITE statement, the actual text to be displayed must be enclosed in quotation marks. For example, if the message "How are you today?" was to be displayed, the following WRITE statement could be used:

WRITE ("How are you today?")

When the values of variables are to be displayed, the names of the variables are listed in the parentheses following the word WRITE, separated by commas. When the statement is executed, the values of these variables, not their names, will be displayed on the output device. For example, if the variable SUM contained the value 253, and the variable NUMBER contained the value 12, the WRITE statement

WRITE (SUM, NUMBER)

would produce the following output:

```
253   12
```

The *assignment statement* is used in a pseudocode program to assign a value to a variable. A constant value may be stored in a variable, as the following indicates:

$$TOTAL \leftarrow 0$$

This statement would store the value 0 in the memory location named TOTAL. The *assignment operator* ($\leftarrow$) can be read as "takes the value of" or "is replaced by." Thus the above example would be read as "TOTAL takes the value of 0."

An expression rather than a constant may appear on the right side of the assignment operator. If this is the case, the expression is first evaluated and then its value is assigned to the variable named on the left side of the $\leftarrow$. For example, given the following assignment statement:

$$AVERAGE \leftarrow SUM \ / \ NUMBER$$

the value of the expression SUM / NUMBER (the / symbol indicates division) would first be calculated and then this result would be stored in the variable AVERAGE.

The following arithmetic operations symbols may be used in pseudocode assignment statements:

Operations symbol	Meaning
+	Addition
−	Subtraction
*	Multiplication
/	Division
^	Exponentiation

There are two *selection statements*. The first is referred to as an *IF-THEN statement*. If the condition following the word IF is true, the statement or statements following the THEN statement are executed. If the condition is false, the statement or statements following the THEN statement and preceding the ENDIF statement are skipped. For example, in the IF-THEN statement:

```
IF HOURS > 40
THEN
      OVERTIME ← HOURS − 40
ENDIF
```

the assignment statement OVERTIME ← HOURS − 40 will be executed if and only if the condition HOURS > 40 is true. If this condition is false (HOURS are less than or equal to 40), the assignment statement will not be executed and the statement following the ENDIF statement will be executed next. The conditions following the word IF may make use of the following logical operators:

Logical operators	Meaning
>	Greater than
<	Less than
>=	Greater than or equal to
<=	Less than or equal to
><	Not equal to

The second type of selection statement that may be used is the *IF-THEN-ELSE statement:*

```
IF SCORE >= 70
THEN
      WRITE ("Congratulations! You passed!")
ELSE
      WRITE ("You need to study harder.")
ENDIF
```

If the condition SCORE >= 70, which follows the word IF, is true, the WRITE statement that displays the message "Congratulations! You passed!" will be executed. If the condition is false (the SCORE is less than 70), the WRITE statement that displays the message "You need to study harder." will be executed. Notice that only one of the messages will be displayed, not both. If the statement or statements following the THEN statement and preceding the ELSE statement are executed because the condition following the word IF is true, the statement or statements following the word ELSE are not executed. The next statement executed in this case will be the statement following the ENDIF statement.

If a statement or group of statements is to be executed more than once in a pseudocode program, a *repetition statement* would be used. The *WHILE statement* causes the statement or group of statements following the WHILE statement and preceding the ENDWHILE statement to be executed repetitively as long as the condition following the word WHILE is true. When the condition becomes false, program execution continues with the statement following the ENDWHILE statement. In the following segment of pseudocode:

```
READ (NAME, HOURS)
WHILE NAME <> "DONE"
    PAY ← HOURS * 3.65
    WRITE (NAME, PAY)
    READ (NAME, HOURS)
ENDWHILE
```

the three statements contained between the WHILE and ENDWHILE statements will continue to be executed as long as the condition NAME <> "DONE" remains true. As soon as a name of DONE, followed by some value for HOURS, is entered in response to either of the READ statements, the condition will no longer be true, and program execution will then continue with the statement following the ENDWHILE statement.

Notice that the first READ statement in the segment of code just given precedes the WHILE statement, so it is executed only once. This necessitates a second READ statement inside the WHILE loop which will be executed repeatedly as long as the condition in the WHILE statement remains true. The first READ statement is referred to as a "priming READ," since it provides an initial value for the variable NAME that is immediately tested in the conditional expression in the WHILE statement (NAME <> "DONE"). If this initial READ statement was omitted, the variable NAME would not have a value yet assigned to it the first time the condition in the WHILE statement is tested for truth or falsity.

The second type of repetition statement in the pseudocode being used is the *FOR-NEXT statement*. This statement also causes repetitive execution of a statement or group of statements, but is usually used for what is called a *determinate*, or counted, loop. For example, if we wished to sum a list of 10 values entered into the computer, we could use the following pseudocode segment:

```
SUM ← 0
FOR COUNT = 1 TO 10
    READ (NUMBER)
    SUM ← SUM + NUMBER
NEXT COUNT
```

The two statements between the FOR and NEXT statements would be executed 10 times before program execution would continue with the statement following the NEXT statement. The variable COUNT is used by the FOR-NEXT statement in this example to monitor the number of times the loop has been executed. COUNT is first set to 1 (the value following the "=" sign in the FOR statement is called the *starting value*) and is incremented by 1 each time the NEXT statement is executed. Notice that the same variable name must follow both the word FOR and the word NEXT. Looping will continue until the value of this variable (COUNT) exceeds the *ending value* that follows the word TO in the FOR statement (in this example the ending value is 10).

As can be seen from the discussion above, there are basically two different situations where repetition or looping structures are used. The first problem situation where a loop is required is when a group of statements is to be repeated a given number of times. For example, if the problem requires that a set of operations be performed five times, we have a counted, or *determinate,* loop. The FOR-NEXT statement is the control structure normally used for this situation. Key phrases appearing in problem statements that provide a hint that this type of loop should be used are: "There will be ten input values . . .", "Process 20 student scores . . .", etc. Whenever the number of repetitions to be performed is known or can be determined *before* the looping statement is executed the first time, a determinate loop is used.

The second type of repetition structure is an *indeterminate* loop. In this situation, the number of times the loop is repeated is dependent upon some condition occurring in the data being processed. This type of loop is most often constructed using the WHILE statement. Key phrases to watch for in problem descriptions that would make use of this type of loop are: "End of input is indicated by an input value of . . .", "Continue processing transactions until a transaction code of . . .", "The process is to continue until . . .", etc. Notice that a *condition* is either stated or implied in each of these key phrases. Looping is to continue until some condition occurs. Exactly *when* this condition will occur—that is, after how many times the loop has been repeated—is uncertain. This may be after three repetitions, 27 repetitions, or even none. This uncertainty is the tip-off that an indeterminate loop will be needed.

When an indeterminate loop is terminated because of the occurrence of a particular input value ("A zero indicates end of input," "End of input is signaled by an employee name of 'DONE'", etc.), this input value is referred to as a "sentinel" or "flag" value. The value itself is not a data item to be processed along with the rest of the input values; it is there to serve as an indicator to mark the end of input.

A Note on Indenting

In the example segments of pseudocode in the previous sections, some statements were indented while others were not. The use of indentation to indicate repetition or selection logic in a program is a technique that should be used consistently. It not only makes programs more attractive, it makes them easier to read and understand. Sample programs throughout this book, both those written in pseudocode and those written in BASIC, will make use of this important aid that makes programs more readable. The following suggestions regarding indentation should be followed when writing pseudocode programs:

Use of Indentation   The following statements should be indented three spaces:

1. Statements after the THEN statement and before the ENDIF statement in an IF-THEN statement.
2. Statements after the THEN statement and before the ELSE statement in an IF-THEN-ELSE statement.
3. Statements after the ELSE statement and before the ENDIF statement in an IF-THEN-ELSE statement.
4. Statements after the WHILE statement and before the ENDWHILE statement in a WHILE loop.
5. Statements after the FOR statement and before the NEXT statement in a FOR-NEXT loop.

Note that indentation has no effect on machine interpretation of statements; it has an effect only on programmer reading and understanding of a program.

Choosing Variable Names

The last topic to be discussed before starting to use pseudocode statements is naming variables. A variable is simply a name for a location in the computer's memory where a value may be stored. The value stored in a particular location may be changed during program execution by storing another value in that location with an assignment statement, or by entering a new value into that location by means of an input statement. A program will be easier to read and understand if names used for these locations are meaningful. For example, if a location is needed to store the sum of a group of numbers, the variable name SUM might be used to refer to that particular location. If it is desired to store a person's address at another location in memory, that location might be named ADDRESS.

The rules to be used for forming variable names in pseudocode are as follows:

Rules for Forming Variable Names

1. Variable names may be up to 255 characters long.
2. Letters, digits, and the period may be used to form variable names.

3. Variable names must start with a letter and cannot contain embedded blanks.
4. Choose variable names that are meaningful.

Several examples of valid and invalid variable names are:

Valid	Invalid
STUDENT.NAME	1ST.VALUE
CITY.STATE	LAST NAME
TOTAL	X*Y*Z

What is wrong with the names in the invalid column? 1ST.VALUE is invalid because it starts with a digit (1), and variable names must start with a letter. The second variable name, LAST NAME, contains an embedded blank, which is not permitted. The last variable name in the invalid column is not allowed because it uses the * symbol in the name, which is not one of the valid characters listed in rule 2 above. It would also be a poor choice for a variable name since it is not a meaningful name.

An Example Pseudocode Solution

Referring to the board length conversion problem one more time, the following shows how the pseudocode statements discussed in the Note on Indenting could be used to state an algorithm that would solve this problem. Obviously, there is more than one correct solution to this problem, but here is one that would be acceptable:

{This section accepts the input and performs the necessary calculations}

{Process the first board}
    WRITE ("Enter the length of the board in feet, inches")
    READ (FEET1, INCHES1)
    *LENGTH.IN.INCHES1 ← FEET1 * 12 + INCHES1*
    *LENGTH.IN.CM1 ← LENGTH.IN.INCHES1 * 2.54*

{Process the second board}
    WRITE ("Enter the length of the board in feet, inches")
    READ (FEET2, INCHES2)
    *LENGTH.IN.INCHES2 ← FEET2 * 12 + INCHES2*
    *LENGTH.IN.CM2 ← LENGTH.IN.INCHES2 * 2.54*

{*Process the third board*}
    WRITE ("*Enter the length of the board in feet, inches*")
    READ (FEET3, INCHES3)
    LENGTH.IN.INCHES3 ← FEET3 * 12 + INCHES3
    LENGTH.IN.CM3 ← LENGTH.IN.INCHES3 * 2.54

{*Process the fourth board*}
    WRITE ("*Enter the length of the board in feet, inches*")
    READ (FEET4, INCHES4)
    LENGTH.IN.INCHES4 ← FEET4 * 12 + INCHES4
    LENGTH.IN.CM4 ← LENGTH.IN.INCHES4 * 2.54

{*This section outputs the headings*}
    WRITE (" Length in   Length in")
    WRITE ("Feet and Inches   Centimeters")
    WRITE ("   ")

{*This section outputs the body of the table*}
    WRITE (FEET1, INCHES1, "   ", LENGTH.IN.CM1)
    WRITE (FEET2, INCHES2, "   ", LENGTH.IN.CM2)
    WRITE (FEET3, INCHES3, "   ", LENGTH.IN.CM3)
    WRITE (FEET4, INCHES4, "   ", LENGTH.IN.CM4)

This solution uses several of the different types of pseudocode statements previously mentioned. Notice they are all sequential statements. The operation of the program begins with the first executable statement, the WRITE statement that follows the comment statement, {*Process the first board*}, and continues right down the list (a comment statement, remember, is not an executable statement—it simply provides information about the program). Blank lines have been inserted to separate the sections of the program and make it more readable. The only types of pseudocode statements used in this solution are WRITE, READ, comment, and assignment statements. No selection or repetition statements are needed.

Both forms of the WRITE statement discussed are used in this solution. The statement WRITE ("*Enter the length of the board in feet, inches*") is used to display a message, and the last four WRITE statements display the values stored in variables. The names of the variables FEET1, INCHES1, LENGTH.IN.CM1, etc., are not enclosed in quotation marks, so rather than the names of these variables being displayed, their values are displayed. The quotation marks in these last four WRITE statements enclose a group of blank spaces that are used to line up the values of the variables under the appropriate headings.

The variable names used in the solution were selected to represent the values they were storing. Other names could have just as well been chosen. For example, instead of using FEET1 to store the length of the first board in feet, another name such as LENGTH.OF.FIRST.BOARD.IN.FEET could have been used. This second name would certainly work, as it definitely is meaningful, but it would get rather cumbersome to type over and over again. There needs to be a trade-off between how meaningful a variable name is and how ungainly it is to use. Common sense is necessary when selecting variable names.

The next section of this chapter is concerned with the process involved in proceeding from a formal problem definition to a completed pseudocode solution to the problem—in other words, the design of a problem solution.

2.5 THE TOP-DOWN DESIGN APPROACH TO PROBLEM SOLUTION

Probably the most natural way to design a solution to a problem is through the process known as *top-down design*. This same approach can be taken to many kinds of problems—problems that will not, necessarily, result in a computer program. Top-down design, then, is a method for solving problems.

The Steps in Top-Down Design

When the top-down design approach is used to solve a problem, the first task is to simply list in English-like phrases, or comments, the steps to be followed in solving the problem. At this initial stage it is not necessary to be concerned with how these steps are to be performed by the computer—that comes later. These steps are stated in very general terms; again, the specificity comes later.

Once a complete list of the steps needed to solve the problem has been developed, the second phase of the top-down design process beings. Each of the steps in the first level is refined into a more specific description of exactly what that step involves. This process continues through a third, fourth, etc., phase until finally all the steps involved in solving the problem have been refined to the point where they are all expressed in pseudocode.

Each completed refinement is referred to as a *level*. The first list of steps is Level I, the second is Level II, etc. The number of times each comment must be refined will be determined by the complexity of the problem and by how easily each comment can be refined into pseudocode. This process of restating each step with more specificity is referred to as *stepwise refinement*.

Performing a Top-Down Design

Let's work through a complete top-down design of a problem together. Given the following formal problem definition, write a complete top-down design of a solution to this problem:

□ **Formal Problem Definition**

General Description

A program is to be written to determine whether the product or the sum of two input values is the larger. The larger of the two is to be displayed, along with an appropriate message.

Input Specifications

Input will consist of two numeric values, both on the same line. This input is to be prompted by the message:

```
Enter two values, separated by a comma:
```

Output Specifications

Output is to consist of a single line, either:

```
The product is larger. It is: <prod>
```

or

```
The sum is larger. It is: <sum>
```

where <prod> is to be replaced by the value obtained by multiplying the two numbers together and <sum> is to be replaced by the value obtained by adding the two numbers together.

Normal Example

Input:

```
Enter two values, separated by a comma:
?4,3
```

Output:

```
The product is larger. It is: 12
```

Unusual or Error Conditions

1. If only one value is entered, no output will be produced, and the message, ?Redo from start, will be displayed by the system.

2. If a comma is not placed between the two values entered, they will be treated as a single value, and the same message as above will be displayed by the system.
3. If more than two values are entered, only the first two will be used.
4. If the sum and product of the two values are equal, the program will still identify one of them as being larger, and one of the two messages will be output.

As was indicated in the previous section, the first step is to write down the steps involved in solving this problem in very general, English-like statements, or comments. This first list of the steps involved in solving the problem, written all in comment form, is referred to as Level I of the top-down design.

Probably the easiest way to determine the steps needed to solve a problem is to look at the normal example given in the formal problem definition first, and then the input specifications and the output specifications. This usually provides enough information to get started. Looking at the input section of the normal example first, it can be seen that the first operation to be performed is to display an input prompt, "Enter two values, separated by a comma:". This is an output task, so the first step might be

{*display an input prompt requesting two values*}

The next event that occurs in the input section of the normal example is that two numbers are entered. A statement of this in comment form would be:

{*enter two numbers*}

Level I would look like this, then, so far:

Level I

{*display an input prompt requesting two values*}
{*enter two numbers*}

The output section of the normal example provides a hint as to what the next step must be. It indicates that a message is to be displayed, along with a value that was calculated. In order to decide which message to output, it will be necessary to compare two values—the sum and the product. Before that can be done, however, they must be calculated. That must be the next step:

{*calculate the sum of the two input values*}
{*calculate the product of the two input values*}

Now these values can be compared and one of the two messages specified in the output specifications section of the formal problem definition displayed:

*{compare the sum and product and display the larger of
the two, appropriately labeled}*

A complete Level I, then, would be

Level I

{display an input prompt requesting two values}
{enter two values}
{calculate the sum of the two input values}
{calculate the product of the two input values}
*{compare the sum and product and display the larger of
the two, appropriately labeled}*

Level I is a complete solution to the problem. Every step necessary to solve the problem is listed, but in too general a form to be considered ready for translation into a programming language. Each comment in Level I must now be refined and more clearly specified in Level II. Remember, the final goal in top-down design is to attain a list of the steps required to solve the problem, all stated in pseudocode.

The first comment in the Level I solution, *{display an input prompt requesting two values}*, obviously becomes a WRITE statement. The exact form of the input prompt to be displayed can be found in the input specifications. The correct refinement of this comment, then, would be

WRITE ("Enter two values, separated by a comma:")

It is also quite easy to see that the second step listed in Level I, *{enter two values}*, will translate into a READ statement, since that is the only statement we have in pseudocode that performs an input operation. The only other question that needs to be answered before the refinement of this comment can be written is what variable names should be used for the two values that are to be input? Selection of these names is completely at the discretion of the programmer; so suppose the names NUM1 and NUM2 are used. Putting all this together yields the following:

READ (NUM1, NUM2)

The third comment to be refined, *{calculate the sum of the two input values}*, is also quite straightforward in its translation. The only type of statement that may be used to perform calculations is the assignment statement; so this must be what is needed here. The calculation to be performed is to find the sum, which would be the result of evaluating the expression, NUM1 + NUM2. Now all that must be decided is in what variable the result of this calculation should be stored. It would seem to make sense to store it in a variable called SUM. Again, the choice of variable name is completely up to the programmer, but a name should be chosen that is meaningful, and SUM would seem to be a good choice. The final form of the assignment statement, then, would be

$$SUM \leftarrow NUM1 + NUM2$$

Remember, the arrow always points to the left, the single variable must appear on the left side of the arrow, and the expression always goes to the right of the arrow.

The next comment to be refined is {*calculate the product of the two input values*}. This should be easy, especially after the last statement. The variable name PRODUCT would seem to be a good choice for the location in which to store the calculation that needs to be performed; so the completed refinement would be

$$PRODUCT \leftarrow NUM1 * NUM2$$

Remember, the asterisk (*) is used to indicate multiplication.

Let's take a look at what Level II now looks like:

Level II

WRITE (*"Enter two values, separated by a comma:"*)
READ (NUM1, NUM2)
SUM ← NUM1 + NUM2
PRODUCT ← NUM1 * NUM2

The last comment, {*compare the sum and product, and display the larger of the two, appropriately labeled*}, presents more of a challenge. Two different operations are involved in this comment—comparison and output. The type of statement needed to perform the comparison will be a selection statement—the only question is which one, an IF-THEN, or an IF-THEN-ELSE? Since in either case, the sum being the larger, or the product being the larger, output needs to be displayed, the IF-THEN-ELSE would appear to be the appropriate choice. The condition to be checked is whether SUM is larger or PRODUCT is larger. It could be written in either of two ways, SUM > PRODUCT or PRODUCT > SUM. Let's use the latter:

> IF PRODUCT > SUM
> THEN
> > {display PRODUCT, *appropriately labeled*}
> ELSE
> > {display SUM, *appropriately labeled*}
> ENDIF

The completed Level II, then, would be

Level II

> WRITE (*"Enter two values, separated by a comma:"*)
> READ (NUM1, NUM2)
> SUM ← NUM1 + NUM2
> PRODUCT ← NUM1 * NUM2
> IF PRODUCT > SUM
> THEN
> > {display PRODUCT, *appropriately labeled*}
> ELSE
> > {display SUM, *appropriately labeled*}
> ENDIF

Has the final goal then been reached, a solution stated completely in pseudocode? Not quite, unfortunately. There are still two comments to be refined, {display PRODUCT, *appropriately labeled*}, and {display SUM, *appropriately labeled*}. Both of these comments indicate output is to be produced; so they will both result in WRITE statements. The first, {display PRODUCT, *appropriately labeled*}, would be translated into

> WRITE (*"The product is larger. It is:"*, PRODUCT)

and the second comment, {display SUM, *appropriately labeled*}, would become:

> WRITE (*"The sum is larger. It is:"*, SUM)

Notice that in both of these WRITE statements, the message part of the statement is enclosed in quotation marks; that is, "The product is larger. It is:", but the name of the variable, PRODUCT, is not. This is because the *value* of the variable, PRODUCT, is to be displayed, not the *name* of the variable. If the second pair of quotation marks were placed after PRODUCT instead of where they are, execution of this statement would produce:

```
The product is larger. It is: ,PRODUCT
```

not:

```
The product is larger. It is: 12
```

which is the output desired.

Inserting these two WRITE statements in place of their respective comments in Level II gives us Level III, the final solution to the problem, all stated in pseudocode:

Level III

WRITE ("Enter two values, separated by a comma:")
READ (NUM1, NUM2)
SUM ← NUM1 + NUM2
*PRODUCT ← NUM1 * NUM2*
IF PRODUCT > SUM
THEN
    WRITE ("The product is larger. It is:", PRODUCT)
ELSE
    WRITE ("The sum is larger. It is:", SUM)
ENDIF

To ensure that the solution works, a *hand trace*, or *walk-through*, may be performed. A hand, or paper-and-pencil, trace of a pseudolanguage solution means to play computer—in other words, perform each statement just as the computer would if it could understand pseudocode. Let's run through the solution quickly and see if it is going to work.

The first pseudocode statement says to display the message, "Enter two values, separated by a comma:", so we do that:

```
Enter two values, separated by a comma:
```

The next statement, *READ (NUM1, NUM2)*, causes a question mark to be displayed, indicating that input is requested, so now the screen would look like this:

```
Enter two values, separated by a comma:
?
```

Now two numbers are entered, as requested, separated by a comma:

```
Enter two values, separated by a comma:
?5,10
```

The value 5 would be stored in the variable NUM1, the first variable listed in the READ statement, and 10 would be stored in NUM2. The next statement, $SUM \leftarrow NUM1 + NUM2$, performs the calculation of adding the value of NUM1 to the value of NUM2 and storing that answer in SUM. Performing this operation, $5 + 10$ equals 15; so 15 is stored in SUM.

The next assignment statement, $PRODUCT \leftarrow NUM1 * NUM2$, assigns the value of 50 to PRODUCT (5 times 10). Now it is time to execute the IF-THEN-ELSE statement. The condition to be examined is PRODUCT > SUM. Using the values for SUM and PRODUCT calculated previously, the question being asked becomes "Is 50 greater than 15?" Since the answer to this question is "yes," the condition is true, and the statement following the THEN statement is executed. This is the WRITE statement,

WRITE ("The product is larger. It is:", PRODUCT)

When this statement is executed, it produces:

```
The product is larger. It is: 50
```

The next statement in the pseudocode program is ELSE, but because the condition in the IF statement is true and the THEN clause has already been executed, the ELSE clause, which is all the statements down to the ENDIF statement, would be skipped. This brings us to the end of the program. A complete picture of how the screen would look then is:

```
Enter two values, separated by a comma:
?5,10
The product is larger. It is: 50
```

Let's try another trace. Suppose the values of 1 and 3 are entered in response to the question mark generated by the READ statement:

```
Enter two values, separated by a comma:
?1,3
```

This means that the value 1 will be assigned to NUM1 and the value 3 to NUM2. The SUM of the two numbers will be 4 $(1 + 3)$, and the PRODUCT will be 3 $(1 *$ 3). Now we come to the IF-THEN-ELSE statement. The answer to the question,

"Is PRODUCT greater than SUM", is "no," so the condition is false. This means that the THEN clause is skipped, and the ELSE clause will be executed. The statement following the ELSE statement, *WRITE ("The Sum is larger. It is:", SUM)*, is executed, and the final screen becomes

```
Enter two values, separated by a comma:
?1,3
The sum is larger. It is: 4
```

You may want to try tracing the third possibility yourself—the case where the sum and product are equal. Input values of 2 and 2 would produce this result. Because of the way we stated the condition, PRODUCT > SUM, the WRITE statement executed would be the one following the ELSE statement, which would indicate that the sum is larger.

Top-Down Design Examples

The top-down design approach to designing a problem solution becomes a natural approach to use only through practice. Once this method is used for a time, it becomes very difficult to write a program in any other manner. Since top-down design has been found to be the best way yet developed to design efficient, structured programs, it is vital that you become comfortable with this technique. For this reason, let's look at a few more examples.

The first problem to be considered can be solved in one of two ways. Both solutions work correctly, but they are very different approaches to the same problem:

Write a program to find the largest of three input values.

The first step is to write a formal problem definition:

☐ Formal Problem Definition

General Description

A program is to be prepared that will determine and display the largest of three values input to the computer. This output is to be appropriately labeled.

Input Specifications

Input will consist of three numeric values, all entered on a single line, separated by commas. This line of input is to be prompted by the message:

```
Enter three values, separated by commas:
```

Output Specifications

A single line of output is to be produced by this program:

    The largest value is: <largest>

where <largest> will be replaced by the value of the largest input value.

Normal Example

Input:

    Enter three values, separated by commas:
    ?35,42,27

Output:

    The largest value is: 42

Unusual or Error Conditions

1. If fewer than three values are entered, no output will occur.
2. If more than three values are entered, only the first three values will be used by the program—the remaining values will be ignored.
3. If two, or all three, of the input values are the largest, a single value will still be displayed and identified as being the largest.

Reading the formal problem definition over carefully, the following Level I solution might be written:

Level I

{enter three numbers}
{determine which of the three numbers is the largest}
{display this largest value, appropriately labeled}

The first comment to be refined is *{enter three numbers}*. Examining the normal example and the input specifications section, it can be seen that an input prompt will also be necessary preceding this input operation. The input statement will need names chosen for three memory locations in which to store the three values to be entered. Level II then, might start out as:

Level II

WRITE ("Enter three numbers, separated by commas:")
READ (NUM1, NUM2, NUM3)

The next comment to be refined, {*determine which of the three numbers is the largest*}, can be seen to involve comparisons, so several selection statements will be needed. There are three numbers to be compared, but only two can be compared at a time. This process might start out:

```
IF NUM1 > NUM2
THEN
     {compare NUM1 to NUM3}
ELSE
     {compare NUM2 to NUM3}
ENDIF
```

The reasoning behind the logic above is: first compare NUM1 and NUM2. If NUM1 is larger than NUM2, then NUM2 no longer needs to be considered, so all that remains to be done is to compare NUM1 to NUM3 to determine which of these two is the larger. If, on the other hand, NUM1 is not larger than NUM2, we proceed to the ELSE clause where NUM2 must be compared to NUM3 to determine which of this pair is the larger. Level II now would look like this:

Level II

```
WRITE ("Enter three numbers, separated by commas:")
READ (NUM1, NUM2, NUM3)
IF NUM1 > NUM2
THEN
     {compare NUM1 to NUM3}
ELSE
     {compare NUM2 to NUM3}
ENDIF
```

The last comment from Level I to be refined is {*display this largest value, appropriately labeled*}. This will obviously be a WRITE statement, and its exact form can be determined by referring to the formal problem definition. The only other decision needed to be made before this WRITE statement can be written is what the variable name should be in which the largest value is to be stored. LARGEST would seem to be an appropriate choice.

```
WRITE ("The largest value is:", LARGEST)
```

The complete Level II then, would be

Level II

WRITE *("Enter three numbers, separated by commas:")*
READ *(NUM1, NUM2, NUM3)*
IF *NUM1 > NUM2*
THEN
    {compare NUM1 to NUM3}
ELSE
    {compare NUM2 to NUM3}
ENDIF
WRITE *("The largest value is:", LARGEST)*

Two comment statements still remain at this level, so a Level III will be needed. The first comment, *{compare NUM1 to NUM3}*, will result in another selection statement. There are two possibilities; either NUM1 will be larger than NUM3, or NUM3 will be larger than NUM1. In the first case, we want to store NUM1 in the variable LARGEST; in the second, we want to store NUM3 in the variable LARGEST. This would indicate that an IF-THEN-ELSE structure will be needed to replace the first comment. The comment, then, could be replaced with:

IF *NUM1 > NUM3*
THEN
    LARGEST ← NUM1
ELSE
    LARGEST ← NUM3
ENDIF

With this replacement made, Level III would look like this:

Level III

WRITE *("Enter three numbers, separated by commas:")*
READ *(NUM1, NUM2, NUM3)*
IF *NUM1 > NUM2*
THEN
    IF *NUM1 > NUM3*
    THEN
        LARGEST ← NUM1
    ELSE
        LARGEST ← NUM3
    ENDIF

```
ELSE
     {compare NUM2 to NUM3}
ENDIF
WRITE ("The largest value is:", LARGEST)
```

Notice that this second IF-THEN-ELSE structure is indented under the THEN clause of the first IF statement. This indicates that this second IF-THEN-ELSE statement is to be executed if and only if the first condition, NUM1 > NUM2, is true.

The second comment to be refined, {compare NUM2 to NUM3}, will also result in an IF-THEN-ELSE statement. The condition this time will need to be NUM2 > NUM3 or NUM3 > NUM2, with the appropriate assignment statements to assign the larger of the pair to LARGEST. If the first condition is chosen, the pseudocode refinement of this comment would be:

```
IF NUM2 > NUM3
THEN
     LARGEST ← NUM2
ELSE
     LARGEST ← NUM3
ENDIF
```

Inserting this in place of the comment it replaces, {compare NUM2 to NUM3}, a final Level III would be:

Level III

```
WRITE ("Enter three numbers, separated by commas:")
READ (NUM1, NUM2, NUM3)
IF NUM1 > NUM2
THEN
     IF NUM1 > NUM3
     THEN
          LARGEST ← NUM1
     ELSE
          LARGEST ← NUM3
     ENDIF
ELSE
     IF NUM2 > NUM3
     THEN
          LARGEST ← NUM2
```

```
        ELSE
            LARGEST ← NUM3
        ENDIF
    ENDIF
    WRITE ("The largest value is:", LARGEST)
```

Notice that this second IF-THEN-ELSE statement is indented under the ELSE clause of the first IF-THEN-ELSE statement, indicating that this comparison is to be made if and only if the first condition, NUM1 > NUM2, is false.

As was mentioned at the beginning of this problem, there are two very different ways to design a solution to the problem. Let's consider a second way. Returning to the previous Level I solution:

Level I

{enter three numbers}
{determine which of the three numbers is the largest}
{display this largest value, appropriately labeled}

the first comment would be refined in the same manner as in the first solution:

WRITE ("Enter three numbers, separated by commas:")
READ (NUM1, NUM2, NUM3)

The second comment, {determine which of the three numbers is the largest}, however, could be refined in a much different manner. Let's assume that the first number input, NUM1, is the largest value. This would be done by assigning the value of NUM1 to LARGEST:

LARGEST ← NUM1

The first part of Level II, then, would look like this:

Level II

WRITE ("Enter three numbers, separated by commas:")
READ (NUM1, NUM2, NUM3)
LARGEST ← NUM1

If in fact NUM1 is the largest value, the solution is completed, except for outputting the value of LARGEST. If, however, NUM2 is larger than the value currently stored in LARGEST, then LARGEST should be assigned the value of NUM2. This can be written as follows:

```
IF NUM2 > LARGEST
THEN
        LARGEST ← NUM2
ENDIF
```

In a like manner, the value of NUM3 needs to be compared to the value of LARGEST, and if it is larger, the value of NUM3 needs to be assigned to LARGEST:

```
IF NUM3 > LARGEST
THEN
        LARGEST ← NUM3
ENDIF
```

Placing these two revisions into our Level II solution and revising the last comment, {*display this largest value, appropriately labeled*}, as we did in the previous solution to the problem, we arrive at the following:

Level II

```
WRITE ("Enter three numbers, separated by commas:")
READ (NUM1, NUM2, NUM3)
LARGEST ← NUM1
IF NUM2 > LARGEST
THEN
        LARGEST ← NUM2
ENDIF
IF NUM3 > LARGEST
THEN
        LARGEST ← NUM3
ENDIF
WRITE ("The largest value is:", LARGEST)
```

This solution, which no doubt was not obvious at first, turns out to be the simpler, which can be easily seen if we look at diagrams of the logic contained in the two solutions. Flowcharts of the two solutions are provided in Figures 2.10 and 2.11 to graphically illustrate the difference between these two solutions. The logic of the second solution as shown in Figure 2.11 is certainly much simpler. The other advantage of this solution is that modifying the solution to work for four or more input values would be a minor addition. Modification of the first solution would be a major undertaking. Let's try another problem.

Given the following formal problem definition, perform a complete top-down design of this problem:

Figure 2.10   Flowchart of solution 1.

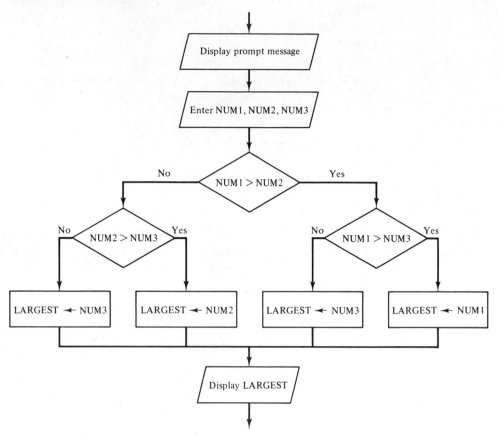

☐ **Formal Problem Definition**

General Description

A program is to be written to compute this year's fuel bill for a fuel oil customer. Also to be computed is next year's predicted bill (last year's bill increased by 10 percent), and the monthly budget payment amount based on next year's predicted bill.

Input Specifications

Input is to be the amounts of the fuel oil bills for this year, one value per line. This input is to be prompted by the message:

```
Enter this year's bills, one value per line.
Enter a value of 0 to indicate end of input.
```

Figure 2.11 Flowchart of solution 2.

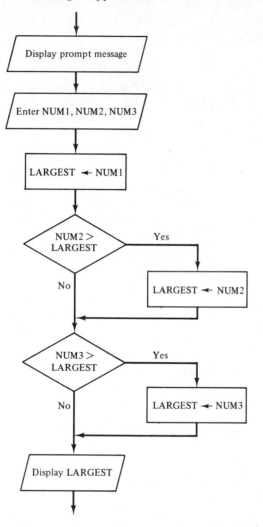

As the second line of the prompt indicates, end of input is indicated by entering a value of 0.

Output Specifications

There are to be three lines of output produced. The first line will be

```
This year's total bill = $ <bill>
```

where <bill> is the sum of the input values. The second line of output is to be

```
Next year's predicted bill = $ <new bill>
```

where <new bill> is next year's predicted bill (this year's bill increased by 10 percent). The third line of output is to be

```
Monthly budget payment amount = $ <budget>
```

where <budget> is the amount of the monthly budget payment, calculated by dividing next year's predicted bill by 12.

Normal Example

Input:

```
Enter this year's bills, one value per line.
Enter a value of 0 to indicate end of input.
?136.82
?185.45
?215.56
?209.63
?149.55
?0
```

Output:

```
This year's total bill = $ 897.01
Next year's predicted bill = $ 986.71
Monthly budget payment amount = $ 82.23
```

Unusual or Error Conditions

1. If more than one bill amount is entered on a line, only the first value will be used.
2. If a zero is not entered after the last bill amount, no output will be displayed.
3. Any bill amounts entered after a zero is entered will be ignored.

After reading over the formal problem definition carefully, and looking at the normal example in particular, it can be seen that the problem is comprised of two distinct parts. The first part involves entering the individual bill amounts and summing them up. Once this has been accomplished, the second part of the problem involves calculating certain values based upon the sum computed and performing some output operations. An appropriate Level I, then, might be

Level I

{enter and sum bill amounts}
{calculate predicted bill and budget payment}
{display results}

Hints as to how the first comment, {*enter and sum bill amounts*}, might be refined can be obtained from the input specifications section of the formal problem definition, as well as the input section of the normal example. Looking at these two sources of information, it can be seen that the first task is to display an input prompt. Then, since the number of bill amounts to be entered will vary, some type of loop will be needed. The appropriate choice of a looping structure for this problem would be a WHILE loop. The reason this type of loop would be selected rather than a FOR-NEXT loop is that an indeterminate loop is needed for this problem since it is not known when the loop is begun how many times it will be executed—it is dependent upon the input data. The loop will continue to be executed until an input value of 0 is encountered. Based upon this discussion and the normal example, a Level II refinement of this first comment might be

Level II

{*display input prompt*}
{*enter bill amount*}
WHILE {*bill amount not equal to zero*}
    {*add bill amount to total*}
    {*enter bill amount*}
ENDWHILE

A bill amount must be entered before the WHILE statement is first executed in order that bill amount has a value to be tested for zero in the conditional portion of the WHILE statement. This is an example of using the "priming read" structure discussed previously in this chapter.

Continuing the refinement of Level I, the next comment to be refined is {*calculate predicted bill and budget payment*}. This comment really involves two separate calculations, so it might be translated into:

{*calculate predicted bill by increasing
this year's bill by ten percent*}
{*calculate budget amount by dividing
predicted bill by 12*}

The last comment from Level I to be refined is {*display results*}. Looking at the output specifications section and the output section of the normal example, it becomes clear that there are really three values to be displayed—the total of this year's bills, the predicted bill for next year, and the budget amount. This last comment, then, could be refined as follows:

{display this year's total bill}
{display next year's predicted bill}
{display the monthly budget amount}

All three of these output lines, of course, would need to be appropriately labeled. The final form of Level II, then, would be

Level II

{display input prompt}
{enter bill amount}
WHILE *{bill amount not equal to zero}*
    {add bill amount to total}
    {enter bill amount}
ENDWHILE
{calculate predicted bill by increasing
 this year's bill by ten percent}
{calculate budget amount by dividing
 predicted bill by 12}
{display this year's total bill}
{display next year's predicted bill}
{display the monthly budget amount}

Progress is being made, but the solution is still not expressed in pseudocode, so another level is needed. The first comment to be refined is *{display input prompt}*. Looking at either the input specifications section or the input section of the normal example, it can be seen that two WRITE statements are needed; two WRITE statements since a two-line input prompt is to be displayed:

WRITE *("Enter this year's bills, one value per line.")*
WRITE *("Enter a value of 0 to indicate end of input.")*

The second comment to be refined is *{enter bill amount}*. A variable name is needed in which to store the bill amount; so we might choose BILL.AMOUNT? The pseudocode statement corresponding to this comment, then, would be

READ *(BILL.AMOUNT)*

The next comment is the condition of the WHILE statement, *{bill amount is not equal to zero}*. Using the variable name chosen for the READ statement above, this comment would become

BILL.AMOUNT <> 0

Placing this condition in the WHILE statement would result in

WHILE BILL.AMOUNT <> 0

{add bill amount to total}, the next comment to be refined, would become an assignment statement. A variable name needs to be selected in which to store the total of the BILL.AMOUNT's, so TOTAL might be used:

TOTAL ← TOTAL + BILL.AMOUNT

This statement means, "The previous value of TOTAL is increased by BILL-.AMOUNT, and the resulting sum is stored in TOTAL" or "TOTAL is replaced by the sum of the previous value of TOTAL and BILL.AMOUNT." This would cause TOTAL to contain a running sum of the values entered into the variable BILL.AMOUNT.

This assignment statement would seem to do what is needed, only there is one slight problem—what is the previous value of TOTAL the first time this statement is executed? In other words, when the first number stored in BILL.AMOUNT is added to TOTAL, what is the value of TOTAL at this point? Obviously, it should be zero; unfortunately, that assumption cannot be made. A modification needs to be made in the design. One of the first things we needed to do was to set TOTAL to 0. Back to Level II. Level II would now look like this, with the needed modification made:

Level II

{set TOTAL to zero}
{display input prompt}
{enter bill amount}
WHILE {bill amount not equal to zero}
    {add bill amount to total}
    {enter bill amount}
ENDWHILE
{calculate predicted bill by increasing
 this year's bill by ten percent}
{calculate budget amount by dividing
 predicted bill by 12}
{display this year's total bill}
{display next year's predicted bill}
{display the monthly budget amount}

Let's see what this corrected Level II looks like with the refinements made thus far:

Level II

{*set TOTAL to zero*}
WRITE (*"Enter this year's bills, one value per line."*)
WRITE (*"Enter a value of 0 to indicate end of input."*)
READ (BILL.AMOUNT)
WHILE BILL.AMOUNT <> 0
      TOTAL ← TOTAL + BILL.AMOUNT

Maybe it would be a good idea at this point, before going on, to refine the first comment just inserted, {*set TOTAL to zero*}, into pseudocode. A refinement of this would be

TOTAL ← 0

The next comment, {*enter bill amount*}, is also the same as a previous comment, so it results in

READ (BILL.AMOUNT)

Let's see how Level II looks now:

Level II

TOTAL ← 0
WRITE (*"Enter this year's bills, one value per line."*)
WRITE (*"Enter a value of 0 to indicate end of input."*)
READ (BILL.AMOUNT)
WHILE BILL.AMOUNT <> 0
      TOTAL ← TOTAL + BILL.AMOUNT
      READ (BILL.AMOUNT)
ENDWHILE
{*calculate predicted bill by increasing
 this year's bill by ten percent*}
{*calculate budget amount by dividing
 predicted bill by 12*}
{*display this year's total bill*}
{*display next year's predicted bill*}
{*display the monthly budget amount*}

The next comment that needs to be refined is {*calculate predicted bill by increasing this year's bill by ten percent*}. Since a calculation is to be performed, an assignment statement must be what is needed. A variable name must be selected in which to store next year's predicted bill. How about PREDICTED.BILL? The percentage of increase, 10 percent, also must be changed to its decimal equivalent, .10:

$$PREDICTED.BILL \leftarrow TOTAL + .10 * TOTAL$$

Another expression that could have been used to perform this calculation is 1.10 * TOTAL (110 percent of TOTAL is the same as TOTAL + 10 percent of TOTAL).

The calculation of the budget amount, which is the process contained in the next comment statement, could be performed by the following assignment statement:

$$BUDGET.AMOUNT \leftarrow PREDICTED.BILL / 12$$

The last three comment statements to be refined are all output statements, so they would all result in WRITE statements. The exact form of each can be determined by examining the output specifications and being sure to use the variable names used in the assignment statements above:

```
WRITE ("This year's total bill = $", TOTAL)
WRITE ("Next year's predicted bill = $", PREDICTED.BILL)
WRITE ("Monthly budget payment amount = $", BUDGET.AMOUNT)
```

The final pseudocode solution to the problem, then, would be

Level II

```
TOTAL ← 0
WRITE ("Enter this year's bills, one value per line.")
WRITE ("Enter a value of 0 to indicate end of input.")
READ (BILL.AMOUNT)
WHILE BILL.AMOUNT <> 0
    TOTAL ← TOTAL + BILL.AMOUNT
    READ (BILL.AMOUNT)
ENDWHILE
PREDICTED.BILL ← TOTAL + .10 * TOTAL
BUDGET.AMOUNT ← PREDICTED.BILL / 12
WRITE ("This year's total bill = $", TOTAL)
WRITE ("Next year's predicted bill = $", PREDICTED.BILL)
WRITE ("Monthly budget payment amount = $", BUDGET.AMOUNT)
```

Let's try a little more difficult problem. Suppose we take the second formal problem definition example from earlier in the chapter.

☐ Formal Problem Definition

General Description

Design and write a program to calculate the average of a set of input values. The number of values to be averaged will be the first input value, followed by the actual values themselves. Output is to consist of the number of values to be averaged and their average, both output values appropriately labeled.

Input Specifications

The first line of input is to be prompted by the message:

```
How many values are to be averaged?
```

The value entered in response to this prompt is to be a single whole number. Following this line will be as many lines of input as the initial whole number indicates. Each of these succeeding entries will be on a separate line, each prompted by the message:

```
Enter value
```

Output Specifications

There will be three lines of output produced. The first line will be:

```
The number of values to be averaged is: <n>
```

where <n> is the number entered in response to the prompt, "How many values are to be averaged?" This line is followed by a blank line, followed by the third and last line of output:

```
The average is: <a>
```

where <a> is the average of the values entered in response to the prompts, "Enter value." The average is calculated by adding these input values together and dividing that sum by the number of values (the first value entered).

Normal Example

Input:

```
How many values are to be averaged?
?4
Enter value
?2
```

```
Enter value
?2.5
Enter value
?-1
Enter value
?10.5
```

Output:

```
The number of values to be averaged is: 4

The average is: 3.5
```

Unusual or Error Conditions

1. If any nonnumeric values are entered, the system will respond with the message, "?Redo from start".
2. If the first input value is not a whole number, the noninteger portion of the value will be truncated.
3. If the first input value is less than one, the following message will be output:

```
Impossible to average fewer than one number!!
```

4. If fewer values are entered to be averaged than the first number entered specifies, no output will occur.
5. If more values are entered to be averaged than the first number entered specifies, the additional values will be ignored.

The first attempt at listing the steps to solve this problem might be as follows:

Level I

{get how many values are to be averaged}
IF {this value is less than one}
THEN
    {display error message}
ELSE
    {continue processing}
ENDIF}

Notice that this initial list of steps is primarily stated as a list of comments (statements enclosed in curly brackets). This list of steps was arrived at by carefully reading over the general description and then looking at the normal example. The first portion of the second statement,

```
IF {this value is less than one}
THEN
     {display error message}
```

was derived from the unusual or error conditions section. The third condition listed in this section indicates that we are to continue processing only if the first value entered is greater than or equal to one. Someone else might come up with a somewhat different list of steps, but they would no doubt be similar. The next step is to refine each of these comments into one or more statements that are more specific than the initial ones. Remember, the final goal is to arrive at a list of steps that is stated using only pseudocode statements.

The first comment, {*get how many values are to be averaged*}, implies the need for an input statement, since that is the type of statement that allows us to enter a number into the computer. A variable in which to store this value will also be necessary. This comment could be replaced with the pseudocode statement, READ (NUMBER.OF.VALUES). Looking at the normal example again, however, it is seen that the message, "How many values are to be averaged?" is to be displayed before the input is requested. This would seem to indicate that the first comment needs to be refined into two pseudocode statements—a WRITE statement followed by a READ statement. Level II, the next revision of the steps in the solution of the problem, therefore, might start out like this:

Level II

```
WRITE ("How many values are to be averaged?")
READ (NUMBER.OF.VALUES)
```

The second comment to be refined, {*this value is less than one*}, is the condition to be evaluated in the IF statement. Since a variable name to store the number of values has been already selected in the previous statement, the READ statement, it is apparent that the variable to be tested in the IF statement condition is the variable, NUMBER.OF.VALUES. The refinement of the comment form of the condition, {*this value is less than one*}, would be, then, NUMBER.OF.VALUES < 1. Putting this condition into the IF-THEN-ELSE structure yields the following refinement of the second comment.

```
IF NUMBER.OF.VALUES < 1
THEN
     {display an error message}
ELSE
     {continue processing}
ENDIF
```

The next comment to be translated into pseudocode is {*display an error message*}. This step is quite straightforward, as the only reasonable solution is a WRITE statement. Examining the third condition listed under Unusual or Error Conditions, we determine that the message to be written is "Impossible to average fewer than one number!!". If this change is included in the solution, Level II will now look like this:

Level II

WRITE ("How many values are to be averaged?")
READ (NUMBER.OF.VALUES)
IF NUMBER.OF.VALUES < 1
THEN
    WRITE ("Impossible to average fewer than one number!!")
ELSE
    {continue processing}
ENDIF

The fourth comment to be refined, {*continue processing*}, means that if a value greater than or equal to one has been entered for the number of values to be averaged, it makes sense to continue with the process of entering a set of values and calculating their average. Since this comment encompasses a rather large number of processes to be performed, it would be difficult to go directly from this extremely general comment right to pseudocode. It would be better to try to refine this comment into several, more specific comments. Looking at the normal example again, it can be seen that the steps involved in {*continue processing*} are:

{enter the values to be averaged and add them together}
{compute the average}
{display the number of values}
{display the average}

A final version of Level II, then, would be:

Level II

WRITE ("How many values are to be averaged?")
READ (NUMBER.OF.VALUES)
IF NUMBER.OF.VALUES < 1
THEN
    WRITE ("Impossible to average fewer than one number!!")

ELSE
    {enter the values to be averaged and add them together}
    {compute the average}
    {display the number of values}
    {display the average}
ENDIF

Another level is definitely going to be needed since all the steps listed in the ELSE clause are still in comment form. The first comment to be refined in Level III then is {enter the values to be averaged and add them together}. This comment implies that an input statement for each value to be entered, along with some type of statement to add the numbers together, is going to be needed. The only problem is, the number of individual input statements needed is going to be dependent upon the value entered in response to the prompt, "How many values are to be averaged?". If the value 4 is entered in response to this question, then 4 input statements will be needed; if the value 16 is entered, 16 input statements will be needed. We seem to have a problem. Perhaps a repetition statement might be the answer. Let's replace the comment, {enter these values and add them together}, with the comments, {repeat NUMBER.OF.VALUES times}, {enter a value}, and {add this value on to the total}. Level III would now look like this:

Level III

WRITE ("How many values are to be averaged?")
READ (NUMBER.OF.VALUES)
IF NUMBER.OF.VALUES < 1
THEN
    WRITE ("Impossible to average fewer than one number")
ELSE
    {repeat NUMBER.OF.VALUES times}
        {enter a value}
        {add this value on to the total}
    {compute the average}
    {display the number of values}
    {display the average}
ENDIF

Remember, since we have a repetition structure in the program, the statements inside the loop need to be indented.

The next comment from Level II to be refined is {compute the average}. Since a calculation is to be performed, this means an assignment statement is needed. This comment could be replaced by

AVERAGE ← {*the total of the numbers*} / NUMBER.OF.VALUES

Since a variable name has not yet been selected to hold the total of the numbers, its place in the formula is held by a comment, {*the total of the numbers*}.

The next comment, {*display the number of values*}, translates into a WRITE statement. Looking at the normal example again, this WRITE statement needs to output the message, "The number of values to be averaged is:", along with how many values were entered. This could be accomplished with the following statement:

WRITE (*"The number of values to be averaged is:"*, NUMBER.OF.VALUES)

The last comment to be refined is {*display the average*}. Again, this would be a WRITE statement that would display both a message and the value of the variable AVERAGE:

WRITE (*"The average is:"*, AVERAGE).

With these refinements included, Level III would now look like this:

Level III

WRITE (*"How many values are to be averaged?"*)
READ (NUMBER.OF.VALUES)
IF NUMBER.OF.VALUES < 1
THEN
    WRITE (*"Impossible to average fewer than one number!!"*)
ELSE
    {*repeat NUMBER.OF.VALUES times*}
        {*enter a value*}
        {*add this value on to the total*}
    AVERAGE ← {*the total of the numbers*} / NUMBER.OF.VALUES
    WRITE (*"The number of values to be averaged is:"*,
        NUMBER.OF.VALUES)
    WRITE (*"The average is:"*, AVERAGE)
ENDIF

Notice that the repetition portion includes only two statements, {*enter a value*}, and {*add this value on to the total*}. These are the only two processes that need to be repeated, so they are indented under the comment {*repeat NUMBER.OF.VALUES times*}. The assignment statement that computes the value of AVERAGE is only to be performed once, after all the values have been entered and summed, so it is not a part of the loop and is not indented. The final goal of a solution to the problem stated all in pseudocode is getting closer, but there are still comments included in Level III, so a fourth level will be needed.

The first comment to be refined for LEVEL IV, {*repeat NUMBER.OF-VALUES times*}, is found following the ELSE statement. The fact that a repetition structure is needed here has already been discussed; so the only question is whether a WHILE statement or a FOR-NEXT statement should be used. Since it is known at this point how many times the loop is to be repeated (NUMBER.OF.VALUES times), a FOR-NEXT statement would probably be best. The FOR statement portion would be

$$FOR\ COUNT\ =\ 1\ TO\ NUMBER.OF.VALUES$$

The variable name COUNT was selected to keep track of how many times the loop is repeated—any other name could have just as well been chosen.

The first comment inside the loop, {*enter a value*}, will be replaced by a READ statement, obviously, but looking at the normal example again indicates that an input prompt is to be provided for each of these inputs. A WRITE statement will also be needed. The comment {*enter a value*}, then, yields the following two pseudocode statements:

$$WRITE\ (\text{``Enter value''})$$
$$READ\ (VALUE)$$

The variable name VALUE was selected to store the input values as they are entered.

The other statement inside the loop, {*add this value on to the total*}, is going to take some work. A variable is needed to hold the total of the numbers. The name TOTAL would seem to be a logical choice. Since a calculation is to be performed (add), the pseudocode statement needed here would appear to be an assignment statement. The form of this statement would be:

$$TOTAL \leftarrow TOTAL + VALUE$$

This statement means, "The previous value of TOTAL is increased by VALUE, and then the resulting sum is stored in TOTAL." This would cause TOTAL to contain a running sum of the values entered into the variable VALUE.

This assignment statement would seem to do what is needed, only there is one slight problem—we forgot to initialize TOTAL to zero before entering the

FOR-NEXT loop. In other words, when the first number stored in VALUE is added to TOTAL, TOTAL needs to contain the value 0 at that point. A modification needs to be made in the design. Back to Level II. Level II would now look like this, with the needed modification made:

Level II

WRITE ("How many values are to be averaged?")
READ (NUMBER.OF.VALUES)
IF NUMBER.OF.VALUES < 1
THEN
    WRITE ("Impossible to average fewer than one number!!")
ELSE
    {set TOTAL to zero}
    {enter the values to be averaged and add them together}
    {compute the average}
    {display the number of values}
    {display the average}
ENDIF

Notice that the comment, *{set TOTAL to zero}*, has been inserted immediately following the ELSE statement. It is not necessary to set TOTAL to zero unless a valid number has been entered for NUMBER.OF.VALUES and the process of computing an average is to occur. This statement, however, could also have been placed anywhere before the IF statement and the program would work correctly. A correspondingly modified Level III, with the appropriate revision of the comment, *{set TOTAL to zero}*, would appear as follows:

Level III

WRITE ("How many values are to be averaged?")
READ (NUMBER.OF.VALUES)
IF NUMBER.OF.VALUES < 1
THEN
    WRITE ("Impossible to average fewer than one number!!")
ELSE
    TOTAL ← 0
    {repeat NUMBER.OF.VALUES times}
        {enter a value}
        {add this value on to the total}
    AVERAGE ← {the total of the numbers} / NUMBER.OF.VALUES

>   WRITE ("*The number of values to be averaged is:*",
>   *NUMBER.OF.VALUES*)
>   WRITE ("*The average is:*", *AVERAGE*)
>   *ENDIF*

Let's see what Level IV would look like with the refinements made thus far:

Level IV

WRITE ("How many values are to be averaged?")
READ (NUMBER.OF.VALUES)
IF NUMBER.OF.VALUES < 1
THEN
        WRITE ("Impossible to average fewer than one number!!")
ELSE
     TOTAL ← 0
     FOR COUNT = 1 TO NUMBER.OF.VALUES
          WRITE ("Enter value")
          READ (VALUE)
          TOTAL ← TOTAL + VALUE
     AVERAGE ← {the total of the numbers} / NUMBER.OF.VALUES
     WRITE ("The number of values to be averaged is:",
                NUMBER.OF.VALUES)
     WRITE ("The average is:", AVERAGE)
ENDIF

Only two things left to do. According to the general form of the FOR-NEXT statement, every time there is a FOR statement, there must be a next statement to indicate the end of the loop. A NEXT statement needs to be inserted just after the statement that adds up the values, *TOTAL ← TOTAL + VALUE*. There is also one comment left in the program that needs to be refined—{*the total of the numbers*}. Since a variable name to hold this value has now been selected, this comment can now be replaced with the variable name TOTAL. The final version of Level IV then would be

Level IV

WRITE ("How many values are to be averaged?")
READ (NUMBER.OF.VALUES)
IF NUMBER.OF.VALUES < 1
THEN

```
              WRITE ("Impossible to average fewer than one number!!")
         ELSE
              TOTAL ← 0
              FOR COUNT = 1 TO NUMBER.OF.VALUES
                   WRITE ("Enter value")
                   READ (VALUE)
                   TOTAL ← TOTAL + VALUE
              NEXT COUNT
              AVERAGE ← TOTAL / NUMBER.OF.VALUES
              WRITE ("The number of values to be averaged is:",
                        NUMBER.OF.VALUES)
              WRITE ("The average is:", AVERAGE)
         ENDIF
```

correct solution to the problem.

2.6 SUMMARY

The process of clearly defining a problem and then designing a solution using a
design language such as pseudocode is the foundation for writing correct, efficient
computer programs. The process of defining a problem can best be accomplished by
writing a formal problem definition, which consists of five parts:

1. A general description
2. Input specificiations
3. Output specifications
4. A normal example
5. Unusual or error conditions

Top-down design is a powerful technique for designing algorithms to solve
problems. This process, by which an initial solution to a problem stated in the form
of comments is restated more specifically at each of several levels through the
process of stepwise refinement is explained and demonstrated. The final level of the
solution is stated in pseudolanguage, which is a design language rather than a
programming language. Elements of programming style, such as the use of
indenting and meaningful variable names, are emphasized and illustrated.

EXERCISES

1. Why is it important to first spend time designing a solution to a problem rather than starting right off writing programming language statements?

2. List and briefly describe each of the five parts of a formal problem definition.

3. What are the only three basic control structures needed to design a solution to any problem that can be solved on a computer?

4. List the pseudocode statements that can be used to design a solution to a problem.

5. In which section of a formal problem definition would the following most likely be found?

    If the input value contains a comma—for example, the value 19,862—only the digits preceding the comma will be read as input.

6. Which of the following is a pseudocode selection statement?
    a. WHILE {condition}
    b. IF {condition} THEN
    c. variable ← expression
    d. READ(variable)
    e. Two of the above are selection statements

7. Which of the following would be a correct refinement of the comment:

    {output NUMBER if NUMBER is greater than zero;
    otherwise output only a zero}?

    a. WRITE (NUMBER)
       IF NUMBER < 0
       THEN
              WRITE ("0")
       ENDIF

    b. IF NUMBER > 0
       THEN
              WRITE (NUMBER − 0)
       ELSE
              WRITE (NUMBER)
       ENDIF

    c. IF NUMBER > 0
       THEN
              WRITE (NUMBER)
       ELSE
              IF NUMBER < 0
              THEN
                     WRITE ("0")
              ENDIF
       ENDIF

    d. IF NUMBER > 0
       THEN
              WRITE (NUMBER)
       ELSE
              WRITE ("0")
       ENDIF

    e. None of the above are correct

8. Which of the following is a correct pseudocode refinement of the comment:

    {compute interest as 12 percent of the unpaid balance}

    a. BALANCE * .12 > INTEREST
    b. READ (.12 * BALANCE)

    c. *IF INTEREST = .12 * BALANCE*
        THEN
            {compute interest}
    d. *INTEREST ← .12 * BALANCE*
    e. More than one of the above is correct

9. Which of the following would be a correct refinement of the comment:

   *{input three numbers, add them together, and
   output their sum}?*

   a. *A ← 10*
      B ← 4
      C ← 16
      SUM ← A + B + C
      WRITE (SUM)

   b. *READ (A)*
      READ (B)
      READ (C)
      D ← A + B + C
      WRITE (D)

   c. *WHILE I <= 2*
        READ (VALUE)
        SUM ← SUM + VALUE
      ENDWHILE
      WRITE (SUM)

   d. *SUM ← 0*
      FOR I = 1 TO 3
        READ (VALUE)
        SUM ← SUM + VALUE
      NEXT I

   e. None of the above are correct

10. Which of the following loops would execute exactly 10 times?

    a. *COUNTER ← 10*
      WHILE COUNTER >= 0
        WRITE ("HERE WE GO ONE TIME")
        COUNTER ← COUNTER − 1
      ENDWHILE

    b. *COUNTER ← 20*
      WHILE COUNTER >= 1
        WRITE ("HERE WE GO ONE TIME")
        COUNTER ← COUNTER − 2
      ENDWHILE

    c. *COUNTER ← 11*
      WHILE COUNTER > 1
        WRITE ("HERE WE GO ONE TIME")
        COUNTER ← COUNTER − 1
      ENDWHILE

11. Which of the following segments of pseudocode would be a correct solution to the
    following?

    Input is a single nonnegative integer that represents the number of directory
    assistance calls placed to the number 555-1212. Compute and display the total
    charges for directory assistance based upon a toll of $0.75 per call after three free
    calls.

    a. *READ ("How many directory assistance calls?")*
      TOTAL.CHARGE ← 0.75 * D.A.CALLS + 3 * FREE.CALLS
      WRITE ("TOTAL.CHARGE")

    b. *FREE.CALLS ← 3*
       READ (D.A.CALLS)
       IF D.A.CALLS > 3
       THEN
           *TOTAL.CHARGE ← 0.75 * (D.A.CALLS − FREE.CALLS)*
       ELSE
           TOTAL.CHARGE ← 0
       ENDIF
       WRITE (TOTAL.CHARGE)
    c. *COUNT ← 1*
       WHILE COUNT <= 3
          READ (FREE.CALL)
          COUNT ← COUNT + 1
       ENDWHILE
       READ (SINGLE.INTEGER)
       IF SINGLE.INTEGER = 555-1212
       THEN
           *TOTAL.CHARGE ← 0.75 * SINGLE.INTEGER*
       ENDIF
       WRITE (TOTAL.CHARGE)

12. The following pseudocode program was designed to be a solution to the following problem:

Write a program to sum a set of input values. The number of values to be added together will be entered first, followed by the values themselves. Output is to be the sum of the input values.

    COUNT ← 0
    SUM ← 0
    READ (HOW.MANY)
    WHILE VALUE >= 0
       READ (VALUE)
       SUM ← SUM + VALUE
       HOW.MANY ← HOW.MANY + 1
    ENDWHILE
    WRITE (COUNT)

There may be several errors in this solution.

  1. The condition in the WHILE statement, *VALUE > = 0* should be:

    a. *VALUE < HOW.MANY*
    b. *VALUE <> 0*
    c. *COUNT < HOW.MANY*
    d. *HOW.MANY > 0*
    e. The condition is correct as written

  2. The statement, *HOW.MANY ← HOW.MANY + 1* should be replaced with:

    a. *HOW.MANY ← HOW.MANY + VALUE*
    b. *HOW.MANY ← HOW.MANY + COUNT*

   d. $COUNT \leftarrow COUNT + 1$
   e. The statement is correct as written

3. The statement, $WRITE\ (COUNT)$, should be replaced with:

   a. $WRITE\ (SUM)$
   b. $READ\ (SUM)$
   c. $WRITE\ (HOW.MANY)$
   d. $READ\ (COUNT)$
   e. The statement is correct as written

13. Write a complete formal problem definition for the following generally stated problem. Supply any additional information needed:

   Read in a series of binary numbers and convert each to its decimal equivalent. Stop when a binary number of 0 is encountered. Display both the binary values and their decimal equivalents.

14. Write a complete formal problem definition for the following generally stated problem. Supply any additional information needed:

   The La Crosse artists club members produce mugs, cups, and flower pots. From time to time the club members put together their products and have a sale. Write an algorithm to determine the amount that each artist earns from the sale, and the total amount earned by the entire club from the sale. Mugs sell for $3.00, cups for $2.00, and flower pots for $1.50.

15. Write a complete formal problem definition for the following generally stated problem. Supply any additional information needed:

   Write a program to enter integer exam scores between 0 and 100, inclusive, and count and display the number of each letter grade assigned. Scores from 91 to 100 are A's, 81 to 90 are B's, 71 to 80 are C's, 61 to 70 are D's, and 0 to 60 are F's.

16. Perform a complete top-down design of the following problem:

General Description

A program is to be designed to help the Corny Seed Company determine and display the amount of seed corn needed by each of its customers, as well as the total bill for each customer. Three types of seed corn are sold by the company. To seed one acre, one would need:

   15 pounds of Type A seed at $1.50 per pound, or
   17 pounds of Type B seed at $1.30 per pound, or
   19 pounds of Type C seed at $1.00 per pound.

Also to be determined and displayed are the total number of pounds of each type of seed corn sold.

Input Specifications

Input consists of one line per customer, each line containing a three-digit customer charge number, a character indicating the seed type ordered (A, B, or C), and an integer indicating the number of acres to be planted in corn. These values are separated by commas. End of input is indicated by a customer charge number of 000.

Output Specifications

Output is to consist of one line per input line, except for the last (customer charge number of 000), containing the customer charge number, total pounds of seed corn needed, and total charge (pounds needed * cost per pound). Totals are to be accumulated for the total number of pounds of Type A, total number of pounds of Type B, and total number of pounds of Type C seed corn sold. These total are to be printed following two blank lines after the last input line has been processed:

```
TYPE A: XXXX
TYPE B: XXXX
TYPE C: XXXX
```

Normal Example

```
Input:                          Output:
  367,B,50                        367    850    1275.00
  294,C,45                        294    855     855.00
  242,A,190                       242   2850    4275.00
  196,A,250                       196   3750    5625.00
  188,F,390                       INVALID TYPE
  113,B,100                       113   1700    2210.00
  142,C,100                       142   1900    1900.00
  000,B,800

                                  TYPE A: 6600
                                  TYPE B: 2250
                                  TYPE C: 2755
```

Unusual or Error Conditions:

1. Extra input values per line are ignored.
2. If the input is entered in the wrong order, the message, "?Redo from start", will be displayed by the system.
3. If any type other than A, B, or C is entered, the error message, "INVALID TYPE", is to be displayed.
4. If negative values are entered for acreage, they will be processed as if correct.

17. Perform a complete top-down design of the following problem:

General Description

Leon County Traffic Court has the following fine schedule for speeders:

MPH over speed limit	Fine	MPH over speed limit	Fine
0–10	$ 35	21–40	105
11–20	65	Over 40	150

Write a program to enter a single value that is the MPH over the speed limit and calculate the fine using the table. Display both the MPH over the speed limit and the amount of the fine, appropriately labeled.

Input Specifications

Input will consist of a single-integer value representing the number of MPH over the speed limit the speeder was going. This input should be prompted by the message:

```
Enter MPH over speed limit:
```

Output Specifications

There will be two lines of output produced by the program. The first line will be:

```
MPH OVER SPEED LIMIT: <MPH over>
```

where <MPH over> is replaced by the input value. The second line of output displayed will be

```
FINE: <fine>
```

where <fine> is replaced by the amount of the fine determined by using the table given in the general description.

Normal Example

Input:

```
Input MPH over speed limit:
?37
```

Output:

```
MPH OVER SPEED LIMIT: 37
FINE: 105
```

Unusual or Error Conditions

1. If more than one value is entered, only the first value will be accepted—the rest will be ignored.
2. If a negative number is entered, it will be processed as though it were in the 0–10 MPH over range.
3. If characters are entered along with the number of MPH over, the system message, "?Redo from start", will be displayed and the MPH over must be reentered.

18. Perform a complete top-down design of the following problem:

General Description

A computer controlled machine tool is making parts that are to be 0.025 ± 0.002 inch in diameter. On a random basis, a part produced by the machine is measured to determine if the diameters of the parts being manufactured still meet specifications. If three parts measured in a row are too large or three parts in a row are too small, the machine is halted so it can be readjusted. At this time, a message indicating why the machine was halted is displayed, as well as the total number of parts sampled before the machine went out of adjustment and was halted. (Note: Three parts in a row must be too large or three parts in a row must be too small before the machine is halted. If parts alternate from too large to too small, the machine is *not* considered out of adjustment.)

Input Specifications

Input will consist of a series of decimal values representing the diameter of each part measured, one value per line.

Output Specifications

Output will consist of two lines. The first line will be one of the following two messages:

```
Machine set too high
```

or

```
Machine set too low
```

The second line will be:

```
Total parts processed = <total parts>
```

where <total parts> is replaced by the number of total parts sampled before three parts in a row larger than 0.027 or three parts in a row smaller than 0.023 were counted.

Normal Example

Input: Output:

```
      .026                              Machine set too low
      .024                              Total parts processed = 13
      .025
      .027
      .029
      .028
      .025
      .022
      .022
      .029
```

```
.021
.022
.020
```

Unusual or Error Conditions

1. If more than one diameter is entered per line, only the first value is processed —the rest are ignored.
2. If character data is entered, the message, "`?Redo from start`", will be output by the computer system, and the diameter must be reentered.

CHAPTER 3

Introduction to BASIC

The last chapter indicated that once a solution to a problem had been designed in pseudocode, it is a relatively simple matter to translate that solution into a particular programming language. This and succeeding chapters will explain the process of converting pseudocode statements into BASIC language statements. The general format used by all BASIC language statements is presented in this chapter, along with an explanation of how the translation of the pseudocode WRITE, assignment, and comment statements into their equivalent BASIC language statements is performed. A number of technical details involved in entering, modifying, and executing programs on a particular computer must also be mastered before the computer becomes a particularly useful tool. The majority of these details will be discussed and illustrated in this chapter; the rest will be covered in subsequent chapters as they are needed.

3.0 OBJECTIVES

After completing this chapter, you should be able to:

1. Write the general form of a BASIC statement.

2. List and use the rules for forming variable names in BASIC.

3. Translate a pseudocode assignment statement into its equivalent BASIC language form.

4. Translate pseudocode WRITE statements into equivalent BASIC language PRINT statements.

5. Translate pseudocode comment statements into equivalent BASIC language REM statements.

6. Make use of the BASIC language interpreter to enter, correct, and execute a BASIC program.

7. Use the BASIC interpreter commands to list, save, retrieve, modify, and delete programs.

3.1A FIRST BASIC PROGRAM

BASIC is a programming language originally developed by John Kemeny and Thomas Kurtz of Dartmouth College in the early 1960s for use on time-shared computer systems. It is easy to use, yet quite powerful, and has become even more popular with the widespread use of microcomputers, since a BASIC language interpreter is furnished with nearly all microcomputers. Unfortunately, BASIC today comes in many different dialects, which means that BASIC programs written to execute on one particular microcomputer may very well not run on some other machine. The Microsoft implementation of BASIC found on the IBM-PC and IBM-PS/2 families of microcomputers is a particularly powerful version of BASIC, with features that permit programs to be written that are truly structured. All program examples in this book are written in Microsoft BASIC.

Let's take a look at a simple BASIC program:

```
100   FEET = 3
110   INCHES = 4
120   LENGTH.IN.INCHES = 12 * FEET + INCHES
130   LENGTH.IN.CM = 2.54 * LENGTH.IN.INCHES
140   PRINT FEET "feet," INCHES "inches equals"
150   PRINT LENGTH.IN.CM "centimeters."
```

This program consists of six instructions, or statements. Each statement is on a separate line and is preceded by a line number. The line numbers tell the computer in what order the instructions are to be performed. The lowest-numbered statement (100) will be executed first, then the next lowest, etc. Two different types of

statements are found in this BASIC program. The first four statements are all
assignment statements—just as in pseudocode, they are used to assign a constant
value or the value of an expression to a variable. The last two instructions in the
program are *output statements*, which are used to display messages and/or the values
of variables on the computer's output device (in the following discussions, it will be
assumed that a CRT screen is the output device being used). The BASIC language
PRINT statement is equivalent to the pseudocode WRITE statement. The
statement,

```
100  FEET = 3
```

assigns the value 3 to the variable FEET. Likewise, the statement,

```
110  INCHES = 4
```

stores the value 4 in the memory location named by the variable INCHES. The
next statement,

```
120  LENGTH.IN.INCHES = 12 * FEET + INCHES
```

performs a calculation and assigns the result to the variable LENGTH.IN.
INCHES. The last assignment statement in the program,

```
130  LENGTH.IN.CM = 2.54 * LENGTH.IN.INCHES
```

performs another calculation, changing a length in inches to a length in
centimeters, and stores this result in LENGTH.IN.CM.

The two PRINT statements display the original length in feet and inches and
its equivalent length in centimeters, appropriately labeled, on the screen. Notice
how quotation marks are used in the PRINT statement just as they are in the
pseudocode WRITE statement to display messages. Parentheses, however, are not
needed around the list of items to be displayed by a PRINT statement as they are in
a pseudocode WRITE statement. The first PRINT statement,

```
140  PRINT FEET "feet," INCHES "inches equals"
```

instructs the computer to display the value of the variable FEET, the message 'feet,',
the value of the variable INCHES, and the message 'inches equals' on the screen.
The second PRINT statement,

```
150  PRINT LENGTH.IN.CM "centimeters."
```

indicates that the second line of output is to be the value of the variable LENGTH.IN.CM, followed by the message 'centimeters.'.

If this program were to be executed by the computer, the following would be displayed on the screen:

```
3 feet, 4 inches equals
101.6 centimeters.
```

As you can see, each PRINT statement causes a separate line of output to be displayed. An automatic carriage return and line feed occur at the end of each PRINT statement.

General Form of a BASIC Statement

All BASIC statements have the following general form:

```
line # [BASIC control word] [constant or expression]
```

Note: the square brackets indicate an item is optional. The *line #* part of the general form of the statement is an integer value that indicates the order in which statements in a BASIC program are to be executed. Normal order of execution is from the lowest-numbered statement through the highest-numbered statement in sequential order.

The *[BASIC control word]* portion of the statement is a single word that states the operation or procedure the instruction is to perform, that is, PRINT, INPUT, etc. In some BASIC statements, the control word is optional, as indicated by the square brackets ([ ]) which enclose this portion of the general form.

The *[constant or expression]* portion of the statement is a constant, variable, or expression upon which the operation or procedure listed in the control word portion of the instruction is to be performed. For example, in the BASIC statement:

```
10  PRINT SUM
```

the BASIC control word PRINT is an operation to be performed on the variable SUM. This particular statement would display (the operation) the value of SUM (a variable) on the screen. The [constant or expression] portion of the general form is also optional, as is indicated by the square brackets.

The BASIC assignment statement has an optional [BASIC control word] in the Mircosoft version of BASIC. The word LET may be included in the assignment statement. Thus the assignment statement, 20 A = 5, may also be written 20 LET A =

5. In this form, the [BASIC control word] is LET and the [constant or expression] portion of the statement is A = 5.

In the statement 45 PRINT the optional [constant or expression] portion of the general form is omitted. This PRINT statement causes a blank line to be displayed on the screen.

A single BASIC statement may be a maximum of 255 characters long, including the line number. Multiple statements may be placed on a single line, separated by colons (:), as long as they do not, collectively, exceed the 255 character maximum statement length. This feature should be used sparingly since it tends to make programs more difficult to read and understand.

Line Numbers

As mentioned in the previous section, each BASIC statement must be preceded by a line number. Line numbers indicate the normal order in which statements in a BASIC program are performed—the statement with the lowest line number first, the statement with the next lowest line number next, etc. Line numbers in Microsoft BASIC must be integers (whole numbers) in the range 0 to 65529, inclusive.

Statements in a BASIC program are often numbered in multiples of 10 (10, 20, 30, etc.) to allow statements to be inserted between the original program statements without the entire program having to be renumbered. For example, if the statements in a program were numbered 1, 2, 3, etc., and it became necessary to insert a statement between the statements numbered 2 and 3, this would not be possible without renumbering the entire program, since line numbers must be whole numbers, and there is no whole number between 2 and 3.

Variable Names

A *variable name* is a string of characters that refers to a location in memory in which a constant may be stored. Variable names in Microsoft BASIC may be up to 255 characters in length. A variable name this long, however, would be of little use. It could not even be used in a BASIC statement since the maximum length of a BASIC statement can only be 255 characters including the line number.

If a variable name is more than 40 characters in length, only the first 40 characters are significant. This means that if two variable names are identical in the first 40 characters of each, and differ only in character positions beyond the 40th character, the BASIC interpreter will not recognize them as being different names. For all practical purposes, this restriction should not cause any difficulties in selecting meaningful variable names.

The only characters that may be used to form variable names are the letters of the alphabet (A through Z), the digits (0 through 9), and the period. Variable names must start with a letter and may not contain any embedded blanks. Variable names may be typed in either upper- or lowercase—the BASIC interpreter automatically shifts all lowercase alphabetic characters in variable names to uppercase.

Certain special characters that identify the type of variable are also allowed as the last character of the name. For example, a variable name with a $ as its last character means that the variable will be used to store characters (letters, punctuation symbols, etc.) rather than numbers. If one of these special characters is not used as the last character of a variable name, the variable is understood to be a numeric variable (a variable that stores numbers).

There are some words or combinations of letters that fit all the above rules and still cannot be used as variable names. These are referred to as *reserved words* and have already been defined by the BASIC language interpreter to serve specific purposes. Examples of reserved words would be INPUT and PRINT. A list of all the reserved words may be found in Appendix A.

Many versions of the BASIC language allow only a single letter, or a single letter followed by a single digit, to be used for variable names. Since Microsoft BASIC permits longer variable names to be used, meaningful variable names may be chosen for use in programs, which makes programs much easier to read and understand. Be sure to take advantage of this useful feature!

3.2 ASSIGNMENT STATEMENTS

Assignment statements in BASIC are of the general form:

```
line# [LET] <variable> = <constant, variable, or
expression>
```

As with all BASIC statements, the first entry must be a line number. The next item in an assignment statement is the optional word LET (remember, square brackets ([ ]) are used to indicate a feature is optional). The word LET, if used, is followed by a variable name, then an = sign, and finally, a constant, variable, or expression. The = sign in the BASIC language assignment statement has the same meaning as the ← in pseudocode, "the value of the variable to the left of the assignment operator is replaced by the value of the constant, variable, or expression on the right." For example, the pseudocode assignment statement:

$$TOTAL \leftarrow NUM1 + NUM2 + NUM3$$

could be replaced by the BASIC statement:

```
100  TOTAL = NUM1 + NUM2 + NUM3
```

In both statements, the value of the variable TOTAL is to be replaced by the value of the expression, NUM1 + NUM2 + NUM3.

Variables may store characters as well as numeric values. If the variable on the left side of the assignment operator is a character string variable (the last character of the variable name is a $), the assignment statement may be used to store a character string constant in that variable. A character string constant is a group of characters enclosed in quotation marks. For example, the assignment statement:

```
110  CITY$ = "La Crosse"
```

stores the character string constant, La Crosse, in the character string variable, CITY$. This character string constant consists of nine characters. The embedded blank in the name of the city is considered to be a character and part of the character string constant. The quotation marks that precede and follow the string are not stored in CITY$. Their purpose is to *delimit* the string (indicate where it begins and ends), and they are not part of the string constant itself.

A particularly useful type of assignment statement often used in programming is one in which the same variable appears on both sides of the assignment operator. For example, the pseudocode assignment statement:

$$NUMBER.OF.SCORES \leftarrow NUMBER.OF.SCORES + 1$$

or its BASIC language equivalent:

```
120  NUMBER.OF.SCORES = NUMBER.OF.SCORES + 1
```

might be used as a "counting statement" in a program. The effect of both of these statements is the same; the value of the variable NUMBER.OF.SCORES is increased by 1 each time the statement is executed.

When a statement such as this is used in a program, it is always necessary to "initialize", or "set the variable which appears on both sides of the assignment operator to zero," early in the program. "Early" means before this assignment statement is executed the first time. Otherwise, the first time this statement is encountered, the variable that is being incremented will not have an initial value assigned to it. How can 1 be added to a value that does not exist?

Some versions of BASIC, including the Microsoft version, automatically assign zero to all variables initially, but it is not good practice to rely on this occurring, particularly since some versions of BASIC, and many other languages, do not perform this automatic initialization. A good rule, then, is to always assign an initial value to all variables that appear on both sides of assignment operators in assignment statements. This assignment of initial values to such variables may be accomplished with either assignment statements or input statements.

3.3 PRINT STATEMENTS

The PRINT statement in BASIC is used to display information on the standard output device. It is the equivalent of the pseudolanguage WRITE statement, and has the following general form:

```
line # PRINT [<constants, variables, and/or expressions>]
```

When this statement is executed, whatever follows the word PRINT is displayed on the screen. Notice that the square brackets indicate that it is optional that anything need follow the word PRINT. As was mentioned before, if nothing follows the word PRINT, a blank line will be output on the display screen by this statement.

If a numeric constant is to be displayed, it may simply be listed following the word PRINT. For example:

```
20  PRINT 7
```

would cause the number 7 to be displayed on the screen, one column to the right of the left screen margin. The first column in the print field is reserved for a negative sign should it be needed. If two or more numeric constants are to be displayed, they would be listed separated by semicolons. Additional spaces between the values in the PRINT statement do not change the spacing when the values are output. For example, the two PRINT statements below would produce exactly the same output:

```
30  PRINT 34;45;56
40  PRINT 34;    45;        56
```

There will be two spaces between the output values regardless of the number of spaces left between the constants.

If a string constant (a group of characters) is to be displayed, the string must be preceded and followed by quotation marks ("). For example, if it was desired to output the message Have a nice day! on the screen, the following PRINT statement could be used:

```
50  PRINT "Have a nice day!"
```

When this statement is executed, the message, without the quotation marks, will be displayed starting in the first column on the left side of the screen. Unlike when numeric constants are output, a column will not be reserved for a possible negative sign.

A string constant can contain digits just as well as letters or other nonnumeric characters. The quotation marks around the digits are what makes a string of digits a string constant rather than a numeric constant. For example, if the following PRINT statement was executed:

```
120  PRINT "123"
```

the characters 123 would be displayed starting in the first column of the screen:

```
123
```

It would not be necessary to reserve the first column for a possible negative sign as is necessary with a numeric constant since in this case the digits 123 are not treated as a number but rather as a group of characters. The major difference between a numeric constant and a string constant consisting of numeric digits is that arithmetic computations may be performed with a numeric constant, but not with a string constant.

If more than one string constant is to be displayed by a single PRINT statement, each string must be enclosed in quotation marks and separated from the other string constants by at least one space and/or a semicolon. Inclusion of several spaces between the strings does not have any different effect than a single space—the space is a separator, not a spacing device. When a PRINT statement containing several string constants is executed, the strings will be displayed without the quotation marks and with no spaces between them. If spaces are desired between the strings, they must be included within the quotation marks that delimit the strings. For example, if the string constants "Joe", "Fred", and "Bill" are to be output on a single line with one PRINT statement, the statement:

```
60  PRINT "Joe" "Fred" "Bill"
```

would cause the display of:

```
JoeFredBill
```

The PRINT statement:

```
70  PRINT "Joe"      "Fred"      "Bill"
```

would still produce:

```
JoeFredBill
```

If two spaces are desired between each name, the two spaces must be included inside the quotations marks, as is done in the PRINT statement below:

```
80  PRINT "Joe  " "Fred  " "Bill"
```

This statement would produce the following line of output:

```
Joe  Fred  Bill
```

Another way to produce this output would be to use the statement:

```
80  PRINT "Joe  Fred  Bill"
```

If the value of a variable is to be displayed rather than constants, the name of the variable must not be enclosed in quotation marks. The following segment of BASIC code:

```
100  TEMPERATURE = -10
110  PRINT TEMPERATURE
```

would produce, when executed:

```
-10
```

If, however, statement 110 read:

```
110  PRINT "TEMPERATURE"
```

the output would be

```
TEMPERATURE
```

The values of more than one variable may be displayed by a single PRINT statement by listing the names of the variables, separated by at least one space, or a semicolon. The short BASIC program that follows:

```
120   EMPLOYEE.NAME$ = "Richard Jones"
130   HOURS.WORKED = 23
140   PAY.RATE = 11.45
150   GROSS.PAY = HOURS.WORKED * PAY.RATE
160   PRINT EMPLOYEE.NAME$; GROSS.PAY
```

would produce the following output:

```
Richard Jones 263.35
```

If it were desired to have more spaces between the name of the employee and the amount of the gross pay, the following PRINT statement could be used in place of the one above:

```
160   PRINT EMPLOYEE.NAME$; "       "; GROSS.PAY
```

This PRINT statement indicates that three items are to be displayed: the employee's name, a string constant consisting of seven blank spaces, and the amount of gross pay. Execution of this statement would cause the following to be displayed:

```
Richard Jones       263.35
```

The PRINT statement can also be used to output the value of an expression. For example, the PRINT statement below:

```
170   PRINT 2 * 3 — 5
```

would output:

```
1
```

As can be seen from the above example, if an expression appears in a PRINT statement, the value of the expression is first calculated and then this value is displayed. More features of the PRINT statement will be discussed in the next chapter.

To briefly review, a pseudocode WRITE statement is converted to its BASIC language equivalent, a PRINT statement, by:

1. Replacing the word WRITE with the word PRINT.

2. Parentheses enclosing the information to be output by a WRITE statement are removed, as they are not needed in a PRINT statement.
3. Items in a PRINT statement are separated by a single space or a semicolon (;) rather than a comma (,) as they are in a WRITE statement.

3.4 REM STATEMENTS—PROGRAM DOCUMENTATION

Another type of BASIC statement frequently used is the REM, or remark, statement. This statement allows the programmer to add explanatory remarks to the program listing without having these comments displayed during program execution. The REM statement, then, is not an *executable statement*—it has no effect on the output produced by the program when the program is executed. There are two general forms of this statement:

```
line # REM [<programmer comments>]
```

and

```
line # ' [<programmer comments>]
```

Examples of remark statements would be

```
180  REM This statement is a remark statement
```

and

```
190  ' This is also a remark statement
```

One situation where this statement is often used is at the beginning of a program to provide a brief description of the purpose and operation of the program. The date the program was written and the name of the programmer are also often included in this initial section. You should decide on a standard format for this identifying information and use it with all programs you write.

Pseudocode comment statements are converted to their BASIC language equivalents, REM statements, by inserting the word REM, or a single quotation mark ('), in front of each pseudocode comment, and deleting the curly brackets ({ }) from around each comment. For example, the pseudocode comment,

{This section of the program computes gross pay}

would become

```
20  REM This section of the program computes gross pay
```

or

```
20  '  This section of the program computes gross pay
```

3.5 THE END STATEMENT

If the computer encounters an END statement in a BASIC program during program execution, program operation halts. The general form of this statement is

```
line # END
```

Microsoft BASIC, unlike many versions of BASIC, does not require that a program have an END statement as the last statement in the program. It is purely optional. If an END statement is not included in a Microsoft BASIC program, when the last statement (the highest-numbered statement) in the program is executed, program execution stops. When a program has finished executing, the prompt "OK" will be displayed on the screen following the last line of output to indicate that program execution has been completed.

3.6 THE PROGRAMMING ENVIRONMENT

A computer program is of little practical use until it is entered into a computer and executed by that computer. As you may recall from Chapter 1, a computer can directly understand and execute only programs written in machine language (a programming language consisting of only 0's and 1's). When programs are written in a high-level language such as BASIC, they must be translated into machine language before they can be executed by the computer. A *BASIC interpreter* performs this translation of BASIC language program statements into equivalent machine language statements for us, one BASIC language instruction at a time, and then executes these equivalent machine language instructions. Different computers use different methods of entering BASIC programs into main memory and executing them. We shall discuss how this process is performed on IBM microcomputers using the BASIC language interpreter.

Using the BASIC Interpreter

A BASIC language interpreter program is furnished with the IBM-PC and the IBM-PS/2. There are actually three different versions of the BASIC interpreter on the IBM: Cassette BASIC, Disc BASIC, and Advanced BASIC. Cassette BASIC resides in ROM (read only memory). If a DOS (Disk Operating System) diskette is not inserted in drive A: before the computer is turned on, the computer system being used is not equipped with at least one diskette drive, or a copy of DOS is not on the hard disk if the computer being used has a hard disk, the computer automatically loads Cassette BASIC into main memory.

Disk BASIC and Advanced BASIC are furnished along with DOS on the DOS diskette. These two more powerful versions of BASIC, which are accessed from DOS, contain the features of Cassette BASIC, plus additional capabilities. For purposes of simplicity, our discussions in the text will assume that Advanced BASIC is being used.

Cassette BASIC, as mentioned above, is the simplest version of the BASIC interpreter furnished with the IBM-PC and IBM-PS/2. This program is permanently stored in ROM (read only memory) and is the only version of BASIC available if the computer being used does not have a diskette drive. Cassette BASIC is entered on this type of system by simply turning on the power to the computer.

On a microcomputer that does have a diskette drive attached, Cassette BASIC is accessed by turning on the computer without having a DOS diskette inserted in drive A: or a copy of DOS on the hard disk. When Cassette BASIC is loaded, the first display on the screen will be a copyright notice followed by the words, "Version C", the release number, and the number of bytes of memory available for use by a BASIC program (a *byte* is the amount of memory needed to store one character of information).

When Cassette BASIC is used, the only storage device that may be used for storing programs and data is a cassette tape recorder. Even if the microcomputer system being used has one or more diskette drives attached to it or a hard disk, once Cassette BASIC has been invoked, the disk drives may not be used for data and program storage or retrieval.

The *Disk BASIC* version of the BASIC interpreter may be used if the microcomputer system being used has one or more disk drives and the IBM Personal Computer Disk Operating System (DOS) has been purchased. The Disk BASIC interpreter program is furnished as one of the programs on the DOS diskette. This program is loaded into the computer's memory in the following manner:

1. First, DOS must be started. This is done by inserting the DOS diskette into drive A: (remember, this is the drive on the left, or the one on the top) and closing the drive door *before* turning on the power to the machine. If your computer has a hard-disk drive, no diskette should be in

the floppy diskette drive when the power is turned on—this causes DOS to be loaded from the hard disk.

2. Once the computer is started, it may request that the current date and time be entered. This information may be entered, or you may respond to these requests by simply pressing the Enter key.

3. The DOS prompt will then be displayed on the screen:

   A> (or C>, if the computer has a hard-disk drive) ·

4. The command BASIC is typed in response to this prompt and the Enter key is pressed:

   A> BASIC (or C> BASIC)

5. Disk BASIC will then be loaded from the DOS diskette or the hard disk and the message, "Version D", the release number, and the number of free bytes will be displayed on the screen.

Disk BASIC allows the user to store and retrieve programs and data to and from diskette and hard disk as well as cassette. Information storage and retrieval is much faster in Disk BASIC using the diskette or hard-disk based storage system than it is with the tape cassette system.

Advanced BASIC contains all the features of Cassette and Disk BASIC plus some additional capabilities such as:

1. *Event trapping*—a program can be written to sense the occurrence of specific events, and branch to a particular program statement upon this occurrence.

2. *Advanced graphics*—additional graphics statements are included that permit more complex graphic designs to be created easily.

3. *Advanced music support*—more sophisticated audio output may be included in programs.

Like Disk BASIC, the Advanced BASIC interpreter program is furnished on the DOS diskette. To start advanced BASIC, DOS must be loaded as explained above for Disk BASIC, and the command BASICA entered in response to the DOS prompt, A> (or C>)

   A> BASICA (or C> BASICA)

When the Enter key is pressed, the system will respond with the message, "Version A", the release number, and the number of bytes available in the work area in which to store a program and/or data.

Once whichever version of BASIC is to be used is loaded, and after the version, release number, and number of free bytes has been displayed, the screen will display the word "Ok". This "Ok" prompt means the system is at command level and is awaiting a command telling it what to do. At this level, two modes of operation are possible: *direct mode* and *indirect mode.*

The *direct mode* of operation causes a statement that is entered to be executed immediately. This mode of operation is specified by *not* using a line number on the statement entered. For example, if the statement:

```
PRINT 3 * 10 + 4
```

were entered, as soon as the Enter key is pressed after this statement is typed, the computer will display 34, the value of the expression. This mode of operation is useful for performing quick computations without having to write a complete program. The major shortcoming of this mode is that the statements entered in this mode are not saved as part of a program, and if needed again, must be typed in again.

The *indirect mode* of operation is indicated to the BASIC interpreter by preceding each statement with a line number. The statements entered in the indirect mode are not executed until the command RUN is entered. For example, the lines below show the sequence of input and output that would occur in indirect mode:

```
20  PRINT 3 * 10 + 4
RUN
  34
Ok
```

The program, which in the above example consists of a single statement, is saved in memory and can be transferred to diskette or cassette storage. It may be executed again by simply typing the RUN command once more.

The Work Area

Regardless of how much random-access memory has been installed on the particular microcomputer you are using, a maximum of 64K bytes of memory may be used by the Microsoft BASIC interpreter. This memory area is used for program and data storage, to hold the values of variables, and to provide a work space for the BASIC interpreter itself to use. This memory area in which BASIC programs can reside is called the *work area.* This is the area into which programs may be entered by typing them in from the keyboard or retrieving them from cassette, diskette, or hard disk storage.

A program that currently resides in the work area may be modified, listed (the statements that comprise the program may be displayed on the screen or printer), or executed. When power to the computer is interrupted, the contents of the work area are lost, so if a program in the work area will be needed later, a copy of it must be saved on the cassette, diskette, or hard disk storage system before the computer is turned off. Instructions as to how this can be done are provided later in this chapter.

Inserting, Deleting, and Replacing Statements

Additional statements may be inserted into a BASIC program by selecting line numbers for these statements which are between the line numbers of the statements where the insertion is desired. For example, suppose we have the following BASIC program:

```
10  NUM1 = 10
20  NUM2 = 20
30  PRODUCT = NUM1 * NUM2
40  PRINT SUM, PRODUCT
```

After this program has been typed in, we notice that we forgot to calculate the value of SUM. It is necessary to compute this value prior to statement 40 where it is to be displayed. Suppose we decide that a statement to compute SUM should be inserted between statement 20 and statement 30. A line number between these two line numbers is chosen for this new statement, perhaps 25, and the needed statement is typed in with this line number. The screen would now show this:

```
10  NUM1 = 10
20  NUM2 = 20
30  PRODUCT = NUM1 * NUM2
40  PRINT SUM, PRODUCT
25  SUM = NUM1 + NUM2
```

If we would now ask the computer to list the program on the screen by typing the command LIST, the program would appear as follows:

```
LIST
10  NUM1 = 10
20  NUM2 = 20
25  SUM = NUM1 + NUM2
30  PRODUCT = NUM1 * NUM2
40  PRINT SUM, PRODUCT
```

As you can see above, the computer has reordered the statements according to the line numbers, and placed the new statement, 25, where it belongs in numeric sequence. Obviously, any number between 20 and 30 could have been chosen for the line number for this new line, but 25 was chosen so that if additional statements need to be inserted between 20 and 30, there is room for them both before and after the new statement.

You may delete statements from a program by typing the line number of the statement to be deleted and pressing the Enter key. For example, if the following program had been entered:

```
10  NUM1 = 10
20  NUM2 = 20
30  SUM = NUM1 + NUM2
40  SUM = NUM1 + NUM2
50  PRODUCT = NUM1 * NUM2
60  PRINT SUM, PRODUCT
```

and you then notice that statements 30 and 40 are identical, the extra statement could be deleted by typing either 30 or 40 and pressing the enter key, as follows:

```
10  NUM1 = 10
20  NUM2 = 20
30  SUM = NUM1 + NUM2
40  SUM = NUM1 + NUM2
50  PRODUCT = NUM1 * NUM2
60  PRINT SUM, PRODUCT
30
```

When the program is then listed, by typing the LIST command, it looks like this:

```
LIST
10  NUM1 = 10
20  NUM2 = 20
40  SUM = NUM1 + NUM2
50  PRODUCT = NUM1 * NUM2
60  PRINT SUM, PRODUCT
```

Statement 30 is no longer included in the program.

A statement in a program may be replaced by another statement by using the same line number for the new statement as was used for the statement it is to replace. For example, suppose we had typed in the following program:

```
10  NUM1 = 10
20  NUM1 = 20
40  SUM = NUM1 + NUM2
50  PRODUCT = NUM1 * NUM2
60  PRINT SUM, PRODUCT
```

When the program is executed, the following output is obtained:

```
20        0
```

Obviously, these are not the answers expected for the sum and product of the values 10 and 20. When the program is reexamined, it is observed that line 20 should have been

```
20  NUM2 = 20
```

not

```
20  NUM1 = 20
```

as had been typed inadvertently. Since NUM2 was not assigned a value, the BASIC interpreter automatically assigned it the value zero. When the value of PRODUCT was then calculated in line 50, PRODUCT was determined to also have a value of zero, which was then displayed by the PRINT statement in line 60. To correct statement 20 it is necessary to simply type the new statement 20:

```
20  NUM2 = 20
```

at the end of the program and the BASIC interpreter will automatically replace the previous statement 20 with this new corrected one. It can be verified that this replacement has been made by listing the program once more:

```
LIST
10  NUM1 = 10
20  NUM2 = 20
40  SUM = NUM1 + NUM2
50  PRODUCT = NUM1 * NUM2
60  PRINT SUM, PRODUCT
```

Statement 20 is now correct, and when the program is executed by typing the RUN command, the output produced is

        30   200

which is the output expected.

Correcting Syntax Errors—Using the BASIC Editor

Another way in which corrections may be made in BASIC program statements is by using the BASIC screen editor. After a program has been entered into the computer, it is executed by typing the command RUN. If the BASIC interpreter encounters a statement containing an error it can recognize (a BASIC control word is misspelled, a statement has an invalid line number, incorrect punctuation has been used, etc.), the statement containing the error will be listed on the screen, an error message given, and the BASIC screen editor invoked.

     The cursor control keys (the keys on the numeric keypad that have the arrows on them, or the separate cursor control keys on the PS/2 keyboard) are used to position the cursor at the position in the statement where the error appears, and then the editing keys are used to make the correction. After the correction has been made in the statement, the Enter key must be pressed to implement the change made. For example, suppose that during the execution of a program the statement

     120 PRNNT SUM

was encountered. The control word PRINT has been misspelled. The BASIC interpreter would recognize that this statement contains an error, halt program execution, list the statement on the screen, and wait for you to correct it. This correction would be made by using the cursor keys to position the cursor under the letter that needs to be *replaced,* the first N in PRNNT, as follows:

     120 PRNNT SUM

The letter "I" is then typed over the "N" that is to be replaced, and the "I" replaces the "N." The corrected statement would now appear like this:

     120 PRINT SUM

Notice that the first letter "N" has been replaced by the "I" and the cursor has automatically moved over one space to the right. To complete this correction, the Enter key is pressed before the cursor is moved to the next statement to be corrected. The Enter key may be pressed with the cursor at any point in the line; the cursor does not need to be moved to the end of the line before the Enter key is pressed.

Corrections that involve *deleting* characters rather than replacing them may also be performed using the BASIC screen editor. Suppose the following statement had been entered in a program:

```
130  PRINT "The the answer is" ANSWER
```

As can be seen, the word "the" was mistakenly typed twice in the message portion of the statement. Although this error would not be detected by the BASIC interpreter during program execution, it can still be corrected using the BASIC screen editor.

To use the BASIC screen editor, you must have the statement to be corrected displayed on the screen. This may be accomplished by using either the LIST or the EDIT command. The EDIT command is used to display a single line on the screen for editing purposes. The general form of the EDIT command is

```
EDIT <line #>
```

where <line #> is replaced by the number of the line to be edited, that is:

```
EDIT 130
```

This would cause line 130 to be displayed on the screen, ready for editing.

The second "the" may be erased from statement 130 above by performing the following series of steps:

1. List the statement on the screen using either the command EDIT 130 or LIST 130.
2. Position the cursor under the first letter of the second "the" by using the cursor control keys.
3. Press the key marked "Del", which is located below the numeric keypad, four times (once for each letter in the word "the" and once to remove the space following the word).
4. Press the Enter key to complete the correction.

As the "Del" key is pressed each time and the character above the cursor is deleted, you will notice that the rest of the statement automatically moves over one space to the left to fill in the position the deleted character occupied. Be careful not to hold the "Del" key down—just tap it—since it, like all keys on the keyboard, repeats when held down, and the entire line may be inadvertently erased.

The third type of correction that may be made with the BASIC screen editor is the situation where characters have been left out of a statement and need to be *inserted.* In the following statement, the letter "I" was omitted in the BASIC control word, PRINT:

```
140  PRNT "Have a nice day"
```

The BASIC interpreter would recognize this error and list the statement on the screen so that it could be corrected. Rather than typing the entire statement over again using the same line number, which is one way of correcting it, the letter "I" may be inserted in the word PRNT by performing the following series of steps:

1. Position the cursor under the character to the immediate right of where the insertion is to be made.
2. Press the "Ins" key, located at the bottom of the numeric keypad, once. The cursor will change from an underline to a large blinking block (■). This means the editor is now in "insert mode," and whatever is typed will be inserted in the line rather than replacing characters in the line, as occurs when the cursor is an underline character.
3. Type the letter "I". The characters to the right (including the character indicated by the cursor) will be slid to the right to make room for the character to be inserted. The editor will remain in "insert mode" until the "Ins" key is pressed again, or the cursor is moved with the cursor control keys or the Enter key.
4. Press the Enter key to complete the correction of the statement.

Statement 140 would now appear as:

```
140  PRINT "Have a nice day"
```

The "Ins" key acts like a toggle switch; when it is pressed once, the cursor changes to the block (■) to indicate "insert mode"; when it is pressed again, it changes back to the underline (_) to indicate "replacement mode."

There are a number of special keys that can be used with the BASIC screen editor to perform special functions easily during the editing process, but they will not be discussed here. If you wish to learn about these keys, refer to the *IBM Personal Computer BASIC Reference Manual* or the *IBM Personal System 2 BASIC Reference Manual.*

Obtaining a Screen Listing

A printed copy of whatever appears on the screen at a given moment may be obtained on the IBM-PC by pressing the PrtSc key while the Shift key is held down.

The PrtSc key is located to the left of the 1 key on the numeric keypad. On PS/2 models, the Print Screen key without the shift is used to perform this operation. This feature is useful for obtaining listings of short programs (programs consisting of 24 lines or less) that will fit in their entirety on the screen. This procedure may also be used to send a copy of a program's output that appears on the screen to the printer.

3.7 SYSTEM COMMANDS

There are a number of commands that may be issued from the BASIC interpreter to manipulate programs. These commands allow programs to be saved on cassette, hard disk, or diskette, retrieved from cassette or diskette storage, listed on the screen or printer, executed, erased from memory or diskette storage, etc. These commands may be issued when the BASIC interpreter is at command level. This occurs when the interpreter has completed a task, and is indicated to the user by the display of the command prompt, "Ok". Before discussing these commands, it is necessary that you understand the conventions used with the BASIC interpreter for assigning names to programs.

Naming Program Files

If programs are to be saved on diskette, cassette, or hard disk, a name must be given to the program before it can be stored. This name is used to retrieve the program from storage later when it is needed again. The complete name of a program is a *file specification*, or *filespec* for short. This file specification consists of two parts, a *device name* and a *filename*. The device name tells BASIC on which storage device to look for the file, and the filename indicates which file or program is being sought. The following names are commonly used:

CAS1: cassette tape player
A: the left diskette drive on a two-drive system, or the only drive on a one-drive system
B: the right, or upper, diskette drive on a two-drive system
C: the hard-disk drive on a hard-disk system

Notice the colon (:), which is the last character in each of the device names given above. The colon is considered to be part of the device name and must always be used, even if a filename is not included. Filenames must conform to the following rules:

For cassette files:

1. The name may not be more than eight characters long.
2. The name may not contain colons, hex `00's or hex FF's.

For diskette or hard-disk files:

1. The name may consist of two parts separated by a period:

   name.extension

   The name may be from 1 to 8 characters long, and the extension may be no more than 3 characters long. The use of the extension is optional. If the extension is omitted and the file is a BASIC program, the BASIC interpreter will automatically append the extension .BAS onto the program name when the program is saved.
2. Only the following characters may be used to form names and extensions:

   A through Z
   0 through 9

Some examples of filenames are:

   SAMPLE   PROG1.BAS   27RTY.TRW   ABC.123

It is suggested that filenames be selected that indicate what is stored in that particular file. When several files are contained on a single diskette or a hard disk and it has been some time since the programs were written, it is helpful if the names "jog" your memory as to what is contained in them. Obviously, the last two filenames shown above are poor choices.

List and Llist

Both of these commands are used to obtain a listing of the statements of the program currently in memory. The LIST command produces this list on the screen, while the LLIST command produces the same list on the printer. Their operation is so similar, except for where the listing appears, that they will be discussed together. The general form of the LIST command is

```
LIST [<line#>] [-[<line#>]]
```

If the optional line number specifications are omitted, the entire program will be listed. When the optional parameters are used, four options are possible:

1. If only a single line number is specified, only that statement will be listed.
2. If a line number followed by a dash (-) is given, that line and all higher-numbered lines are listed.
3. If a dash followed by a line number is typed, all the statements from the beginning of the program through the line number specified are listed.
4. If a line number is followed by a dash followed by another line number, all statements from the first line number specified through the second line number specified, inclusive, are listed.

As mentioned previously, the LLIST command operates in the same fashion as the LIST command, except that it produces the listing on the printer rather than on the screen. Examples of the use of these commands are

```
LIST
```

would produce a complete listing on the screen of the program currently in memory. The command

```
LLIST - 100
```

would produce a list of the statements from the beginning of the program up to and including the statement with line number 100 on the printer. The command

```
LIST 200
```

would list statement 200 on the screen. The command

```
LLIST 50 -
```

would list all statements in the current program starting with line 50 through to the end of the program, on the printer. The command

```
LIST 30 - 100
```

lists statements 30 through 100, inclusive, on the screen.

Delete

The DELETE command may be used to erase program statements. The general form of this command is

```
DELETE [line#] [- line#]
```

This command is generally used when several statements in sequence are to be deleted. It can also be used to delete a single statement by specifying only the first line number. For example:

```
DELETE 60
```

would delete line 60 from the program currently in memory. Generally, however, it is easier to delete a single statement by typing the line number of the statement to be deleted, followed by the Enter key, than it is to type the entire DELETE command. A group of sequential statements may be deleted if the second line number is also specified. The command

```
DELETE 60 - 140
```

would delete all statements numbered from 60 to 140, inclusive. A last example shows how all statements up to and including line 200 could be deleted:

```
DELETE - 200
```

Renum

This command is used to renumber the statements in a BASIC program. The general form of the command is

```
RENUM [newnum] [,[oldnum] [,increment]]
```

where

newnum   is the first line number to be used in the new line-numbering sequence. If a value is not specified for newnum, the first line in the new numbering sequence will be 10.

oldnum   is the line number in the current program where renumbering is to begin. The default is the first line of the program.

increment   is the increment to be used in the new line-number sequence. If not specified, the increment will be 10.

The RENUM command not only changes the line numbers preceding each statement according to the specifications given in the particular form of the command used, it also makes corresponding changes in the line-number references contained in statements such as the GOTO, GOSUB, and IF-THEN. Examples of using this command are

```
RENUM
```

This form of the command renumbers the entire program. The first line number of the program will now be 10, and line numbers will be incremented by 10. The command:

```
RENUM 100, 30, 20
```

renumbers the statements from line 30 on up. The old line 30 will now be numbered 100, and succeeding statement numbers will be incremented by 10.

Run

The RUN command is used to instruct the computer to begin execution of a program. There are three general forms of this statement:

```
RUN
RUN <line#>
RUN <filespec>
```

The first and simplest form of the RUN command begins execution of the program currently in memory starting with the statement having the lowest line number.

The second form of the RUN command also begins execution of the program currently in memory, but execution begins with the statement having the line number specified. For example:

```
RUN 50
```

would start execution of the program currently in memory at the statement having the line number 50.

The third form of the RUN command can be used to perform two functions at once. When this form of the command is issued, the current contents of memory are deleted, the program specified by <filespec> is loaded from diskette, cassette, or hard-disk storage into memory, and execution of this program begins. An example of this form of the command is

```
RUN "B:progl"
```

This command would cause the computer to load the program called "progl" from diskette storage on drive B: and begin executing it. Notice that in the above example, lowercase letters were used in typing the program name. The BASIC interpreter does not care whether uppercase or lowercase is used to enter commands and/or filenames.

Save

The SAVE command causes a copy of a BASIC program to be stored on cassette, diskette, or hard disk. The three general forms of this command are as follows:

```
SAVE <filespec>
SAVE <filespec>, A
SAVE <filespec>, P
```

The first form of the SAVE command above writes a copy of the program currently in memory to cassette, diskette, or hard-disk storage. The name under which the program will be saved is specified in <filespec>. For diskette and hard-disk files, if the name specified is eight characters or less in length, the extension .BAS is added to the name automatically by the system. If a program having the same name already exists on the diskette or hard disk, it will be replaced by the program currently in memory when the SAVE command is issued. For example, the command

```
SAVE "SAMPLE
```

would save a copy of the program currently in memory under the name SAMPLE on cassette or diskette storage. Notice that no quotation marks need follow the program name—only the quotation marks preceding the program name are required. If Cassette BASIC were being used when the above command was issued, the program would automatically be saved on the cassette tape, since that is the only storage device that may be used from Cassette BASIC. If Disk or Advanced BASIC were being used, the program would be stored on the diskette in disk drive A:, which is the default drive if no device designator is given on a floppy diskette based system. On a system containing a hard disk, the program would be saved on drive C:, the drive designator of the hard disk, which is the default drive on this type of system.

The second form of the SAVE command above directs the storage of the program specified to a storage device in the same manner as the first form—the only difference is that this form of the command specifies that the prorgram is to be saved in ASCII format rather than the normal compressed binary format in which BASIC programs are normally saved. The ASCII format requires more storage space, but some applications require that the program be saved in this format. For example, if the MERGE command were to be used to combine this program with another program currently in memory, the program to be merged must be stored in ASCII format. The following command stores the program PART2 on drive B: in ASCII format:

```
SAVE "B:PART2", A
```

Notice that when the option ‘,A’ is used, quotation marks are needed both before and after the program name.

The third form of the SAVE command saves the program in an encoded binary format. The ‘,P’ stands for “protected.” The command:

```
SAVE "TEST.BAS" ,P
```

stores the program TEST.BAS on the default drive in a protected format. A program saved in this format may not be later LISTed or EDITed. If a program is saved in this format, it is essential that an unprotected version of the program be kept on another diskette as there is no way provided to “unprotect” a protected program. If at a later time it is desired to make changes in a program that has been protected, and no unprotected version of the program exists on another diskette, the entire program will have to be typed in again in order that the changes may be made.

Load

The LOAD command loads a copy of a program from the specified storage device into memory, and optionally, runs it. All variables and program statements currently in memory are erased before the requested program is loaded. The general form of this command is

```
LOAD <filespec>[,R]
```

The R option causes the program to be executed automatically after it is loaded. This option is equivalent to the RUN command option, RUN <filespec>.

Files

This command may be used to obtain a listing of the names of all files residing on a diskette or hard disk. It may not be used in Cassette BASIC to obtain a listing of the names of the files on a cassette. The general form of the command is

```
FILES [<filespec>]
```

If the <filespec> option is not used, the names of the files on the default drive will be listed. The names of the files on the diskette in drive B: can be obtained by typing

```
FILES "B:"
```

A listing of a selected group of the files on a given diskette or on the hard disk may be displayed by using the asterisk (*) in place of the filename or extension in the <filespec> option of the FILES command. For example, if the following FILES command were issued:

```
FILES "B:*.BAS"
```

only the names of those files on the diskette in drive B: which had an extension of .BAS would be listed.

New

The NEW command erases the program currently in memory. This command is commonly used to clear memory before a new program is entered. It is vital that a copy of the program currently in memory be saved on cassette, diskette, or hard disk before this command is issued if the current program may be wanted again later. Once the NEW command is typed and the Enter key pressed, the only way to recover the program that was in memory without typing it in again is if a copy of it had previously been saved.

Kill

This command deletes a program from a diskette or hard disk. It may be used only with Disk or Advanced BASIC. The general form of this command is

```
KILL <filespec>
```

The <filespec> must include the extension, if there is one, or the program named will not be deleted from the diskette or hard disk; the computer will simply respond with the message, File not found. The FILES command is useful in determining whether or not a particular program name contains an extension. The KILL command affects only the copy of the program that is on the diskette or hard disk—it has no effect on a program in memory. The command

```
KILL "PROG1.BAS"
```

deletes the BASIC program PROG1 from the default drive. If the program to be deleted is on a diskette in drive B:, then the drive designator B: must be included as part of the <filespec>.

3.8 ENTERING YOUR FIRST BASIC PROGRAM

Let's briefly review at this time the steps involved in entering, listing, correcting, executing, and saving a BASIC program. For the purpose of this discussion, we'll use the following BASIC program:

```
10  LET NUM1 = 20
20  LET NUM2 = 10
30  DIFFERENCE = NUM1 − NUM2
40  QUOTIENT = NUM1 / NUM2
50  PRINT "The difference of the two numbers is" DIFFERENCE
60  PRINT "The quotient of the two numbers is" DIFFERENCE
70  END
```

The first step is to load the version of the BASIC interpreter that is to be used: Cassette BASIC, Disk BASIC, or Advanced BASIC. Refer back to Section 3.6 if you have forgotten how this is done.

Once this has been accomplished, the interpreter will display the "Ok" prompt on the screen, which means that you may begin typing in your program. Type in the statements in the program given above, one statement per line. Be sure to press the Enter key at the end of each statement.

At this point you may wish to list the program on the screen by typing the LIST command so you can see just how your program was accepted by the interpreter. You may notice that all variable names and BASIC control words in the program are now uppercase, even though you may have typed them in using lowercase letters. This automatic capitalization of variable names and BASIC control words is always done by the interpreter. String constants (characters enclosed in double quotation marks), however, are left just the way you typed them in.

Any errors in statements noticed at this point should be corrected by using the BASIC screen editor or by typing the statements containing errors over again correctly.

Once any obvious errors have been corrected, attempt to execute the program by typing the RUN command. If any *syntax errors* (misspelled BASIC control words, invalid line numbers, incorrect punctuation, etc.) are detected by the BASIC interpreter, the statement containing the first error encountered will be displayed on the screen along with an error message. Use the BASIC screen editor to correct the error and type RUN again. Continue this process until the program runs to completion without any errors being detected.

Examine the output to see if it is what was expected. Just because the program finished executing without any syntax errors being discovered by the BASIC interpreter doesn't necessarily mean that the program is producing correct output. It may still contain *logic errors*. These errors are errors in the algorithm developed to solve the problem. It is a good idea to run a program several times with data values for which the correct answer is known to ensure that the program is working correctly.

If you entered the program exactly as shown, you should have the following on your screen:

```
The difference of the two numbers is 10
The quotient of the two numbers is 10
Ok
```

The word 'Ok' appearing at the end of the output indicates that the program has completed execution. The second answer, however, is not correct. The quotient of the two numbers is given as 10, but we know that 20 divided by 10 should be 2. If we examine the program by listing it, we see that statement 60 is incorrect. This statement currently reads

```
60  PRINT "The quotient of the two numbers is" DIFFERENCE
```

The computer has done exactly what we told it to do—display the message, "The quotient of the two numbers is", followed by the value of the variable DIFFER-ENCE. Unfortunately, we want the value of the quotient of the two numbers displayed, not their difference again. This statement needs to be modified so that it reads:

```
60  PRINT "The quotient of the two numbers is" QUOTIENT
```

Use the BASIC screen editor to correct this statement, and try running the program again. If you make the correction properly, the screen should now display

```
The difference of the two numbers is 10
The quotient of the two numbers is 2
Ok
```

Once all the logic errors in a program, if there are any, have been identified and corrected, the program should be saved on cassette, diskette, or hard-disk storage by use of the SAVE command. This will ensure that the program will not be lost if power to your computer is interrupted. A name must be chosen under which to store the program. It must be a name not already used for a program currently stored on your secondary storage device. Saving a new program under the same name already used for a program in storage will cause the previous program to be lost. The FILES command may be used to check the names of the programs currently stored on your diskette or hard disk.

Let's use the name PROG1 for the current program. Type the following command to store the program on your diskette:

```
SAVE"B:PROG1
```

or, if you are using cassette storage, type

```
SAVE"CAS1:PROG1
```

or, if you are using hard-disk storage, type

```
SAVE"C:PROG1
```

The computer should respond with the prompt "Ok".

If you are using Disk or Advanced BASIC, a good way to double check that the program has indeed been saved is to type the FILES command again to see if the name PROG1 appears in the list of program names displayed by this command. Remember, the program was saved on drive B: or drive C:, so the appropriate form of the FILES command that will check the files on drive B: or drive C: must be used. If the name PROG1 does appear, the program has been saved. If not, try the SAVE command again after checking that you have typed the command exactly as shown above.

Even though a copy of the current program has been saved on cassette, diskette, or hard-disk storage, the program is also still in the work area. If you want a printed copy of the program, type the command LLIST. Be sure the printer is turned on before you type this command.

A printed copy of the screen output from the program can be produced by running the program and then sending a copy of the screen display to the printer by pressing the PrtSc key while the Shift key is held down (print screen with no shift on PS/2 models).

If another program is to be entered during this session at the computer, type the NEW command before starting to enter the statements for the next program. The NEW command, as you may remember, erases the work area. Before this command is issued, however, be certain that you have already saved your previous program, or it will be lost when the NEW command is entered.

When you have finished with the computer, turn the power off to the computer, screen, and printer and remove your diskettes or cassettes from the drives. Be sure to keep them in a safe place where they cannot be damaged, and your programs will be available to you the next time you need them.

3.9 SUMMARY

All BASIC statements have the general form of: a line number, followed by a BASIC control word, followed by a constant, variable, or expression. The assignment statement, which may use the optional control word LET, is used to assign a value to the variable. The PRINT statement is used to display output on the screen. The REM statement permits the inclusion of explanatory remarks in a program listing without affecting the output from the program. The END statement, which is optional in Microsoft BASIC, halts program execution.

The following table lists the pseudocode statements for which BASIC language equivalent statements have been discussed in this chapter:

BASIC Statements Introduced in Chapter 3

Pseudocode statement	Equivalent BASIC statement

`<variable> ← <constant,`
`            variable,`
`         or expression>`
	`line# [LET] <variable> = <constant,`
	`                            variable,`
	`                         or expression>`

`WRITE (<variables` `       and/or constants>)`	`line# PRINT [<constants, variables,` `                and/or expressions>]`

`{<programmer comment>}`	`line# REM <programmer comment>`
	`                    or`
	`line# ' <programmer comment>`

The IBM-PC and IBM-PS/2 families of computers have three different BASIC interpreters available for use. Cassette BASIC is stored in ROM and automatically loaded into memory when the power is turned on to the machine. Disk BASIC and Advanced BASIC, which are more powerful versions of BASIC, may be used with computers that have diskette or hard-disk storage available.

A BASIC program that is currently in memory is said to be in the BASIC work area, and can be modified by use of the BASIC screen editor or by line editing. Statements may be inserted, deleted, or modified. Two modes of operation are available in the BASIC interpreter—direct mode and indirect mode. A copy of what is currently appearing on the screen may be printed on the printer by use of the PrtSc or Print Screen key.

A number of BASIC system commands are available that list, store, retrieve, modify, and erase BASIC programs. A brief summary of the commands discussed in this chapter follows:

BASIC System Commands

Command	Description
`DELETE [line1] [-line2]`	Deletes specified program lines
`FILES [<filespec>]*`	Lists the names of the files and programs contained on the specified diskette or hard disk
`KILL <filespec.ext>†`	Erases the named file or program from the diskette or hard disk in the specified drive
`LIST [line1] [-[line2]]`	Lists the specified program lines on the screen
`LLIST [line1] [-[line2]]`	Lists the specified program lines on the printer
`LOAD <filespec> [,R]`	Loads a program from diskette or hard disk into the work area in main memory
`NEW`	Erases the current program and variables from the work area
`RENUM [newnum] [,[oldnum] [,increment]]`	Renumbers program lines
`RUN [<filespec>]`	Executes a program
`SAVE <filespec>`	Saves the program currently in memory on the diskette or hard disk under the selected filename

*[ ] indicates the parameters are optional.

<filespec> contains a double quote followed by the program name. The extension is not required on these commands; that is, "SAMPLE.

†<filespec.ext> contains a double quote followed by the program name, followed by a period and a three-letter extension (in the case of a BASIC program, the extension would be BAS); that is, "SAMPLE.BAS.

EXERCISES

1. What are the three parts of any BASIC statement?

2. Indicate whether each of the following BASIC variable names is valid or invalid. Also indicate for the invalid names why they are invalid.

   a. TOTAL   h. A
   b. SUM.OF.SCORES   i. STAR**
   c. NAME$ j. FIRST.NAME$
   d. RATE_OF_PAY   k. "DONE"
   e. READY123   l. HOURS*RATE
   f. LARGEST VALUE   m. #.OF.LINES
   g. 23SKIDOO   n. 43

3. Write BASIC language assignment statements to perform each of the following. Choose meaningful variable names to use where needed.

   a. Add five test scores together and store their sum in the variable SUM.
   b. Compute GROSS.PAY by multiplying HOURS by RATE.
   c. Calculate the INTEREST on an AMOUNT by multiplying the AMOUNT by the RATE by the DAYS divided by 360.
   d. Find the CIRCUMFERENCE of a circle by multiplying the RADIUS by 3.14159.
   e. Subtract EXPENSES from GROSS.PROFIT to give NET.PROFIT.

4. Write BASIC language PRINT statements that would produce the following output:

   a. Display the value of the variable BIGGEST.
   b. Print the message, "The answer is:", followed by the value of the variable ANSWER.
   c. Produce the message, "Have a nice day!", followed by two blank lines, followed on the next line with the value of the variable STUDENT-.NAME$.
   d. Print the values of the variables CUSTOMER.NAME$, ADDRESS$, and CITY.STATE$ on three separate lines, each line of output starting five spaces to the right of the left margin.
   e. Print the following:

   START
        H
        ENGINE

5. Use REM statements to draw a box composed of asterisks (*) around the title, "P A Y R O L L   P R O G R A M", which is to be displayed as the first lines of a program when it is listed.

6. Convert each of the following pseudocode statements to its equivalent BASIC language statement. Supply your own line numbers:

   a. *SUM ← SUM + NUMBER*
   b. *WRITE ('The answer is', ANSWER)*
   c. *AVERAGE ← (NUM1 + NUM2 + NUM3) / 3*
   d. *{Convert the weight in pounds to kilograms}*
   e. *WRITE (NAME$, ADDRESS$, CITY.STATE$)*

7. List the steps to be followed to erase the statement at line 30 from a BASIC program currently in the work area.

8. A statement to display the value of AVERAGE is to be inserted in a BASIC program between lines numbered 110 and 120. Write the needed BASIC statement with an appropriate line number to accomplish this.

9. List the steps that would need to be followed to insert the character 'A' in the variable name AVERGE in the position preceding the letter G in the statement:

   ```
   100 AVERGE = SUM / 5
   ```

10. Write the BASIC system commands to perform the following operations:

    a. Obtain a listing on the screen of the program currently in the work area.
    b. Produce a listing on the printer of the statements numbered from 100 to 300, inclusive, contained in the program currently in the work area.
    c. Erase all statements in the current program between lines 40 and 80, inclusive.
    d. Renumber the current program starting with the first statement, which is to be renumbered 100, and have the new line numbers incremented by 20.
    e. Execute the program that is currently in the work area beginning with the statement numbered 200.
    f. Execute a program named "PROG1" which is stored on the diskette in drive B:.
    g. Save the program currently in memory on the diskette in drive A: under the name "SAMPLE1".
    h. Store a protected version of the current program on the hard disk (drive C:) using the name "PROG2".
    i. Retrieve a copy of the program "TEST.TXT" from the cassette tape storage.
    j. Obtain a list of the names of the BASIC program stored on the diskette in drive A:.
    k. Erase the program currently in the work area.
    l. Erase the BASIC program "ASSGN1" from the hard disk (drive C:).

11. Corrections need to be made to the program PROG2 which is currently stored on the diskette in drive B:. Indicate the sequence of steps and the commands that would be needed to load this program into the work area, make the needed corrections, and store a corrected copy of the program back on the diskette in drive B: under the same name, PROG2.

12. Type the following short BASIC program in on your computer, get it running,

obtain a printed copy of it, and save it on your cassette, diskette, or hard disk under the name PROGRAM1:

```
10   WEIGHT.IN.LBS = 150
20   WEIGHT.IN.KGS = 2.2046 * WEIGHT.IN.LBS
30   PRINT "A weight of"; WEIGHT.IN.LBS; "pounds"
40   PRINT "is equivalent to"; WEIGHT.IN.KGS;
"kilograms."
```

13. Once you have successfully entered and run the above program, modify it to convert your weight in pounds to kilograms. Save this version of the program on your diskette, cassette, or hard disk under the name PROGRAM2.

CHAPTER 4

Input/Output—
Numeric Expressions

This chapter continues the discussion of sequential BASIC statements begun in Chapter 3. The BASIC language INPUT, READ, and DATA statements, which permit data entry in a program, are introduced. The WIDTH statement, which allows the screen display width to be set to either 40 or 80 characters, is explained, and additional features of the PRINT statement are discussed. The chapter concludes with an explanation of the formation and evaluation of numeric expressions.

4.0. OBJECTIVES

After studying the material in this chapter, you should be able to:

1. Translate a pseudocode READ statement into an equivalent BASIC language INPUT or READ statement.
2. Produce output in a desired format by using the appropriate punctuation and/or functions in PRINT statements.

3. List the BASIC language arithmetic operators.

4. Indicate the order in which arithmetic operations will be performed when a given expression is to be evaluated.

5. Evaluate a BASIC language arithmetic expression.

6. Use the BASIC language arithmetic operators and/or parentheses to form arithmetic expressions to perform needed calculations.

4.1 THE INPUT STATEMENT

The READ statement is the only sequential pseudocode statement for which we do not as yet have an equivalent BASIC language statement. As you may recall from Chapter 2, the pseudocode READ statement is used to indicate the point in an algorithm at which data values are to be entered into one or more variables during program execution. This same process may be accomplished in BASIC by use of an INPUT statement.

General Form of the INPUT Statement

The general form of the BASIC language INPUT statement is

```
line #  INPUT ["prompt",] <variable>[,<variable>] . . .
```

As the general form indicates, a single INPUT statement may be used to obtain a value for a single variable, or values for several variables. If more than one variable is contained in an INPUT statement, the variable names are separated by commas.

When the computer encounters an INPUT statement during execution of a BASIC program, a question mark (?) is displayed on the screen. Program execution then pauses until a data value is typed in and the Enter key pressed.

Data entered in response to an input prompt must correspond as to type (numeric or character) and number with the variable or variables listed in the INPUT statement. For example, if the following INPUT statement was encountered during execution of a BASIC program,

```
40  INPUT COLOR$, SIZE, COST
```

the computer would display a question mark on the screen and wait for data to be entered. The user would need to enter three data values, separated by commas. The first value would need to be a character string and the second and third items numeric values if the data were to correspond in type and number to the variables listed in the INPUT statement:

```
? red, 10, 12.95
```

Entry of incorrect data would cause the error message, "?Redo from start", to be displayed, and the data would need to be reentered:

```
? 15, 8.98, green
  ? Redo from start
? green, 15, 8.98
```

The above example illustrates the entry of character data for a numeric variable. The entry of too many or too few data items for the number of variables listed in the INPUT statement would also cause a data entry error, and the correct number of data items would need to be reentered. If numeric data is entered into a character string variable, this does not cause rejection of the input, however, since numeric digits are valid characters.

As shown in the general form, an optional prompt and comma may follow the word INPUT in the INPUT statement. The prompt may be any message to be displayed on the screen prompting the user as to what data is to be entered. The message is enclosed in quotation marks. If only the quotation marks (" "), followed by a comma, are used, this has the effect of suppressing the ? normally displayed by an INPUT statement. Once a data value or values have been entered, and the Enter key has been pressed, program execution continues.

Entering Numeric Data

A common use of the INPUT statement is to assign numeric values to numeric variables. A numeric variable, as you may recall from Chapter 3, is a variable that may be used to store a number. The advantage of using an INPUT statement to perform this task rather than an assignment statement is that the values stored in numeric variables can be easily changed each time the program is run without modifying any program statements.

Suppose we wished to calculate the sale price of a number of items for our store's yearly sale. Various items are discounted different percentages. We could write a short BASIC program to compute these sale prices:

```
100   INPUT PRICE
110   INPUT DISCOUNT
120   SALE.PRICE = PRICE — PRICE * DISCOUNT / 100
130   PRINT "The sale price is $" SALE.PRICE
140   END
```

For each item, then, we would simply enter the current price of the item, press the Enter key, and then type the percentage it is to be discounted. Once the Enter key is pressed a second time, the sales price would be computed and displayed on the screen. An example would be

```
? 59.95
? 20
The sale price is $ 47.96
OK
```

One improvement that might be made in this program is to insert PRINT statements before the INPUT statements in the program to inform the user as to the order in which data values are to be entered. Suitable statements would be

```
90   PRINT "Enter the price of the item"
```

and

```
105  PRINT "Enter the percent of discount"
```

The program listed would now look like this:

```
 90  PRINT "Enter the price of the item"
100  INPUT PRICE
105  PRINT "Enter the percent of discount"
110  INPUT DISCOUNT
120  SALE.PRICE = PRICE - PRICE * DISCOUNT / 100
130  PRINT "The sale price is $" SALE.PRICE
140  END
```

and a sample run like this:

```
Enter the price of the item
? 59.95
Enter the percent of discount
? 20
The sale price is $ 47.96
Ok
```

PRINT statements such as these are referred to as *input prompts,* as they inform, or prompt, the user as to what data to enter in response to the question mark prompts displayed by INPUT statements. It is a good idea to always use input prompts in programs you write, since they will make the programs easier to use.

One common error often made when entering numeric data is to include dollar signs or other nonnumeric characters as part of the numeric value being entered. This will cause an error message to be displayed, and the data will need to be reentered. If the following INPUT statement was contained in a program,

```
50   INPUT VALUE
```

some examples of valid and invalid data entries that might be made in response to the input prompt produced by this statement are given in the following table:

Valid and Invalid Data Values for a Numeric Variable

Valid data entries	Invalid data entries
36675	133,980
47.86	15%
− 13.9	$86.75

The first item in the invalid column, 133,980, would be invalid because the number would be taken as two data values: 133 and 980. Remember, a comma is used to separate items in the data entered in response to an INPUT statement. The second item in the column is invalid because of the inclusion of a nonnumeric character as part of the entry—the percent sign (%). The third item in the column is invalid for the same reason as is the second; a nonnumeric character, in this case a dollar sign ($), is included as part of the entry.

Entering Character Data

The INPUT statement may also be used to assign character string constants to character string variables. For example, the following section of pseudocode:

```
10   WRITE  ("Enter your first name")
20   READ (FIRST.NAME$)
     .
     .
     .
```

could be expressed in BASIC as:

```
10  PRINT "Enter your first name"
20  INPUT FIRST.NAME$
         .
         .
         .
```

When executed, this program segment would cause the following to be displayed on the screen:

```
Enter your first name
? _
```

If the name Jack was typed in response to this input prompt and the Enter key pressed, the character string constant Jack would be stored in the variable FIRST.NAME$.

Notice that double quotation marks are not required around the name Jack when it is entered in response to an INPUT statement as they are when a character string constant is assigned to a character string variable in an assignment statement, that is,

```
100  FIRST.NAME$ = "Jack"
```

Quotation marks may be used with an INPUT statement if so desired but are usually not necessary. If I had responded "Jack" to the above INPUT statement instead of Jack, the same result would have occurred—the four characters, Jack, would have been assigned to FIRST.NAME$. The quotation marks would not have been taken as part of the character string constant; they simply delimit it (define where the character string begins and ends).

There are two situations where the double quotation marks are necessary when entering a character string constant in response to an INPUT statement.

The first situation is where the character string constant contains a comma (,). Since the comma is normally used to separate data items in a response to an INPUT statement, some indicator must be used to inform the computer that the comma is part of the actual character string and not a delimiter. This is accomplished by enclosing the character string constant in double quotation marks. For example, if we wished to enter the name of a city and state into a single character string variable, double quotation marks would be placed before the first character of the name of the city and after the last character of the state, that is,

```
"La Crosse, Wisconsin"
```

The second situation where double quotation marks would be needed to delimit an input string is the case in which leading or trailing blanks are to be retained as part of the entering string. Normally, BASIC deletes leading and trailing blanks from a character string when it is entered. For example, if the string "   yes " was entered in response to an INPUT statement prompt, without the quotation marks around it,

```
?^^^yes^^
```

(the character ^ indicates that a blank space was entered) only the three characters 'yes' would be assigned to the character string variable. If you wish to include the three leading and two trailing spaces, respond to the input prompt as follows:

```
? "^^^yes^^"
```

This would assign the eight characters consisting of three spaces, yes, and two spaces to the character string variable.

Embedded spaces (spaces preceded and followed by nonblank characters), on the other hand, are always retained during an input operation—only leading and trailing blanks are discarded. The following program segment illustrates this:

```
10  PRINT "Enter your first and last name"
20  INPUT FULL.NAME$
        .
        .
        .
```

Execution of this program segment and entry of the name John Smith would result in the following appearing on the screen:

```
Enter your first and last name
? John Smith
        .
        .
        .
```

The name John Smith, which consists of 10 characters counting the embedded space between the first and last name, would be assigned to the variable FULL.NAME$.

When responding to an INPUT statement by entering a character string constant, remember that the maximum length of a character string constant is 255 characters. This means that your entry cannot exceed this number of characters.

4.2 THE READ AND DATA STATEMENTS

Another type of input statement available in BASIC is the READ statement. It performs the same function as the INPUT statement (assigns values to variables), and therefore may also be used to translate a pseudocode READ statement into BASIC. It differs from the INPUT statement, however, in the manner in which data entry is handled. The actual data values to be used by the READ statement are placed in a DATA statement and are used by the program when a READ statement is encountered during program execution.

The READ and DATA statements will be discussed together in this section, since whenever a program contains a READ statement, it must also contain at least one DATA statement to hold the data values that are to be used by the READ statement.

The general form of the READ statement is

```
line #  READ  <variable> [,<variable>] . . .
```

As with the INPUT statement, values may be assigned to one or more variables by a single READ statement. If more than one variable name is listed after the word READ, they are separated by commas.

The DATA statement has the general form:

```
line #  DATA  <constant> [,<constant>] . . .
```

The DATA statement contains one or more constants that are to be assigned to the variable or variables in a READ statement. If several constants are contained in a DATA statement, they are separated by commas. Character string constants in DATA statements need to be delimited by double quotation marks only if they contain a comma or have leading and/or trailing blanks that are to be retained as part of the strings.

The DATA statement is a nonexecutable statement in the sense that it does not matter where it is placed in the program. The input operation occurs when the computer encounters a READ statement in the program. At that time the first data value in the first (lowest-numbered) DATA statement will be used. DATA statements are commonly grouped at the end of a program, immediately following the READ statement that uses them, or at the beginning of the program. Any one of these placements is acceptable.

Let's examine a sample program containing READ and DATA statements:

```
10  READ NUM1, NUM2, NUM3
20  SUM = NUM1 + NUM2 + NUM3
30  AVERAGE = SUM / 3
40  PRINT "The average of the three numbers is" AVERAGE
50  DATA 10,20,30
```

If we were to execute this program by typing the command RUN, the screen would display the following:

```
The average of the three numbers is  20
Ok
```

One difference from a program using an INPUT statement is immediately obvious; no question mark appeared on the screen, and it was not necessary to enter the data values for NUM1, NUM2, and NUM3. This seems reasonable, of course, when we recall that the purpose of the DATA statement is to hold the data values to be used by the READ statement. Since the data values are already available to the READ statement in the DATA statement, there is no reason to enter them again.

If you would wish to compute the average of three different values, it would be necessary to change the data values in the DATA statement at line 50. This would be accomplished by using the BASIC screen editor, just as is done with any BASIC statement we wish to modify. Once the values in the DATA statement are changed, typing RUN would cause the average of the new set of values to be computed and displayed. For example, if we modified line 50 to be

```
50  DATA 20, 60, 100
```

and then typed RUN, the output displayed on the screen would be

```
The average of the three numbers is  60
Ok
```

If a READ statement contains more variables than there are constants in the first DATA statement in a program, the computer simply uses data values from the next and succeeding DATA statements until all variables have been assigned values. An example of this would be the following:

```
10  READ VALUE1, VALUE2, VALUE3, VALUE4
20  DATA 20
30  DATA 30, 40
40  DATA 50
50  PRINT VALUE1; VALUE2; VALUE3; VALUE4
```

When executed, this program would display the following on the screen:

```
20  30  40  50
Ok
```

If, on the other hand, there are more data values in a DATA statement than are needed by a READ statement, only as many values as are needed are used. The remaining data values may either be used by a READ statement encountered later in the program, or they may not be used at all.

The computer maintains a *data pointer* to keep track of which data values have been used in a program and which data value is to be used next. This data pointer always points to the next data value to be read. When a READ statement is encountered in a program, the first variable following the word READ will be assigned the value being pointed to by the data pointer.

Two types of errors are possible when READ and DATA statements are used in a program. The first error will occur when the variables in a READ statement do not correspond in data type with the constants in the DATA statement. If the following segment of code were to be executed,

```
10  READ EMPLOYEE$, HOURS, PAYRATE
20  DATA 38, 5.85, John Jones
         .
         .
         .
```

the value 38 would be assigned to EMPLOYEE$, 5.85 to HOURS, and then the following would be displayed on the screen:

```
Syntax error in 20
20  DATA 38, 5.85, John Jones
```

This rather cryptic error message is produced when the computer attempts to assign the third value in the DATA statement, 'John Jones', to the third variable in the READ statement, PAYRATE. There is a conflict in data types (38 is assigned to EMPLOYEE$ without an error occurring since digits are legal characters). 'John

Jones' is a character string constant, however, and the variable PAYRATE is a numeric variable. Numeric variables cannot store character data, so the BASIC interpeter displays the error message above, as well as the DATA statement that contains the invalid data value, on the screen. The interpreter has automatically placed the program in edit mode, so the BASIC screen editor may be used to rearrange the order of the data items in the DATA statement (place the employee name first in the list of data constants).

The second possible error that may occur with READ and DATA statements is when there are more variables in the READ statements in a program than there are data values in the DATA statements. A segment of program code containing this type of error would be

```
10  READ NAME1$, NAME2$, NAME3$
20  DATA Judy, Mary
    .
    .
    .
```

When this segment of code is executed, the following error message would be displayed on the screen:

```
Out of DATA in 10
```

This message is a little more descriptive of the error that has occurred than the error message displayed when a data type error occurs. When the READ statement in line 10 was being executed, there were not enough data values in the DATA statements in the program to satisfy all the variables listed in the READ statement. This error could be corrected in one or two ways. Either statement 20 could have another name added to it, or another DATA statement could be inserted in the program containing a third name.

The READ statement is typically used in a BASIC program rather than an INPUT statement in two situations. The first situation occurs when a large number of data items need to be entered in a program. If an INPUT statement is used and an error is made in entering even a single data item, it will be necessary to halt program execution and reenter all the data items again. This can be very time-consuming. If an error is made in entering one of the values into a DATA statement, however, only that one value needs to be changed, which may be done with the BASIC screen editor. The rest of the values do not need to be reentered.

The second situation in which a READ statement might be preferred is a program in which a number of variables need to be initialized at the beginning of the program. If every time the program is run, the same data values need to be assigned to a group of variables, it is much more efficient to have this done by READ and DATA statements rather than having to enter the values each time in response to INPUT statements.

An example of this would be a program in which a table of tax rates needs to be initialized at the beginning of the program. These rates would stay the same for a period of time and when they do change could be easily modified by simply changing the values in the DATA statements. A listing of this section of such a program is shown below:

```
10    REM This program computes the amount to be withheld
20    REM from an employee's weekly paycheck for state tax.
30    REM J. Castek, 7/27/87
40    REM
50    REM *** Load the tax tables from DATA statements
60    REM
70    READ PAY1, TAX1
80    READ PAY2, TAX2
90    READ PAY3, TAX3
100   READ PAY4, TAX4
110   DATA 60, .05, 100, .07, 150, .10, 200, .12
        .
        .
        .
```

Four pairs of data values are read in. The first member of each pair is the weekly pay amount, and the second member of each pair is the percent to be withheld, expressed as a decimal value. In other words, if employees make $60.00 or more a week but less than $100.00, 5 percent of their gross pay is to be withheld for taxes. If they make at least $100.00 but less than $150.00 a week, 7 percent is to be withheld, etc. An employee making $200.00 or more a week would have 12 percent of the weekly paycheck withheld. The rest of the program would make use of this tax table information to compute and display the employees's gross pay, tax withheld, and net pay.

4.3 THE RESTORE STATEMENT

A statement that permits data values in DATA statements to be reused in a program is the RESTORE statement. The general form of this statement is

```
line #  RESTORE [<line number>]
```

If the statement is used without the optional line number following the word RESTORE, execution of the statement causes the data pointer to be reset to the first data value in the first (lowest-numbered) DATA statement in the program. For example:

```
100   READ A, B
110   READ C, D
120   RESTORE
130   READ E, F
140   DATA 3,5,7,9
150   PRINT "A = ";A;"B = ";B;"C = "C;"D = ";D;"E = ";E;"F = ";F
        .
        .
        .
```

If this segment of a BASIC program is executed, the PRINT statement at line 150 would cause the following output to be displayed on the screen:

```
A = 3 B = 5 C = 7 D = 9 E = 3 F = 5
```

The execution of the program segment can be traced through as follows: Statement 100 assigns the value 3 to A and the value 5 to B. The data pointer is now pointing to the third item in the DATA statement, the value 7. Statement 110 assigns 7 to C and 9 to D. When the RESTORE statement at line 120 is executed, the data pointer is reset to point to the first data item in the first DATA statement, the value 3 in the DATA statement at line 140. Then when statement 130 is executed, E is assigned the value 3 and F the value 5.

If the optional line number following the word RESTORE is used, execution of this form of the RESTORE statement causes the data pointer to be set to the first data item in the DATA statment having the line number specified. An example of this would be

```
10   READ A, B
20   RESTORE 80
30   READ C, D
40   RESTORE 70
50   READ E
60   DATA 2
70   DATA 4, 6
80   DATA 8, 10
90   PRINT "A = ";A;"B = ";B;"C = ";C;"D = ";D;"E = ";E
       .
       .
       .
```

When this program segment is executed, the PRINT statement at line 90 would produce the following:

```
A = 2 B = 4 C = 8 D = 10 E = 4
```

A trace of this code segment is as follows: Line 10 assigns the value 2 to A and the value 4 to B. The data pointer is now pointing to the second item in the DATA statement at line 70, the value 6. When the next statement, RESTORE 80, is executed, the data pointer is reset to point to the first data item in the DATA statement at line 80, the value 8. When statement 30 is then executed, READ C, D, the variable C is assigned the value 8, and D the value 10. Statement 40, RESTORE 70, resets the data pointer to the first item in the DATA statement at line 70, the value 4. Execution of the READ statement at line 50 assigns the value 4 to E. As we leave this segment of code, the data pointer is left pointing to the second data item in line 70, the value 6. A subsequent READ statement in the program would begin with this value.

4.4 THE WIDTH STATEMENT

When the BASIC interpreter is started on the IBM-PC or IBM-PS/2, the screen width is initially set to display up to 80 characters per line. If a line of output being displayed is longer than this, BASIC will automatically insert a carriage return and line feed in the output line, and continue the rest of the output on the next line. The WIDTH statement may be used to change the number of characters to be displayed on a line.

The general form of this statement is

```
line # WIDTH <n>
```

where <n> may be a value of either 40 or 80, one of the two screen widths permitted in BASIC. When the width statement is encountered in a program, the screen display will be erased, and the next PRINT statement in the program will display its output line in the new screen width. When a screen width of 40 is selected, a maximum of 40 characters will be displayed on a line, and the characters will be larger, in both height and width:

```
10  WIDTH 40
20  PRINT "These are width 40 characters"
```

results in:

These are width 40 characters

4.5 MORE ABOUT THE PRINT STATEMENT

As you are well aware, the PRINT statement is used in BASIC to display constants and the values of variables on the screen. In this section of the chapter we discuss how to have more control over the placement of output on the screen.

Punctuation

One way to control the horizontal spacing of output is to make use of different punctuation marks in a PRINT statement. If a list of variables or constants in a PRINT statement is separated by either semicolons or spaces, output will be placed close together across the output line. In the case of character string variables and constants, there will be no spaces between items when they are displayed. In the case of numeric values, one or two spaces will separate items depending upon whether or not a leading sign needs to be printed. Examples of this are as follows:

```
10   A = 3
20   B = -17
30   C = 467
40   A$ = "BASIC"
50   B$ = "programming"
60   PRINT A;B;C
70   PRINT A$; B$
80   PRINT A A$ B B$ C
```

When executed, this program would produce the following output, spaced as shown:

```
 3 -17  467
BASICprogramming
 3 BASIC-17 programming 467
Ok
```

The first line of output begins in column 2, one space over from the left edge of the screen, leaving one blank space in case a negative sign is needed. One blank space is left in column 3 to separate the first item, 3, from the next item. The number −17 is printed, followed by one blank space for a separator and one space reserved for the sign of the next number, 467, even though the space is not needed since 467 is a positive value. Lastly, the digits 467 are actually printed in columns 9, 10, and 11.

In the second line of output, both items printed are the values of character string variables, so no spaces are left between them. The first string, BASIC, begins in column 1, since no space need be reserved for a possible negative sign when a character string is being printed.

The third line of output begins in the second column again since the first column must be reserved for a possible negative sign. One space follows the number 3 to separate it from the next item, the value of the character string variable A$, BASIC. The next item, −17, which is the value of B, starts immediately after the word BASIC. There are no blank spaces between BASIC and −17 since character strings never have spaces printed after them, and the sign position for the number −17 is used. One space follows the number −17 to separate it from the next item, programming. The single space that separates the word programming from the number 467 is the column reserved for a possible negative sign before the number 467.

If a comma is used to separate items in a PRINT statement rather than a semicolon or a space, horizontal spacing is quite different. The comma indicates to the BASIC interpreter that *zone printing* is to be used. Zone printing divides the output line into a number of print zones, each of which is 14 columns wide. The actual number of print zones that will be established for an output line is dependent upon whether a screen width of 40 or 80 characters is being used. Each item in a PRINT statement that makes use of commas as separators begins printing at the beginning of the next available print zone. For example,

```
10  A = 3
20  B = -17
30  A$ = "BASIC"
40  PRINT A,B,A$
50  PRINT "The answer to this is", A
```

would produce the following screen display:

```
| <zone 1>       | <zone 2>   | <zone 3> | <zone 4> |
|                |            |          |          |
| 3              | -17        | BASIC    |          |
| The answer to  | this is    | 3        |          |
| Ok             |            |          |          |
```

In the first line of output produced, each item starts at the beginning of a separate print zone—column 1, column 15, and column 29. In the second line of output, the character string constant, The answer to this is, is more than 14 characters long so it extends into the second print zone. This causes the value of A, which is 3, to be printed in the next zone since the comma means, "Move to the beginning of the next print zone."

As mentioned earlier in this chapter, if a line of output produced by a PRINT statement will not fit on a single line, BASIC prints as much of it as will fit on the line, and then continues the rest of the output on the next line, starting in column 1. If the following PRINT statement were to be executed,

```
20  PRINT "This","is","an","example","of","a","long","line."
```

the output produced, on a screen set to an 80-character display width, would be

```
This        is          an          example         of              a
long        line.
```

The first character of each item displayed starts in the first position of a new print zone. An 80-character screen width permits 6 print zones to be established across the screen (the last zone will be only 10 characters in width). When the seventh item is to be printed, BASIC automatically inserts a carriage return and line feed into the print line, causing the seventh and eighth items in the print list to be displayed on the next line, in the first two print zones of that line.

A carriage return and line feed are normally produced at the end of each PRINT statement, so the next line of output always starts at the beginning of the next line. This automatic carriage return/line feed feature may be suppressed by placing a semicolon or a comma at the end of the list of variables or constants following the word PRINT. This will cause the next PRINT statement to begin printing where the previous PRINT statement finished. An example of this would be:

```
10  PRINT "Hello ";
20  PRINT "there, ";
30  PRINT "Joe."
```

When executed, this program would produce:

```
Hello there, Joe.
Ok
```

The spaces that separate the three character string constants are the last character in each of the first two string constants, so when the PRINT statements are executed, these characters are printed and serve to separate the strings.

This suppression of carriage return/line feed can be used quite effectively in providing input prompts. The following segment of code demonstrates this:

```
10  PRINT "What is your first name";
20  INPUT FIRST.NAME$
     .
     .
     .
```

When executed, the following screen display would result:

```
What is your first name? _
```

The semicolon at the end of the PRINT statement suppresses carriage return and line feed, so the question mark prompt generated by the INPUT statement appears on the same line as the prompting message. The data value entered in response to the question mark is then entered on the same line as the message:

```
What is your first name? Jack
```

The optional comma following an input prompt in the INPUT statement that suppresses the question mark may be used in conjunction with an input prompt to generate a gramatically correct prompt:

```
10  PRINT "Enter your first name:";
20  INPUT "", FIRST.NAME$
```

yields:

```
Enter your first name:_
```

which is better form than:

```
Enter your first name:?_
```

which is what would appear if the " ", in the INPUT statement were omitted.

The TAB and SPC Functions

Two useful functions furnished in the BASIC language are the TAB and SPC functions. Both may be used in PRINT statements to control the horizontal spacing of items on the output line. Their general forms are:

```
TAB(n)    and    SPC(n)
```

where n is a constant or numeric expression which evaluates to a number from 1 to the width of the output line.

The TAB function is used to indicate the column to which the cursor is to be moved before the next item in a PRINT statement is printed. For example:

```
10  PRINT TAB(9) "Hello!"
```

causes the display of 'Hello!' starting in column 9 on the current output line. If the cursor is already beyond the specified column in the current line, the cursor moves to the specified column of the next line. For example:

```
10  PRINT TAB(12) "Hi" TAB(8) "there!"
```

would result in the following screen display:

```
        Hi
    there!
Ok
```

The reason for two lines of output in the above example is as follows: Once the character string constant "Hi" has been printed, starting in column 12 as the TAB function preceding it indicates, the cursor will be in column 14. When it is time for the second TAB function to be executed, the cursor is well beyond column 8, which is where the second TAB indicates the cursor is to move. Because the cursor is unable to move backward in a line, the only way in which the second item in the PRINT statement can be printed in column 8 is if a new line is used. This causes the second character string constant, "there!", to be printed on the next line, beginning in column 8.

The SPC function causes a specified number of spaces to be skipped in a PRINT statement before the next item in the print list is displayed. An example of its use would be

```
10  PRINT "Hi" SPC(4) "there!"
```

When executed, this statement results in the following output:

```
Hi    there!
Ok
```

Both of these functions can be very useful in specifying exactly where output is to appear on the screen.

The LPRINT Statement

The LPRINT statement functions in a manner similar to the PRINT statement; the only difference is that output produced by this statement is displayed on the printer rather than on the screen. The general form of this statement is

```
line #  LPRINT [<constants, variables, and/or expressions>]
```

This statement is useful in producing hard-copy output from a program. All the features of the PRINT statement discussed earlier in this chapter operate in the same manner when used in the LPRINT statement as they do in the PRINT statement.

Let's examine a sample problem whose solution makes effective use of the LPRINT statement. I'm sure you have seen, if not received, a computer-generated form letter. This is a letter that has been printed by a computer and uses information about you to "personalize" the letter. By this, I mean that your name and perhaps address have been inserted by the computer into the body of the letter to make it appear that the letter was personally written by someone just for you.

Let's suppose that we wish to write a letter of application to a number of companies applying for a summer position. Rather than having to write an individual letter to each company, we wish to design a program to generate a computerized form letter that will permit us to enter information about the particular company and the particular job on the screen, and then have the computer print the letter on the printer.

The first step is to decide just what information it will be necessary to enter about each company so that when the letter is printed, it will contain the information specific to that particular company. Certainly the name of the company, the street address, and the city, state, and zip code are three items that will need to be entered. Another needed item is the name and title of the particular person in the company to whom the letter is to be sent. Since not all the companies to which we will be sending the letter will have the same job opening, we will also need to enter the name of the particular job for which application is being made.

The statements necessary to request and accept entry of the above information are as follows:

```
100  REM Program to generate a job application form letter
110  REM J. Castek, 7/29/87
120  REM
130  REM This section of the program requests the
140  REM information needed to prepare a job application
150  REM form letter.
160  REM
170  PRINT "Enter the name of the company:";
```

```
180   INPUT "", COMPANY.NAME$
190   PRINT "Enter the street address:";
200   INPUT "", STREET.ADDRESS$
210   PRINT "Enter the city, state, and zip code. Enter this"
220   PRINT " information in double quotation marks:";
230   INPUT "", CITY.STATE$
240   PRINT "Enter the title to be used in the salutation of"
250   PRINT " the letter (Mr., Ms., etc.):";
260   INPUT "", TITLE$
270   PRINT "Enter the first name of the person to whom the"
280   PRINT " letter is to be addressed:";
290   INPUT "", FIRST.NAME$
300   PRINT "Enter their last name:";
310   INPUT "", LAST.NAME$
320   PRINT "Enter their position title:";
330   INPUT "", POSITION.TITLE$
340   PRINT "Enter the job for which you are applying:";
350   INPUT "", JOB$
```

Notice that PRINT statements are used in the above section of code since the entry of the information needed to prepare the letter is to be performed in response to input prompts displayed upon the screen. The use of the optional " ", immediately following the word INPUT in the INPUT statements suppresses the question mark prompt normally produced by an INPUT statement.

The next section of the program, which will actually print the letter, uses LPRINT statements, since we wish to have the letter printed on paper and not on the screen:

```
360   REM
370   REM This section produces the requested letter on paper
380   REM
390   LPRINT TAB(30); "1535 Main Street"
400   LPRINT TAB(30); "La Crosse, WI 54601"
410   LPRINT TAB(30); "April 10, 1987"
420   LPRINT
430   LPRINT
440   LPRINT
450   LPRINT
460   LPRINT TITLE$ SPC(1) FIRST.NAME$ SPC(1) LAST.NAME$
470   LPRINT POSITION.TITLE$
480   LPRINT COMPANY.NAME$
490   LPRINT STREET.ADDRESS$
500   LPRINT CITY.STATE$
510   LPRINT
520   LPRINT "Dear ";TITLE$ SPC(1) LAST.NAME$;":"
530   LPRINT
540   LPRINT "     I would like to apply for a summer position"
```

```
550  LPRINT "as ";JOB$;" with your company. I have had"
560  LPRINT "experience working at a job similar to this for"
570  LPRINT "the last two summers, and am certain I could do"
580  LPRINT "the work satisfactorily."
590  LPRINT
600  LPRINT "      I would be able to come for an interview on"
610  LPRINT "any afternoon after 2:00 p.m. that is convenient"
620  LPRINT "for you. I will be available to start work any"
630  LPRINT "time after Friday, May 24, as this is my last"
640  LPRINT "day of school for the spring."
650  LPRINT
660  LPRINT "      I would like to work for ";COMPANY.NAME$ "as"
670  LPRINT JOB$;" very much, and would appreciate"
680  LPRINT "hearing from you as soon as possible. Thank you"
690  LPRINT "for your consideration."
700  LPRINT
710  LPRINT TAB(30);"Sincerely yours,"
720  LPRINT
730  LPRINT
740  LPRINT
750  LPRINT TAB(30);"John Richards"
760  END
```

This second portion of the program uses many features of the PRINT statement (or, in this case, LPRINT statement). Notice the use of the TAB function in lines 390 through 410 which causes the address and date to be printed on the right side of the page. The SPC function is used in lines 460 and 520 to cause a single blank space to be printed to separate the character strings being printed by these two statements.

When executed, the first section of the program produces output on the screen. Output from the last section, lines 360 through 740, would be sent directly to the printer. A sample run of the first section appears below:

```
Enter the name of the company: Lee Gas Company
Enter the street address: 1002 Academy Street
Enter the city, state, and zip code. Enter this
   information in double quotation marks: "Elroy, WI 53929"
Enter the title to be used in the salutation of
   the letter (Mr., Ms., etc.): Mr.
Enter the first name of the person to whom the
   letter is to be addressed: Charles
Enter their last name: Huschka
Enter their position title: Operations Manager
Enter the job for which you are applying: a meter reader
```

Notice that each data item entered above is entered on the same line as its prompt. This occurs because a semicolon has been placed after each PRINT statement that precedes one of the input statements. No question mark prompts are generated by the INPUT statements since the optional " ", preceding the list of input variables has been used in each INPUT statement.

Once the above information has been entered, the computer prints the letter on the printer. The finished letter would appear as follows:

```
                                          1535 Main Street
                                          La Crosse, WI 54601
                                          April 10, 1987




        Mr. Charles Huschka
        Operations Manager
        Lee Gas Company
        1002 Academy Street
        Elroy, WI 53929

        Dear Mr. Huschka:

            I would like to apply for a summer position
        as a meter reader with your company. I have had
        experience working at a job similar to this for
        the last two summers, and am certain I could do
        the work satisfactorily.

            I would be able to come for an interview on
        any afternoon after 2:00 p.m. that is convenient
        for you. I will be available to start work any
        time after Friday, May 24, as this is my last
        day of school for the spring.

            I would like to work for Lee Gas Company as
        a meter reader very much, and would appreciate
        hearing from you as soon as possible. Thank you
        for your consideration.

                                          Sincerely yours,



                                          John Richards
```

As you can see, the letter above appears as though it has been "personally" written to a particular person at a particular company to apply for a particular job. Entry of different data when the program is run again would produce just as personal a letter seeking a completely different job at another company.

4.6 NUMERIC EXPRESSIONS

There are many problem situations in which it is necessary to instruct the computer to perform arithmetic calculations in order to solve a problem. This next section of the chapter describes the symbols that may be used in BASIC programs to form the numeric expressions needed to perform arithmetic calculations, and the manner in which the computer will perform these calculations.

Arithmetic Operators

There are a number of different symbols that are used in BASIC to instruct the computer to perform particular calculations. Some of these we have already used in designing pseudocode solutions to problems; some of the others that are available we have not. The symbols that may be used to form arithmetic expressions are given in the following table.

The Arithmetic Operators in BASIC

Operator	Meaning	Example
^	Exponentiation	3^2
−	Negation	−7
*	Multiplication	5*6
/	Real number division	6 / 4
\	Integer division	6 \ 4
MOD	Modulo arithmetic	12 MOD 5
+	Addition	3 + 4
−	Subtraction	7 − 2

Most of these symbols are no doubt quite familiar to you. Others, however, may not be. Let's briefly review them.

The ^ symbol, which is called a *circumflex*, indicates that a number is to be raised to a power. The expression 3 ^ 2 would be read as "3 raised to the second power" or "3 squared." In either case, it indicates that 3 is to be multiplied by itself, giving the resulting value of 9. This notation is used rather than the more common

3^2, since there is no easy way to write the power 2 as a small number slightly above and to the right of the base 3 on the display screen.

The negative symbol, $-$, simply means that the negative of a value is to be computed. If, for example, the variable X contains the value -3, the negation of X, or $-X$, would be equal to 3.

The * (asterisk) is used in BASIC to indicate multiplication. The expression 5 * 6 means to multiply 5 by 6 giving 30.

The symbol / is used to indicate real number division. This means that when the division is performed, the answer, or quotient, is to be expressed as a decimal value, correct to as many decimal places as the computer can calculate it. The expression 6 / 4 , for example, would yield the result 1.5.

The symbol \ also indicates that division is to be performed, but it is to be what is known as *integer division*. This operation may only be performed on integers; so if the value preceding the symbol and the value following the symbol are not integers (whole numbers), they will first be rounded to integers. The division is then performed, and the quotient truncated (rounded down) to a whole number. 6 \ 4 results in a value of 1. The expression 3.84 \ 2.123 would first be converted to 4 \ 2, which would then result in an answer of 2.

The operator MOD performs what is referred to as *modulo arithmetic*. The expression 12 MOD 7 would evaluate to 5. This would be the same value obtained for the remainder if integer division were performed (12 divided by 7 is 1 with a remainder of 5). This operation is also permitted only on integers, so the *operands* (values preceding and following the word MOD) are first rounded to integer values before the MOD operation is performed.

The $+$ symbol obviously indicates addition. The expression 3 + 4 yields 7 when it is evaluated.

The symbol $-$ may also be used to indicate subtraction when it appears between two constants and/or variables. The expression 7 $-$ 2 means, "subtract 2 from 7," yielding 5.

Order of Operations

When several arithmetic operations occur in an arithmetic expression, there is a particular order in which these operations are performed by the computer. This order is referred to as the *order of precedence* and is the same as the order in which operations are performed in algebra. The following table indicates the order in which operations will be performed by the computer when an arithmetic expression is evaluated. Operators are listed in the table in order from highest precedence (performed first) to lowest precedence (performed last):

Order of Precedence of the Arithmetic Operators

Operator	Meaning
^	Exponentiation
−	Negation
*,/	Multiplication, real number division
\	Integer division
MOD	Modulo arithmetic
+ ,−	Addition, subtraction

When two operators have the same level of precedence, as, for example, do the Addition and Subtraction operators, they are performed in left-to-right order as they are encountered in an arithmetic expression. Parentheses may also be used to indicate the order in which operations are to be performed. Operations within parentheses are always performed first.

Evaluating Arithmetic Expressions

The following examples illustrate the application of the rules given above for evaluating BASIC arithmetic expressions:

☐ **Example 1**

      2 + 3 * 2 − 4 = ?

This expression would be evaluated as follows:

1. There are no parentheses in the expression, so the first step is to determine which operator has the highest precedence.
2. Looking at the table above, we can see that the multiplication (*) operator has the highest precedence of any operator contained in the expression being evaluated.
3. Evaluating this part of the expression, 3 * 2 = 6, so we are left with 2 + 6 − 4 to evaluate.
4. The two remaining operations, addition (+) and subtraction (−), are at the same level of precedence, so they are performed in order, from left to right. 2 + 6 = 8, and 8 − 4 = 4, which is the value of the expression.

☐ **Example 2**

```
(3 + 2) * 2^3 + 5 - 6 * 3 = ?
```

Evaluation of this expression would be performed as follows:

1. This expression does contain parentheses, so the first operation performed would be $(3 + 2) = 5$. The expression would now look like this:

```
5 * 2^3 + 5 - 6 * 3 = ?
```

2. The exponentiation operator (ˆ) in the expression has the highest order of precedence of the operators remaining, so it would be performed next. $(2ˆ3 = 2 * 2 * 2 = 8$. Now we have

```
5 * 8 + 5 - 6 * 3 = ?
```

3. There are two multiplication operators (*) in the expression, so they are performed in order from left to right, $5 * 8 = 40$ and $6 * 3 = 18$. The expression is now

```
40 + 5 - 18 = ?
```

4. The two remaining operators, addition (+) and subtraction (−), have the same order of precedence, so they are performed in order from left to right, $40 + 5 = 45$, and $45 - 18 = 27$, the value of the expression.

☐ **Example 3**

```
19 MOD 14 \ 3 + 3 = ?
```

This last expression to be evaluated contains two of the less commonly used operators, MOD and integer divide (\). It would be evaluated as follows:

1. There are no parentheses in the expression, so we can immediately perform the operation having the highest level of precedence, the integer division (\) operation; $14 \setminus 3 = 4$. The expression would now be

```
19 MOD 4 * 3 = ?
```

2. The next operation to be performed is the MOD operation. $19 \text{ MOD } 4 = 3$ (19 divided by 4 is 4 with a remainder of 3). The expression is now

```
3 + 3 = ?
```

3. All that remains to be done is to perform the addition, 3 + 3, which gives a final result of 6 for the expression.

A problem that requires some rather extensive calculations is the problem of making change using the fewest possible number of coins. Given the following formal problem definition, let's perform a complete top-down design, and then write a BASIC program to solve this problem:

□ Formal Problem Definition

General Description

A program is to be prepared to calculate and output the fewest number of coins that may be used to make change for a purchase.

Input Specifications

Input to the program will be two values. The first, and smaller of the two values, will be the amount of the purchase. The second, and larger of the two values, will be the amount tendered to pay for the item. Both values will be whole numbers and less than or equal to 100. The first value will be entered in response to the input prompt:

```
Enter the amount of the purchase: <cost>
```

The second value will be prompted by the message:

```
Enter the amount tendered: <amount>
```

Output Specifications

The first line of output will be the amount of change. This amount (<change>) is calculated by subtracting the cost of the item (<cost>) from the amount tendered (<amount>). This value will be displayed as follows:

```
The amount of change due the customer is: <change>
```

This line of output will be followed by a blank line, followed by several lines listing the number of quarters, dimes, nickels, and pennies given in change. Each of these lines will have the following form:

```
<n> quarter(s)
<n> dime(s)
      .
      .
      .
```

Normal Example

Input:

```
Enter the amount of the purchase: 34
Enter the amount tendered: 100
```

Output:

```
The amount of change due the customer is: 66

2 quarter(s)
1 dime(s)
1ˑ nickel(s)
1 penny(ies)
```

Unusual or Error Conditions

1. If the first value entered is larger than the second, a negative amount of change will be computed and the number of coins will be incorrect.
2. If decimal values are entered, the amount of change will be calculated correctly, but the number of coins will be incorrect.
3. If negative values are entered, the amount of change will be incorrect, as well as the number of coins.

The first level of the top-down design might be

Level I

{enter the cost of the item}
{enter the amount tendered}
{compute the amount of change}
{display the amount of change}
{compute the number of each coin}
{display the number of each coin}

If we examine the input specifications of the formal problem definition, we see that the first comment, *{enter the cost of the item}*, results in two pseudocode statements:

WRITE ("Enter the amount of the purchase:")
READ (COST)

and likewise, the next comment, *{enter the amount tendered}*, is refined to be

WRITE ("Enter the amount tendered:")
READ (AMOUNT)

The next comment, {*compute the amount of change*}, would result in an assignment statement:

CHANGE ← AMOUNT − COST

The comment, {*display the amount of change*}, would translate into a WRITE statement, the exact format of which may be found in the output specifications:

WRITE (*"The amount of change due the customer is:"*, CHANGE)

The next statement at this point, according to the output specifications, is to display a blank line:

WRITE

Grouping together the pseudocode statements we have thus far, Level II would look like this:

Level II
WRITE (*"Enter the amount of the purchase:"*)
READ (COST)
WRITE (*"Enter the amount tendered:"*)
READ (AMOUNT)
CHANGE ← AMOUNT − COST
WRITE (*"The amount of change due the customer is:"*, CHANGE)
WRITE

The next comment to be refined, {*compute the number of each coin*}, is not yet specific enough to be converted to pseudocode, so it needs to be refined into one or more comments. This comment might be replaced by the following comments:

{*compute the number of quarters*}
{*compute the number of dimes*}
{*compute the number of nickels*}
{*compute the number of pennies*}

A completed Level II, then, might be as follows:

Level II
WRITE (*"Enter the amount of the purchase:"*)
READ (COST)

WRITE (*"Enter the amout tendered:"*)
READ (*AMOUNT*)
CHANGE ← AMOUNT − COST
WRITE (*"The amount of change due the customer is:"*,*CHANGE*)
WRITE
{*compute the number of quarters*}
{*compute the number of dimes*}
{*compute the number of nickels*}
{*compute the number of pennies*}
{*display the number of each coin*}

The first comment to be refined in Level III is {*compute the number of quarters*}. How can the number of quarters be computed? Suppose the amount of change that had been calculated for a specific pair of input values was 83 cents. We can see that there would be 3 quarters in this amount. The question is, how do we instruct the computer as to how to determine this? One way in which this could be done is to divide the amount of change by 25, the value of one quarter, and take the whole number, or integer, part of the answer.

Fortunately we have a BASIC language operator that will perform an integer division, the backward slash (\). The number of quarters then, would be given by CHANGE \ 25. Therefore the comment, {*compute the number of quarters*}, could be replaced with:

QUARTERS ← CHANGE \ 25

Once we have given the customer 3 quarters in change, there remains 8 cents to be given in change (3 quarters is 75 cents, and 83 − 75 = 8 cents). In order to determine how many of the next coins are needed, the amount paid out so far needs to be subtracted from the total amount of change with which we started. This could be accomplished in several ways. One way is to subtract the number of quarters multiplied by 25 from the original amount of change:

CHANGE ← CHANGE − QUARTERS * 25

The other way in which this could be done is to use the MOD function. The remainder obtained when the original amount of change was divided by 25 can be calculated by using the MOD function, CHANGE MOD 25. This method would also result in an assignment statement:

CHANGE ← CHANGE MOD 25

Either method would work fine and produce the same result; CHANGE now contains the amount of change remaining to be paid after the quarters have been paid out.

The number of each of the remaining coins would be calculated in a similar manner. Translating these remaining comments into pseudocode would yield the following Level III:

Level III

```
WRITE ("Enter the amount of the purchase:")
READ (COST)
WRITE ("Enter the amount tendered:")
READ (AMOUNT)
CHANGE ← AMOUNT − COST
WRITE ("The amount of change due the customer is:", CHANGE)
WRITE
QUARTERS ← CHANGE \ 25
CHANGE ← CHANGE MOD 25
DIMES ← CHANGE \ 10
CHANGE ← CHANGE MOD 10
NICKELS ← CHANGE \ 5
CHANGE ← CHANGE MOD 5
PENNIES ← CHANGE
{display the number of each coin}
```

Notice that the number of pennies will be equal to the amount of change remaining after the nickels have been taken out. We could have divided CHANGE by 1 if we wanted to continue the pattern used for the previous coins, but it would produce the same result, so it was not done. All that remains to be done is refine the last comment, {display the number of each coin}, into a series of WRITE statements that will produce the output shown in the output specifications section of the formal problem definition. A final pseudocode solution to the problem, then, would be

Level III

```
WRITE ("Enter the amount of the purchase:")
READ (COST)
WRITE ("Enter the amount tendered:")
READ (AMOUNT)
CHANGE ← AMOUNT − COST
WRITE ("The amount of change due the customer is:", CHANGE)
```

```
WRITE
QUARTERS ← CHANGE \ 25
CHANGE ← CHANGE MOD 25
DIMES ← CHANGE \ 10
CHANGE ← CHANGE MOD 10
NICKELS ← CHANGE \ 5
CHANGE ← CHANGE MOD 5
PENNIES ← CHANGE
WRITE (QUARTERS, "quarter(s)")
WRITE (DIMES, "dime(s)")
WRITE (NICKELS, "nickel(s)")
WRITE (PENNIES, "penny(ies)")
```

The translation of this to BASIC would be quite simple. First, each pseudocode statement is assigned a line number:

```
10     WRITE ('Enter the amount of the purchase:')
20     READ (COST)
30     WRITE ('Enter the amount tendered:')
40     READ (AMOUNT)
50     CHANGE ← AMOUNT − COST
60     WRITE ('The amount of change due the customer is:',CHANGE)
70     WRITE
80     QUARTERS ← CHANGE \ 25
90     CHANGE ← CHANGE MOD 25
100    DIMES ← CHANGE \ 10
110    CHANGE ← CHANGE MOD 10
120    NICKELS ← CHANGE \ 5
130    CHANGE ← CHANGE MOD 5
140    PENNIES ← CHANGE
150    WRITE (QUARTERS, 'quarter(s)')
160    WRITE (DIMES, 'dime(s)')
170    WRITE (NICKELS, 'nickel(s)')
180    WRITE (PENNIES, 'penny(ies)')
```

Each pseudocode statement is then translated into a corresponding BASIC statement as follows:

```
10    PRINT "Enter the amount of the purchase:";
20    INPUT "", COST
30    PRINT "Enter the amount tendered:";
```

```
40    INPUT "", AMOUNT
50    CHANGE = AMOUNT - COST
60    PRINT "The amount of change due the customer is:";CHANGE
70    PRINT
80    QUARTERS = CHANGE \ 25
90    CHANGE = CHANGE MOD 25
100   DIMES = CHANGE \ 10
110   CHANGE = CHANGE MOD 10
120   NICKELS = CHANGE \ 5
130   CHANGE = CHANGE MOD 5
140   PENNIES = CHANGE
150   PRINT QUARTERS;"quarter(s)"
160   PRINT DIMES;"dime(s)"
170   PRINT NICKELS;"nickel(s)"
180   PRINT PENNIES;"penny(ies)"
```

Let's examine one final topic in this section, the conversion of algebraic expressions to equivalent BASIC expressions. Given the following algebraic expression, how would it be expressed in BASIC?

$$\frac{3X + Y}{X - Y} + 7$$

As we examine this expression, we can see that the quantity $3X + Y$ is to be divided by the quantity $X - Y$, and then 7 is to be added to this result. This could be expressed in BASIC as:

```
(3 * X + Y) / (X - Y) + 7
```

Two observations should be made concerning this solution. Parentheses need to be placed around the quantities $3 * X + Y$ and $X - Y$ so that these operations are performed before the division is done. The second observation is that implied multiplication ($3X$ in algebra means 3 times X) is not allowed in BASIC as it is in algebra; the computer must be specifically instructed to perform the multiplication of X by 3 by writing it as $3 * X$.

One final caution that should be mentioned regarding the formation of numeric expressions in BASIC; two arithmetic operators cannot occur together in an expression; for example, the expression

```
3 * + 4
```

would be invalid since the multiplication and addition operators occur together between the constants 3 and 4.

4.7 SUMMARY

Both the INPUT and READ statements may be used to enter values into variables in a BASIC program. Either may serve as the BASIC language translation of the pseudocode READ statement. If a BASIC READ statement is used in a program, one or more DATA statements must be included in the program to hold the data values to be used by the READ. The RESTORE statement may be used to direct the READ statement as to which DATA statement from which to select values.

Microsoft BASIC permits screen displays to be of either 40 or 80 characters in width. The WIDTH statement may be used to instruct the computer as to which length of line to use to display information.

Horizontal placement of values in an output line may be controlled by the use of semicolons and commas as separators in the print list of a PRINT statement. The TAB and SPC functions may also be used in PRINT statements to format output.

The LPRINT statement is used to direct output to a printer rather than the screen. It may use punctuation marks and the TAB and SPC functions to control the appearance of a printed line just as the PRINT statement does with a line on the screen.

When arithmetic expressions in BASIC are evaluated, the order in which operations are performed is determined by the order of precedence of the arithmetic operators. Operations within parenthesis are always performed first.

A table summarizing the conversion process for the pseudocode READ statement to its BASIC language equivalent statements is given in the following table.

The Pseudocode READ statement and Its BASIC Language Equivalents

Pseudocode	BASIC
READ (<variable> [, <variable>])	line # INPUT ["prompt",] <variable> [,<variable>]
or	
	line # READ <variable> [,<variable>]

EXERCISES

1. Write appropriate PRINT statements to provide input prompts and INPUT statements to accept data entry for each of the following situations. Appropriate variable names will also need to be selected:

   a. Enter a temperature in degrees Celsius.
   b. Enter your favorite color.

    c. Enter a date such as July 12, 1986, all into a single variable.

    d. Enter a person's weight in pounds and ounces.

    e. Enter an employee's name, hours worked, and hourly pay rate.

    f. Enter the city and state in which you live.

    g. Enter the string consisting of two blank spaces followed by the letter x followed by three blank spaces.

2. What is a numeric variable in BASIC? a character string variable? How do you name these two types of variables so that the computer can tell which is which?

3. Write appropriate READ and DATA statements to perform the following:

    a. Enter the value 3 into the variable A.

    b. Enter the value 6 into the variable B and the value 7 into the variable C.

    c. Read the names of three grocery items into the variables ITEM1$, ITEM2$, and ITEM3$, and then their respective prices into PRICE1, PRICE2, and PRICE3.

    d. Read the name of a grocery item into ITEM1$ and its price into PRICE1, then read the name of a second grocery item into ITEM2$ and its price into PRICE2, and lastly the name and price of a third item into ITEM3$ and PRICE3.

4. What values would be stored in the variables A, B, C, D, and E by each of the following segments of program code?

```
a. 100   READ A, B          b. 100   READ A, B
   110   READ C                110   READ C
   120   READ D, E             120   RESTORE
   130   DATA 3,4,5            130   READ D
   140   DATA 8,2             140   READ E
   150   DATA 7,1             150   DATA 2,4,6,8
                              160   DATA 3,5,7

c. 100   READ A             d. 100   RESTORE 180
   110   RESTORE 190           110   READ A, B, C
   120   READ B, C             120   READ B, C
   130   RESTORE 180           130   RESTORE 170
   140   READ D                140   READ D, E
   150   RESTORE               150   READ A
   160   READ E                160   DATA 2,4
   170   DATA 2,4,6            170   DATA 6
   180   DATA 3,5              180   DATA 8,10
   190   DATA 7,9              190   DATA 3,5,7,9
   200   DATA 1
```

5. Describe the output that would be produced by each of the following PRINT statements. Indicate what values would be printed and exactly where they would appear on the screen.

```
a. 10   PRINT "Hi";"there!"
b. 10   PRINT "Hi","there!"
c. 10   PRINT "Hi",,"there!"
d. 10   PRINT A; B; C
        (A = 45 B = -33 and C = 123456)
```

e. 10   PRINT A, B, C
             (A = 45 B = −33 and C = 123456)
f. 10   PRINT TAB(10) "Hello" TAB(20) "Mary"
g. 10   PRINT SPC(10) "Hello" SPC(20) "Mary"
h. 10   PRINT TAB(30) "***" TAB(20) "***"

6. Determine what output would be produced by each of the following short program segments. Indicate what values would be printed and exactly where they would appear on the screen (A = 10 B = 20 C = − 19).

a. 100   PRINT A,
      110   PRINT B; C

b. 100   PRINT A TAB(2) B;
      110   PRINT TAB(12) C

c. 100   PRINT A;
      110   PRINT B;
      120   PRINT C

d. 100   WIDTH 40
      110   PRINT TAB (35) A, B, C

7. If A = 3, B = 4, C = 2, and D = 6, evaluate each of the following BASIC assignment statements for the value of X.

a. 30   X = A * B + D / A
b. 30   X = B + D / C + A
c. 30   X = (B + D) / (C + A)
d. 30   X = C ^ A / B + D
e. 30   X = C ^ A ^ B / B * C
f. 30   X = (D \ B) * A − C
g. 30   X = B MOD A + C
h. 30   X = (A + B * (D − B) ^ C) MOD (A ^ C + C)

8. Translate each of the following algebraic expressions into equivalent BASIC assignment statements.

a. $A = \dfrac{B + C}{D}$ **b.** $X = \dfrac{A}{B} + \dfrac{C}{D}$

c. $M = \dfrac{(Y2 - Y1)}{(X2 - X1)}$ **d.** $A = \dfrac{(B1 + B2)H}{2}$

e. $Y = 2X^2 + 3X - 7$ **f.** $V = B \times H \times L$

9. Write a program to input a length in yards, feet, and inches and output the equivalent length in inches. Provide appropriate prompts for the input values and label your answer.

10. Write a program to input the miles traveled and the gallons of gasoline used in your car and compute and output the miles per gallon you obtained. Miles per gallon is equal to miles traveled divided by gallons of gasoline used.

11. Write a program to input the radius of a circle and compute the circumference and area of the circle. The formulas needed are:

$$\text{Circumference} = 2 \times \text{pi} \times \text{radius}$$

and

$$\text{Area} = \text{pi} \times \text{radius} \times \text{radius}$$

Use 3.14159 for the value of pi.

12. Write a program to compute the interest (I) earned on a sum of money (P) deposited for a number of days (T) at an interest rate (R). Values for P, T, and R are to be input. The formula for calculating I is

$$I = P \times R \times T/360$$

Be sure that your input prompt for R, the interest rate, indicates that R must be entered as a decimal value (8 percent is to be entered as .08).

13. Write a program to compute the value of the change you have in your pocket. Input will be the number of quarters, dimes, nickels, and pennies. Output is to be the total value of this change in dollars and cents. For example, if you had 5 quarters, 3 dimes, 4 nickels, and 7 pennies, the computer should output that the total value of your change is $1.82. Provide input prompts for the number of each coin you have, and label the answer appropriately.

14. Write a program to input a person's first and last name and then output it in the form:

    last name, first name

When the output is produced, the comma should immediately follow the person's last name, followed by a single space, followed by the person's first name.

15. Write a program to generate a form letter requesting a campaign donation for Senator Snort's campaign for the United States Senate. Request appropriate input from the screen so that the letter can be "personalized" for each contributor, and then have the letter output on the printer.

CHAPTER 5

Selection Statements

Problem situations frequently occur in which choices must be made. One action must be performed when a certain condition exists and another action, or no action, performed when the condition does not exist. Selection statements are typically used to design solutions to this type of problem. This chapter discusses how to write the expressions used in selection statements to describe the condition that determines the set of actions to be performed under a given condition. The translation of the pseudocode selection statements, IF-THEN and IF-THEN-ELSE, into their BASIC language form is also explained. Using these statements in writing problem solutions concludes the chapter.

5.0 OBJECTIVES

Upon completion of this chapter, you should be able to:

1. Write simple conditional expressions using the relational operators.
2. Write compound conditional expressions using AND, OR, and NOT.

3. Determine the truth value of compound conditional expressions.

4. Convert pseudocode IF-THEN statements into equivalent BASIC language IF-THEN statements.

5. Convert pseudocode IF-THEN-ELSE statements into equivalent BASIC language IF-THEN-ELSE statements.

6. Design BASIC language solutions to problems using the appropriate selection statements.

5.1 THE RELATIONAL OPERATORS

The relational operators are the symbols that can be used in both pseudocode and BASIC statements to express the relationship between two variables, constants, and/or expressions. A list of these operators and their meanings is provided below.

Relational Operators

Symbol	Meaning
$<$	Less than
$>$	Greater than
$=$	Equal to
$<>$ or $><$	Not equal to
$>=$ or $=>$	Greater than or equal to
$<=$ or $=<$	Less than or equal to

These symbols are a shorthand notation used to write conditional expressions that describe the relationship between two values.

5.2 CONDITIONAL EXPRESSIONS

A conditional expression is a statement of the relationship between two values. For example, if the value stored in a variable named NUM1 is 6 and the value stored in a second variable named NUM2 is 4, a statement describing the relationship between these two variables could be "NUM2 is less than NUM1." A shorthand method of expressing this condition is "NUM2 < NUM1." The symbol '<' means "less than," as can be seen in the table of relational operators in the previous section.

The general form of a simple conditional expression is

$$\left(\begin{array}{c}\text{variable, constant}\\\text{or expression}\end{array}\right) \quad \left(\begin{array}{c}\text{relational}\\\text{operator}\end{array}\right) \quad \left(\begin{array}{c}\text{variable, constant}\\\text{or expression}\end{array}\right)$$

Notice that only one relational operator can be used in a conditional expression. Expressions such as $3 < X < 10$, which are common in mathematics, may *not* be used in either pseudocode or BASIC.

If a conditional expression is contained in a BASIC language statement, when the statement is evaluated by the BASIC interpreter, the conditional expression is assigned a value of either "TRUE" or "FALSE". This is referred to as the *truth value* of the expression. For example, suppose the conditional expression HOURS.-WORKED > 40 is contained in a program, and when this expression is encountered by the BASIC interpreter during program execution, HOURS.-WORKED has the value 53. The expression, HOURS.WORKED > 40 will be assigned a value of "TRUE" by the interpreter. If this expression is encountered again later in the program, and the value of HOURS.WORKED is now 35, the expression would be evaluated this time as "FALSE".

Examples of simple conditional expressions are

```
SUM < 100
NUM1 + 3 < NUM2 + 6
DAY$ = "Monday"
```

The first example, SUM < 100, will be assigned either the value "TRUE" or "FALSE", depending upon the value of SUM at the time the expression is evaluated. The second example, which compares two numeric expressions, is evaluated in the following manner: First, the arithmetic calculations are performed; 3 is added to the value of NUM1 and 6 is added to the value of NUM2. Next the comparison is made—if the value of the first expression is less than the value of the second expression, the condition is assigned the value of "TRUE"; if not, the conditional expression is evaluated as "FALSE".

The third example illustrates the fact that the relationship between character strings can also be expressed. The conditional expression, DAY$ = "Monday", will be true only if the variable DAY$ contains the value "Monday" when the expression is evaluated. One other important point should be made with regard to the comparison of character strings; two strings are equal if and only if they contain *exactly* the same characters in the same order. For example, "Monday" is not equal to "MONDAY", nor is "Monday" equal to "Mnoday". For now we will use only the relational operators $=$ (equal to) and $<>$ (not equal to) for string comparisons.

The discussion of how one string may be greater than or less than another string will be postponed until Chapter 7.

5.3 LOGICAL OPERATORS—AND, OR, AND NOT

More complex relationships can be expressed in conditional expressions using the logical operators AND, OR, and NOT. When AND and OR are used in forming conditional expressions, these expressions are referred to as *compound conditional expressions.*

The *AND* operator is used to describe a situation in which two or more simple conditions must all be true in order for a certain action to be performed. If one or more of the simple conditions is false, the value of the entire compound expression is "FALSE". Suppose the statement is made, "Let's go to the beach if the sun is shining and the wind is not blowing." There are two simple conditions expressed in this statement: "the sun is shining" and "the wind is not blowing." If both of these simple conditions are true, we will go to the beach. If either one is false, that is, if the sun is *not* shining, or the wind is blowing, we will not go to the beach. If both conditions are false, we definitely won't go!

Examples of compound conditional expressions using the AND operator are:

```
          MONTH$ = "January" AND YEAR = 1988
          (AVERAGE >= 80) AND (AVERAGE < 90)
BILL > 100 AND DAYS.OVERDUE > 30 AND DEFERRED.ACCOUNT = "NO"
```

The first example is a compound conditional expression that compares the equality of two character strings in the first simple condition and performs a numeric comparison in the second simple condition. This is certainly permissible. What cannot be done is mix character strings and numbers in the same simple conditional expression. The second example above has parentheses around the simple conditions, which may be used to make the expression easier to read. In the third example, which contains three simple conditions, all three conditions must be true for the entire compound condition to be evaluated as "TRUE".

The possible truth values of the general form of a compound conditional expression that contains an AND operator:

```
<condition 1> AND <condition 2>
```

can be summarized in a table as follows:

The AND Operator in a Compound Conditional Expression

condition 1	condition 2	condition 1 AND condition 2
TRUE	TRUE	TRUE
TRUE	FALSE	FALSE
FALSE	TRUE	FALSE
FALSE	FALSE	FALSE

As the table indicates, the only situation in which the compound condition is "TRUE" is when both of the simple conditions are "TRUE".

The above table is often referred to as a *truth table*. It is a shorthand method of listing all the possible combinations of true and false conditions for the simple conditions, <condition 1> and <condition 2>, and what the resulting truth value will be for a compound condition composed of these two simple conditions. For example, if we consider the second row in the table, we see that if the first simple condition, <condition 1>, is TRUE, and the second simple condition, <condition 2>, is FALSE, the compound condition, <condition 1> AND <condition 2>, will be FALSE.

The *OR* operator is used to write compound conditional expressions that describe situations in which only one of two or more simple conditions need be true for the compound condition to be true. For example, suppose the following statement is found in the operator's manual for your automobile, "Change the engine oil if it has been 2000 miles, or if it has been 60 days since the last oil change." Again, there are two simple conditions; "it has been 2000 miles (since the last oil change)", and "it has been 60 days since the last oil change." In this situation, however, the action, "Change the engine oil" is to be performed if *either* of the two simple conditions is true. If both are true, the engine oil definitely needs changing, but only one need be true to cause the action to be performed.

Examples of compound conditional expressions using the OR operator are:

```
              MILES > 2000 OR DAYS > 60
TRANS.CODE$ = "D" OR TRANS.CODE$ = "W" OR TRANS.CODE$ = "I"
              ANSWER$ = "Y" OR ANSWER$ = "y"
```

The first example is a BASIC language version of the conditions discussed in the previous paragraph. The second example illustrates that more than two simple conditions may be combined into a compound conditional expression with the OR operator. Only one of the three simple conditions need to be true for the compound expression to be true. The last example is a reminder that string comparisons need to consider the case of the characters being compared as well as the characters themselves.

A truth table summarizing the possible outcomes of the compound conditional expression:

```
<condition 1> OR <condition 2>
```

is:

The OR Operator in a Compound Conditional Expression

condition 1	condition 2	condition 1 OR condition 2
TRUE	TRUE	TRUE
TRUE	FALSE	TRUE
FALSE	TRUE	TRUE
FALSE	FALSE	FALSE

As can be seen in the table, the only situation in which a compound conditional expression containing an OR operator evaluates to "FALSE" is when both simple conditions are false. This same outcome is true if more than two simple conditional expressions are combined with OR operators: all must be false in order for the compound conditional expression to be false; if at least one simple condition is true, the compound condition is true.

The *NOT* operator is used for a different purpose than the AND and OR operators. It is used to *reverse* the meaning of a conditional expression rather than to combine simple conditional expressions into compound conditional expressions. For example, the conditional expression, SUM = 0, will be true if the variable SUM contains the value 0. If SUM contains any other value, the expression will evaluate to "FALSE". The conditional expression NOT (SUM = 0) evaluates exactly the opposite; if the variable SUM contains the value 0, the expression NOT (SUM = 0) evaluates as "FALSE". If SUM contains a value other than 0, NOT (SUM = 0) will be "TRUE".

When the NOT operator is used as shown above to reverse the meaning of a conditional expression, the expression following the word NOT must be enclosed in parentheses—the expression NOT SUM = 0 has an entirely different meaning to the BASIC language interpreter than does NOT (SUM = 0).

The NOT operator should be used sparingly. It is always better to state a condition directly than to state its opposite, and then reverse it by use of NOT. A major goal of this book is to encourage the reader to write programs that are easy to read and understand—conditional expressions that make use of the NOT operator do not, in most cases, advance this goal.

Obviously, the three logical operators AND, OR, and NOT can all appear in a single compound conditional expression. The order of precedence, that is, the order in which the simple conditions are evaluated to arrive at a single truth value of "TRUE" or "FALSE" for the compound expression, is as follows:

Order of Precedence for Evaluation of Conditional Expressions

1. Arithmetic calculations in conditional expressions are performed before any relational conditions are evaluated.
2. Conditional expressions inside parentheses are evaluated next.
3. The relational operations ($<$, $>$, $=$, etc.) are evaluated next.
4. The logical operations are evaluated in this order:

   a. NOT
   b. AND
   c. OR

Let's try an example. Given the compound conditional expression:

```
A > B AND B > C OR C > B AND C > A
```

and the values of A, B, and C as 6, 3, and 1, respectively, the truth value of the expression would be determined as follows:

1. There are no arithmetic calculations to be performed, so rule 1 is not applied.
2. There are no parentheses in the expression, so 2 does not need to be applied.
3. The four simple conditional expressions are evaluated next:

   $\textcircled{3}$
T		T		F		F
A > B	AND	B > C	OR	C > B	AND	C > A

4. Next, applying rule 4 above, the AND's are evaluated:

   $\textcircled{4}$
T		F

   $\textcircled{3}$
T	AND	T		F	AND	F
A > B	AND	B > C	OR	C > B	AND	C > A

   T AND T yields T and F AND F yields F.

5. Last of all, the OR is evaluated:

   $\textcircled{5}$
T

   $\textcircled{4}$
T	OR	F

(3) ___T___ AND ___T___ OR ___F___ AND ___F___

      A > B   AND   B > C   OR   C > B   AND   C > A

T OR F yields T, so the final truth value of the expression, then, is "TRUE".

Let's try one more, this time with an expression containing parentheses and a NOT:

    NOT (X > Y) AND ((X < Z + 2) OR (Z > Y))

and the values of X, Y, and Z being 4, 4, and 3, respectively.

(1) **1.** First, perform the arithmetic calculations:

$$3 + 2 = 5$$

    NOT (X > Y) AND ((X < Z + 2) OR (Z > Y))

(the value of Z, 3, is substituted for Z in the condition $(X < Z + 2)$, giving $(X < 3 + 2)$, or $(X < 5)$, expressed in its simplest form)

(2) **2.** Next, assign the truth values to the simple conditional expressions:

    NOT ___(F)___   ___(T___   ___F)___

    NOT (X > Y)   AND   ((X < 5)   OR   (Z > Y))

3. Since the compound condition on the right side of the expression is contained inside parentheses, it must be evaluated next:

                                   (3)   _____T_____

    NOT ___(F)___   ___(T___ OR ___F)___

    NOT (X > Y)   AND   ((X < 5) OR (Z > Y))

4. According to the order of precedence for the logical operators, next the NOT must be evaluated:

(4) ___T___   (3)   _____T_____

(2) NOT ___(F)___   ___(T___ OR ___F)___

    NOT (X > Y)   AND   ((X < 5) OR (Z > Y))

As can be seen, NOT (F) evaluates as T.

5. The last step is to evaluate the AND:

⑤ $\underline{\hspace{5cm} \text{T} \hspace{5cm}}$

④ $\underline{\hspace{1cm} \text{T} \hspace{1cm}}$ AND $\underline{\hspace{4cm} \text{T} \hspace{4cm}}$

② NOT $\underline{\hspace{1cm} \text{(F)} \hspace{1cm}}$ $\underline{\hspace{0.5cm} \text{(T}} \hspace{0.3cm} \text{OR} \hspace{0.3cm} \underline{\text{F)}}$

   NOT   (X > Y)   AND   ((X < 5)   OR   (Z > Y))

Since we have a T and a T, combined by an AND operator, the entire expression evaluates to T, or "TRUE".

Now that we know how to write and evaluate conditional expressions, they can be used in selection statements needed in problem solutions. As you may recall from Chapter 2, there are two basic types of selection statements—the IF-THEN and the IF-THEN-ELSE. Let's consider the simpler one first—the IF-THEN statement.

5.4 THE IF-THEN STATEMENT

The IF-THEN statement is used in problem solutions to perform a sequence of actions when a particular condition is true. If the condition is false, the actions are not performed and program execution continues with the statement following the ENDIF statement. This may be diagramed as is shown in Figure 5.1. If the condition is true, Action 1, Action 2, etc., are performed. If the condition is false, these actions are omitted and program execution continues with the statement following the IF-THEN structure in the program. An example of a pseudolanguage comment which would result in an IF-THEN statement would be

> {If employee works more than 40 hours, compute overtime pay
> as 1.5 times the regular pay rate for all hours over 40}

The first refinement of this comment might be

> IF HOURS.WORKED > 40
> THEN
>   {compute overtime pay}
> ENDIF

A further refinement might produce:

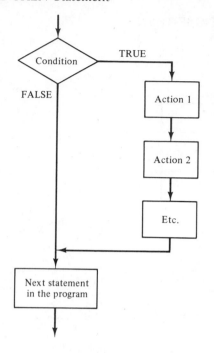

Figure 5.1 Flowchart of an IF-THEN control structure.

$$IF\ HOURS.WORKED > 40$$
$$THEN$$
$$\qquad OVERTIME.PAY \leftarrow 1.5 * PAYRATE * (HOURS.WORKED - 40)$$
$$ENDIF$$

Now that this statement is written in pseudocode, all that remains is to convert it to BASIC.

Converting Pseudocode to BASIC

The general form of the IF-THEN statement in BASIC is

```
line# IF <condition> THEN <statementl> ELSE <statement2> *
```

The execution of this general form occurs as indicated in the flowchart in Figure 5.2. The operations illustrated in this flowchart may be described as follows:

---

*Note: This is really the general form of the IF—THEN—ELSE statement but is the statement that will be used to convert both IF—THEN and IF—THEN—ELSE pseudocode control structures to a structured BASIC form.

Figure 5.2 Flowchart of the BASIC IF-THEN-ELSE statement.

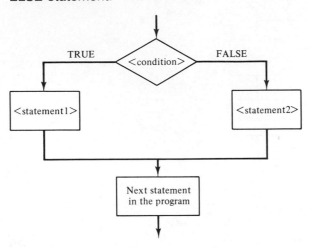

1. The conditional expression, <condition>, following the word IF evaluates as either "TRUE" or "FALSE".
2. If the <condition> is "TRUE", (statement1), which follows the word THEN, is executed.
3. If the <condition> is "FALSE", (statement2), which follows the word ELSE, is executed.

This is quite different from the pseudocode form of the IF-THEN statement we have been using. The following example illustrates how this BASIC statement will be used to implement the pseudocode IF-THEN structure we have been using. Let's use the IF-THEN pseudocode example from the previous section:

```
IF HOURS.WORKED > 40
THEN
        OVERTIME.PAY ← 1.5 * PAYRATE * (HOURS.WORKED − 40)
ENDIF
```

The first step is to assign line numbers to each pseudocode statement, selecting numbers that would place it in the proper position in our program. Suppose line number 100 is where this segment of code needs to begin:

```
100   IF HOURS.WORKED > 40
110   THEN
```

```
120        OVERTIME.PAY ← 1.5 * PAYRATE * (HOURS.WORKED
           − 40)
130    ENDIF
```

The second step is to convert statements numbered 110 through 130 to their BASIC language equivalents. There is no BASIC language THEN statement, so line 110 is converted to a remark statement by placing a single quote (') before the word THEN. This is also the case for line 130, ENDIF; it is also changed to a remark statement by placing a single quote mark before the word ENDIF. Line 120 is an assignment statement and, as has already been shown, is translated into BASIC by changing the pseudocode assignment operator (←) to an equal sign (=). The segment of code would now look like this:

```
100    IF HOURS.WORKED > 40
110    'THEN
120       OVERTIME.PAY = 1.5 * PAYRATE * (HOURS.WORKED − 40)
130    'ENDIF
```

The only pseudocode statement left to convert to BASIC is line 100, the IF statement. Referring back to the general form:

```
line# IF <condition> THEN <statement1> ELSE <statement2>
```

the conversion of a pseudocode IF-THEN statement is performed as follows:

1. Replace <statement 1>, which follows the word THEN, with the statement, GOTO <line#1>, where <line#1> is the line number of the 'THEN statement.
2. Replace <statement 2>, which follows the word ELSE, with the statement, GOTO <line#2>, where <line#2> is the line number of the 'ENDIF statement.

Performing these steps on statement 100 of the pseudocode segment results in:

```
100  IF HOURS.WORKED > 40 THEN GOTO 110 ELSE GOTO 130
110 'THEN
120    OVERTIME.PAY = 1.5 * PAYRATE * (HOURS.WORKED − 40)
130 'ENDIF
```

If this code is examined, along with the discussion of how the general form of the IF-THEN statement performs, it can be seen that this translation will operate exactly as desired. If the condition is true (HOURS.WORKED is greater than 40), statement 100 states that program control is to be passed to line 110 (GOTO 110), which is the 'THEN statement. Statement 120 will be executed next, followed by 130, etc. If the condition is false (HOURS.WORKED is not greater than 40), the ELSE portion of line 100 (GOTO 130) directs program control to line 130, the 'ENDIF statement, which causes program execution to skip over the THEN portion of the program code.

Let's summarize the steps, then, for converting a pseudocode IF-THEN statement to BASIC:

1. Number each statement of the pseudocode IF-THEN structure.
2. Convert the THEN and ENDIF pseudocode statements to BASIC remark statements by placing a single quote mark (') in front of the words THEN and ENDIF.
3. Replace the pseudocode IF statement:

line# IF <condition>

with the BASIC statement:

```
line# IF <condition> THEN GOTO <line#1> ELSE GOTO <line#2>
```

where <line#1> is replaced by the line number of the 'THEN statement, and <line#2> is replaced by the line number of the 'ENDIF statement.

An option in Microsoft BASIC is that the GOTO <line#> statement following the words THEN and ELSE in the BASIC language form of the IF statement can be replaced with just the line number, so the BASIC language translation of

line# IF <condition>

can also be

```
line# IF <condition> THEN <line#1> ELSE <line#2>
```

where <line#1> refers to the line number of the 'THEN statement and <line#2> corresponds to the line number of the 'ENDIF statement.

Use of the IF-THEN Statement

Let's examine some problem situations where the IF-THEN statement would be used:

Suppose we are writing a payroll program in which an employee name, hours worked, and hourly pay rate are entered, and gross pay is calculated and output. Gross pay is calculated by multiplying pay rate by hours worked for the first 40 hours, and multiplying pay rate by 1.5 by hours worked for any overtime work over the regular 40 hours. Sound familiar? O.K., here's the difference—suppose we are concerned that the person operating the program might enter incorrect data inadvertently. We know that no hourly employee of the company currently makes more than $12.50 an hour, nor is anyone normally allowed to work more than 55 hours per week. We would like our program to output warning messages to the operator if either or both of these unusual conditions occur. A top-down design of this problem might begin with:

Level I

{prompt and enter employee name, hours worked,
  and pay rate}
{if hours worked > 55, display warning message}
{if pay rate > 12.50, display warning message}
{compute gross pay}
{display employee name and gross pay}

The first three comments are the only ones with which we need be concerned right now, so let's just work on them for now:

Level II

WRITE ("Enter employee name:")
READ (EMPLOYEE.NAME)
WRITE ("Enter hours worked:")
READ (HOURS.WORKED)
WRITE ("Enter hourly pay rate:")
READ (PAY.RATE)
IF HOURS.WORKED > 55
THEN
        {display warning message}
ENDIF
IF PAY.RATE > 12.50

THEN
    {display warning message}
ENDIF
{compute gross pay}
{display employee name and gross pay}

And a final level, with the first part of the solution all in pseudocode:

Level III
WRITE ("Enter employee name:")
READ (EMPLOYEE.NAME)
WRITE ("Enter hours worked:")
READ (HOURS.WORKED)
WRITE ("Enter hourly pay rate:")
READ (PAY.RATE)
IF HOURS.WORKED > 55
THEN
    WRITE ("Warning!!! Value greater than 55 entered")
    WRITE ("for hours worked. This may be an error!!!")
ENDIF
IF PAY.RATE > 12.50
THEN
    WRITE ("Warning!!! Pay rate greater than $12.50")
    WRITE ("entered. This may be an error!!!"
ENDIF
{compute gross pay}
{display employee name and gross pay}

Now to convert the pseudocode portion of this solution to BASIC. The first step is to assign a line number to each pseudocode statement:

```
100   WRITE ("Enter employee name:")
110   READ (EMPLOYEE.NAME)
120   WRITE ("Enter hours worked:")
130   READ (HOURS.WORKED)
140   WRITE ("Enter hourly pay rate:")
150   READ (PAY.RATE)
160   IF HOURS.WORKED > 55
170   THEN
180       WRITE ("Warning!!! Value greater than 55 entered")
190       WRITE ("for hours worked. This may be an error!!!")
```

```
200  ENDIF
210  IF PAY.RATE > 12.50
220  THEN
230      WRITE ("Warning!!! Pay rate greater than $12.50")
240      WRITE ("entered. This may be an error!!!")
250  ENDIF
         .
         .
         .
```

Next, each pseudocode statement is converted to its BASIC language equivalent:

```
100  PRINT "Enter employee name:";
110  INPUT "", EMPLOYEE.NAME$
120  PRINT "Enter hours worked:";
130  INPUT "", HOURS.WORKED
140  PRINT "Enter hourly pay rate:";
150  INPUT "", PAY.RATE
160  IF HOURS.WORKED > 55 THEN 170 ELSE 200
170  'THEN
180      PRINT "Warning!!! Value greater than 55 entered"
190      PRINT "for hours worked. This may be an error!!!"
200  'ENDIF
210  IF PAY.RATE > 12.50 THEN 220 ELSE 250
220  'THEN
230      PRINT "Warning!!! Pay rate greater than $12.50"
240      PRINT "entered. This may be an error!!!"
250  'ENDIF
         .
         .
         .
```

Notice that this final BASIC version of the problem solution is a line-by-line conversion of the final level of pseudolanguage. The quotation marks and comma following the word INPUT in the INPUT statements suppresses the question mark normally produced by an INPUT statement. This produces a grammatically correct input prompt in each case. There is a one-to-one correspondence between the pseudocode and the BASIC. It is left to you to complete the rest of the program if you wish—computing gross pay and displaying it, along with the employee name.

As another example of the use of the IF-THEN statement in a problem solution, let's use the second method developed in Section 2.5 to find the largest of three input values. This method, if you recall, was to assume the first value input was the largest, and then compare the second and third input values to this largest value, making a reassignment to largest if a larger value was found. The final pseudocode developed was:

Level II

WRITE *("Enter three numbers, separated by commas:")*
READ *(NUM1, NUM2, NUM3)*
LARGEST ← *NUM1*
IF *NUM2 > LARGEST*
THEN
    LARGEST ← *NUM2*
ENDIF
IF *NUM3 > LARGEST*
THEN
    LARGEST ← *NUM3*
ENDIF
WRITE *("The largest value is:", LARGEST)*

There are two IF-THEN statements in this solution—one that compares the second input value to LARGEST, and one that compares the third input value to LARGEST. Let's convert this pseudocode solution to BASIC. The first step is to assign a line number to each pseudocode statement:

200   WRITE *("Enter three numbers, separated by commas:")*
210   READ *(NUM1, NUM2, NUM3)*
220   LARGEST ← *NUM1*
230   IF *NUM2 > LARGEST*
240   THEN
250   LARGEST ← *NUM2*
260   ENDIF
270   IF *NUM3 > LARGEST*
280   THEN
290   LARGEST ← *NUM3*
300   ENDIF
310   WRITE *("The largest value is:", LARGEST)*

Statements 200 through 220 are easily converted:

```
200  PRINT "Enter three numbers, separated by commas:"
210  INPUT "", NUM, NUM2, NUM3
220  LARGEST = NUM1
```

Lines 230 through 260 comprise the first IF-THEN structure to be converted. Line 230, following the rules given in the previous section, would become

```
230  IF NUM2 > LARGEST THEN GOTO 240 ELSE GOTO 260
```

This statement indicates that if the condition is "TRUE", program control is to pass to line 240, the THEN statement. If, however, the condition is "FALSE", program execution will continue at line 260, the ENDIF statement. Lines 240 through 260 would be translated as:

```
240  'THEN
250     LARGEST = NUM2
260  'ENDIF
```

The next four statements to be converted, lines 270 through 300, form the second IF-THEN structure in the program. Statement 270:

270   IF NUM3 > LARGEST

would be converted to

```
270  IF NUM3 > LARGEST THEN GOTO 280 ELSE GOTO 300
```

The remaining three statements in the IF-THEN control structure would become

```
280  'THEN
290     LARGEST = NUM3
300  'ENDIF
```

The last statement in the pseudocode solution:

310   WRITE ("The largest value is:", LARGEST)

is translated into

```
310  PRINT "The largest value is:"; LARGEST
```

A completed BASIC language translation of this problem solution would then be

```
200  PRINT "Enter three numbers, separated by commas:"
210  INPUT "", NUM, NUM2, NUM3
220  LARGEST = NUM1
230  IF NUM2 > LARGEST THEN GOTO 240 ELSE GOTO 260
240 'THEN
250     LARGEST = NUM2
260 'ENDIF
270  IF NUM3 > LARGEST THEN GOTO 280 ELSE GOTO 300
280 'THEN
290     LARGEST = NUM3
300 'ENDIF
310  PRINT "The largest value is:"; LARGEST
```

The next section contains a discussion of the second type of selection control structure, the IF-THEN-ELSE statement, and how it is translated from pseudocode to BASIC.

5.5 THE IF-THEN-ELSE STATEMENT

The IF-THEN-ELSE statement is used in problem solutions to perform one set of actions when a given condition is true and a different set of actions when the condition is false. It is similar to the IF-THEN statement, but there are differences, as the flowchart in Figure 5.3 indicates. If the condition is true, Action 1 will be performed, then the next statement in the program executed. If the condition is

Figure 5.3 Flowchart of the IF-THEN-ELSE control structure.

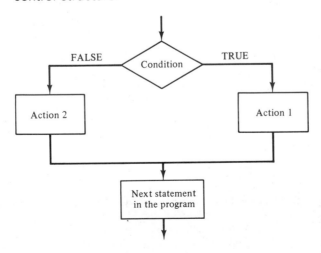

false, however, Action 2 will be performed instead, followed by execution of the next statement in the program.

An example of a pseudocode comment that would result in an IF-THEN ELSE statement is

{*Compare the student's answer to the correct answer, and
output an appropriate response*}

A refinement of this comment might yield the following pseudocode:

IF STUDENT.ANSWER = CORRECT.ANSWER
THEN
    WRITE (*"Correct!!! Good work!!!"*)
ELSE
    WRITE (*"No, the correct answer is "* , CORRECT.ANSWER)
ENDIF

Once the solution is in pseudocode, it may be converted to BASIC.

Converting Pseudocode to BASIC

Conversion of an IF-THEN-ELSE pseudocode statement to BASIC uses the same general form of the BASIC language IF-THEN-ELSE statement as was used to convert IF-THEN pseudocode statements to BASIC:

```
line# IF <condition> THEN <statementl> ELSE <statement2>
```

The only difference in the way in which this general form is used in the translation of an IF-THEN-ELSE pseudocode structure is how the line number reference made in <statement2> is used. Rather than <statement2> referencing the line number of the 'ENDIF statement, it is used to direct program control to the 'ELSE statement. Let's examine how this works using the pseudocode segment given at the end of the previous section:

IF STUDENT.ANSWER = CORRECT.ANSWER
THEN
    WRITE (*"Correct!!! Good work!!!"*)
ELSE
    WRITE (*"No, the correct answer is "*,CORRECT.ANSWER)
ENDIF

The first step is to assign line numbers to each line:

```
40   IF STUDENT.ANSWER = CORRECT.ANSWER
50   THEN
60        WRITE ("Correct!!! Good work!!!")
70   ELSE
80        WRITE ("No, the correct answer is ",CORRECT.ANSWER)
90   ENDIF
```

The translation, then, proceeds pretty much as it did with the IF-THEN statement, keeping in mind the difference mentioned above. Statement 40 would become

```
40  IF STUDENT.ANSWER = CORRECT.ANSWER THEN 50 ELSE 70
```

Statements 50 and 60 would be translated as

```
50 'THEN
60     PRINT "Correct!!! Good work!!!"
```

Statement 70, ELSE, is translated as the THEN statement is—the word ELSE must be preceded by a single quotation mark:

```
70 'ELSE
```

Statements 80 and 90 are converted to BASIC just as they would be in an IF-THEN statement:

```
80     PRINT "No, the correct answer is ";CORRECT.ANSWER
90 'ENDIF
```

The translation thus far would be as follows:

```
40  IF STUDENT.ANSWER = CORRECT.ANSWER THEN 50 ELSE 70
50 'THEN
60     PRINT "Correct!!! Good work!!!"
70 'ELSE
80     PRINT "No, the correct answer is ";CORRECT.ANSWER
90 'ENDIF
```

Only one step remains to be performed. If the program is left as is shown above, what happens when the condition in statement 40 is "TRUE"? Program control will be sent to line 50, the 'THEN statement, line 60 will be performed next, then line 70, line 80, and line 90. This is not what we wish to have happen. If the condition is "TRUE", line 50 and line 60 are to be executed, and the ELSE portion of the code—lines 70 and 80—is to be skipped. In order to force the program code to behave as an IF-THEN-ELSE structure should, it is necessary to insert the statement, GOTO 90, in the program between lines 60 and 70. This can be done by selecting a line number between 60 and 70 for this statement and placing it in its proper location:

```
40  IF STUDENT.ANSWER = CORRECT.ANSWER THEN 50 ELSE 70
50 'THEN
60     PRINT "Correct!!! Good work!!!"
65     GOTO 90
70 'ELSE
80     PRINT "No, the correct answer is ";CORRECT.ANSWER
90 'ENDIF
```

This added statement at line 65 would cause the above program segment to implement the IF-THEN-ELSE structure as desired. Let's summarize the steps, then, involved in translating a pseudocode IF-THEN-ELSE statement into its BASIC language equivalent:

1. Number each statement of the pseudocode version of the IF-THEN-ELSE structure.
2. Convert the THEN, ELSE, and ENDIF pseudocode statements to BASIC remark statements by placing a single quotation mark (') in front of the words THEN, ELSE, and ENDIF.
3. Replace the pseudocode IF statement:

   line# IF <condition>

   with the BASIC statement:

   line# IF <condition> THEN <line#1> ELSE <line#2>

   where <line#1> is replaced by the line number of the 'THEN statement and <line#2> is replaced with the line number of the 'ELSE statement.
4. Insert a GOTO <line#> statement in the program as the statement immediately preceding the 'ELSE statement, where <line#> is replaced by the line number of the 'ENDIF statement.

Notice that the option of using <line#> rather than GOTO <line#> has been used in the BASIC language IF-THEN-ELSE statement form. Either option may be used with Microsoft BASIC.

Use of the IF-THEN-ELSE Statement

The IF-THEN-ELSE statement is used in problem situations where either one or another set of actions is to be performed based upon the truth value of a given condition. Let's take a look at an example problem that would make use of this control structure:

Given the cost of two different sizes of a product, determine and display which is the better buy in terms of cost per unit.

The first step is to write a Level I solution that is expressed all in comment form:

Level I

{prompt and enter first cost, first size}
{prompt and enter second cost, second size}
{determine and display which is a better buy,
 and its cost per unit}

Refining these comments yields:

Level II

WRITE ("Enter the cost and size of the first choice:")
READ (COST1, SIZE1)
WRITE ("Enter the cost and size of the second choice:")
READ (COST2, SIZE2)
IF (COST1 / SIZE1) < (COST2 / SIZE2)
THEN
     {display cost per unit of SIZE1 as being the better buy}
ELSE
     {display cost per unit of SIZE2 as being the better buy}
ENDIF

There are still two statements in comment form, so another level is needed:

Level III

WRITE ("Enter the cost and size of the first choice:")
READ (COST1, SIZE1)
WRITE ("Enter the cost and size of the second choice:")
READ (COST2, SIZE2)

```
IF (COST1 / SIZE1) < (COST2 / SIZE2)
THEN
     WRITE (SIZE1, "is a better buy at a cost of")
     WRITE (COST1 / SIZE1, "per unit")
ELSE
     WRITE (SIZE2, "is a better buy at a cost of")
     WRITE (COST2 / SIZE2, "per unit")
ENDIF
```

Now that the solution is all in pseudocode, the steps listed in the previous section can be applied to convert this solution to BASIC. The first step is to assign line numbers to each pseudocode statement:

```
500  WRITE ("Enter the cost and size of the first choice:")
510  READ (COST1, SIZE1)
520  WRITE ("Enter the cost and size of the second choice:")
530  READ (COST2, SIZE2)
540  IF (COST1 / SIZE1) < (COST2 / SIZE2)
550  THEN
560      WRITE (SIZE1, "is a better buy at a cost of")
570      WRITE (COST1 / SIZE1, "per unit")
580  ELSE
590      WRITE (SIZE2, "is a better buy at a cost of")
600      WRITE (COST2 / SIZE2, "per unit")
610  ENDIF
```

The next step is to begin translating the pseudocode statements into BASIC statements. The first four statements become PRINT and INPUT statements:

```
500  PRINT "Enter the cost and size of the first choice:"
510  INPUT "", COST1, SIZE1
520  PRINT "Enter the cost and size of the second choice:"
530  INPUT "", COST2, SIZE2
```

The next statement, line 540, is the IF-THEN-ELSE statement. It would be converted as follows:

```
540  IF (COST1 / SIZE1) < (COST2 / SIZE2) THEN 550 ELSE 580
```

Remember, the line number following the word THEN in this statement is the line number of the THEN statement, and the line number following the word ELSE is the line number of the ELSE statement.

Lines 550, 580, and 610 need single quote marks (') inserted following their line numbers and preceding the words THEN, ELSE, and ENDIF. Lines 560, 570, 590, and 600, which are all WRITE statements, become PRINT statements. If these changes are made, the program from line 550 through 610 would look like this:

```
550 'THEN
560     PRINT SIZE1; "is a better buy at a cost of"
570     PRINT COST1 / SIZE1; "per unit"
580 'ELSE
590     PRINT SIZE2; "is a better buy at a cost of"
600     PRINT COST2 / SIZE2; "per unit"
610 'ENDIF
```

The only step remaining is to insert a GOTO statement before line 580 'ELSE to transfer control from this point to line 610, the ENDIF statement. Line 575 then, would be GOTO 610. Placing this statement in the program results in the following for the final BASIC language translation:

```
500  PRINT "Enter the cost and size of the first choice:"
510  INPUT "", COST1, SIZE1
520  PRINT "Enter the cost and size of the second choice:"
530  INPUT "", COST2, SIZE2
540  IF (COST1 / SIZE1) < (COST2 / SIZE2) THEN 550 ELSE 580
550  'THEN
560     PRINT SIZE1; "is a better buy at a cost of"
570     PRINT COST1 / SIZE1; "per unit"
575     GOTO 610
580  'ELSE
590     PRINT SIZE2; "is a better buy at a cost of"
600     PRINT COST2 / SIZE2; "per unit"
610  'ENDIF
```

If this program is compared to the Level III pseudocode solution, it can be observed that the pseudocode statements translated line for line into BASIC language statements. The only additional BASIC language statement is the GOTO 610 at line 575, needed to force the program to skip the ELSE clause if the THEN clause has been executed.

Let's try another example:

Write a program to determine the amount to be deducted from an employee's wages for health insurance. Prompt for input, which is to be the employee name and marital status. Output is to consist of the employee name and amount to be deducted for health insurance. An amount of $27 is to be deducted if the employee is married, and $15 is to be deducted if the employee is single.

The first general solution, written in comment form, might be

Level I

{display prompt message}
{enter employee name and marital status}
{determine which amount is to be deducted}
{display employee name and amount to be deducted}

A refinement of this level might result in the following:

Level II

WRITE ("Enter employee name and marital status:")
READ (EMPLOYEE.NAME, MARITAL.STATUS)
IF MARITAL.STATUS = "MARRIED"
THEN
    AMOUNT.DEDUCTED ← 27.00
ELSE
    AMOUNT.DEDUCTED ← 15.00
ENDIF
WRITE ("Name: ", EMPLOYEE.NAME)
WRITE ("Amount to be deducted:", AMOUNT.DEDUCTED)

Since the solution is now in pseudocode, we can proceed right to BASIC at this point. The first step is to assign line numbers:

```
100   WRITE ("Enter employee name and marital status:")
110   READ (EMPLOYEE.NAME, MARITAL.STATUS)
120   IF MARITAL.STATUS = "MARRIED"
130   THEN
140       AMOUNT.DEDUCTED ← 27.00
150   ELSE
160       AMOUNT.DEDUCTED ← 15.00
170   ENDIF
180   WRITE ("Name: ", EMPLOYEE.NAME)
190   WRITE ("Amount to be deducted:", AMOUNT.DEDUCTED)
```

The first pseudocode statement becomes a PRINT statement:

```
100  PRINT "Enter employee name and marital status:"
```

Statement 110, obviously, becomes an INPUT statement:

```
110  INPUT "", EMPLOYEE.NAME$, MARITAL.STATUS$
```

Notice that it is necessary to append a ' $ ' to both variable names to indicate to the BASIC interpreter that the variables are to accept character data as input values, not numbers.

Statement 120 must have line numbers after the conditional expression to direct program control to the next statement to be performed based upon the truth value of the expression:

```
120  IF MARITAL.STATUS$ = "MARRIED" THEN 130 ELSE 150
```

Statements 130, 150, and 170 must be converted to comments by preceding the word in each with a single quotation mark:

```
        .
        .
        .
130 'THEN
        .
150 'ELSE
        .
170 'ENDIF
        .
        .
```

The two pseudocode assignment statements at lines 140 and 160 are each translated to BASIC by replacing the assignment operator (←) with an equal sign (=):

```
        .
140     AMOUNT.DEDUCTED = 27.00
        .
160     AMOUNT.DEDUCTED = 15.00
        .
        .
```

Incorporating all these changes, the program would look like this so far:

```
100   PRINT "Enter employee name and marital status:"
110   INPUT "", EMPLOYEE.NAME$, MARITAL.STATUS$
120   IF MARITAL.STATUS$ = "MARRIED" THEN 130 ELSE 150
130   'THEN
140      AMOUNT.DEDUCTED = 27.00
150   'ELSE
160      AMOUNT.DEDUCTED = 15.00
170   'ENDIF
              .
              .
```

At this point it is probably a good idea to insert the needed GOTO statement preceding the ELSE statement at line 150 so it is not forgotten. Assigning line number 145 to this statement, the program would now be

```
100   PRINT "Enter employee name and marital status:"
110   INPUT "", EMPLOYEE.NAME$, MARITAL.STATUS$
120   IF MARITAL.STATUS$ = "MARRIED" THEN 130 ELSE 150
130   'THEN
140      AMOUNT.DEDUCTED = 27.00
145      GOTO 170
150   'ELSE
160      AMOUNT.DEDUCTED = 15.00
170   'ENDIF
              .
              .
```

The only two statements remaining to be converted to BASIC are the two WRITE statements, lines 180 and 190 of the pseudocode program. They both become PRINT statements, resulting in the final BASIC language version of the program:

```
100   PRINT "Enter employee name and marital status:"
110   INPUT "", EMPLOYEE.NAME$, MARITAL.STATUS$
120   IF MARITAL.STATUS$ = "MARRIED" THEN 130 ELSE 150
130   'THEN
140      AMOUNT.DEDUCTED = 27.00
145      GOTO 170
150   'ELSE
160      AMOUNT.DEDUCTED = 15.00
170   'ENDIF
180   PRINT "Name: ";EMPLOYEE.NAME$
190   PRINT "Amount to be deducted:";AMOUNT.DEDUCTED
```

As long as the process illustrated by these two examples of converting pseudocode programs that contain IF-THEN-ELSE statements to their BASIC language equivalents is followed, program structure is maintained. The selection statement control structure operates in this BASIC language form just as it does in pseudocode, and as diagramed in the flowchart that introduced the previous section.

It is certainly true that the program above would produce the same output if the line number following the word THEN in the IF statement at line 120 sent program control to line 140 rather than line 130. The reason this is not done, however, is in case program modifications need to be made. Suppose it was determined that another statement was needed inside the THEN clause, which currently encompasses lines 130 up to 145 (from the 'THEN statement up to but not including the GOTO 170 statement), and this new statement was inserted with a line number of 135. If the IF statement directed program control to line 140, line 135 would never be executed. This type of error is avoided by always sending program control to the 'THEN statement from the IF statement. The same argument holds for always having the line number following the word ELSE in the IF statement always be the line number of the 'ELSE statement.

The next section of this chapter examines more problem situations that require selection statements.

5.6 USING SELECTION STATEMENTS IN PROBLEM SOLUTIONS

There are many problems that require the use of one or more selection statements. Anytime a decision needs to be made as to which action to perform based upon a particular condition, a selection statement is probably going to be needed. Let's take a look at some problem examples in which decisions occur inside decisions —referred to as "nested selection statements."

Given the following problem:

A program is to be written which determines which form of address—Mr., Mrs., or Miss—is to be used in the salutation line of a form letter, based upon the sex and marital status of the customer. Input to the program will be the last name, marital status, and sex of a customer. Output will be the correct salutation, "Dear <xxx> <lastname>;", with <xxx> replaced by the correct title, and <lastname> replaced with the customer's last name.

The first step, of course, is to write a pseudocode solution in comment form. The first level might look like this:

Level I

{*display an input prompt*}
{*enter customer's last name, sex, and marital status*}
{*determine correct title based on sex and marital status*}
{*display salutation line*}

The first two comments, as well as the last comment, can be quite easily refined into pseudocode. The first comment will become a WRITE statement, the second comment a READ statement, and the last comment a WRITE statement. It is the third comment that is going to take some work. Level II might look like this:

Level II

WRITE ("Enter last name, sex, and marital status:")
READ (LAST.NAME, SEX, MARITAL.STATUS)
{*determine correct title based on sex and marital status*}
WRITE ("Dear ", TITLE, " ", LAST.NAME, ";")

Notice that provision is made in the last WRITE statement for inserting spaces and punctuation marks in the appropriate places. A space is included inside the quotation marks after the word "Dear" to insert a space between that word and the person's title. A space is printed after the value of the variable TITLE and before the value of the variable LAST.NAME to separate the person's title from their last name. Lastly, a semicolon (;) is printed after the person's last name to end the salutation.

To refine the third comment, {*determine correct title based on sex and marital status*}, a selection structure will be needed. Two conditions need to be examined —sex and marital status. Either condition could be examined first. Let's choose sex. If the customer is a male, the correct title will be "Mr." Otherwise, we know that the customer is a female, and marital status will need to be examined to determine the correct title to be used. This can be expressed as an IF-THEN-ELSE statement, and gives us for Level III:

Level III

WRITE ("Enter last name, sex, and marital status:")
READ (LAST.NAME, SEX, MARITAL.STATUS)
IF SEX = "MALE"
THEN
    TITLE ← "Mr."

```
ELSE
     {determine if Miss or Mrs. should be used}
ENDIF
WRITE ("Dear ", TITLE, " ", LAST.NAME, ";")
```

A single comment, {*determine if Miss or Mrs. should be used*}, remains to be refined into pseudocode. This comment will result in another IF-THEN-ELSE statement to examine the person's marital status. Notice that this second IF-THEN-ELSE statement will be performed only if the value of the variable SEX is not "MALE", which causes the ELSE clause of the IF statement, IF SEX = "MALE", to be executed. This second IF-THEN-ELSE statement, which will be used to examine the marital status of the person, is said to be "nested" within the first IF-THEN-ELSE statement. Notice in the next level of the solution how the indenting of this second IF-THEN-ELSE statement is used to indicate that it is contained inside the ELSE clause of the first IF-THEN-ELSE statement:

Level IV

```
WRITE ("Enter last name, sex, and marital status:")
READ (LAST.NAME, SEX, MARITAL.STATUS)
IF SEX = "MALE"
THEN
     TITLE ← "Mr."
ELSE
     IF MARITAL.STATUS = "MARRIED"
     THEN
          TITLE ← "Mrs."
     ELSE
          TITLE ← "Miss"
     ENDIF
ENDIF
WRITE ("Dear ", TITLE, " ", LAST.NAME, ";")
```

See if the logic of this solution doesn't make sense. If the sex of the customer is "MALE", it is immediately known that the title to be used with the customer is "Mr.", so the value "Mr." is assigned to TITLE, and no further conditions need to be examined. After this assignment is performed (the THEN clause of the first IF statement has been executed), the next statement encountered in the program is ELSE, which causes a jump to the ENDIF statement that corresponds to the first IF statement. The way to determine which of the two ENDIF statements this is is by the indenting—the ENDIF lined up with the first IF statement is the one to which control would be sent.

Only if the condition SEX = "MALE" is "FALSE" will the second IF-THEN-ELSE statement be executed—in this case it is assumed that the customer's sex is female, and it must then be determined whether the title of "Mrs." or "Miss" is to be used. This is determined by examining the value of MARITAL-.STATUS. If the person is married, the title used will be "Mrs."—if not, the title "Miss" will be assigned to the variable TITLE.

Now that the solution is all in pseudocode, it can be translated to BASIC. First, assign the line numbers:

```
200   WRITE ("Enter last name, sex, and marital status:")
210   READ (LAST.NAME, SEX, MARITAL.STATUS)
220   IF SEX = "MALE"
230   THEN
240       TITLE ← "Mr."
250   ELSE
260       IF MARITAL.STATUS = "MARRIED"
270       THEN
280           TITLE ← "Mrs."
290       ELSE
300           TITLE ← "Miss"
310       ENDIF
320   ENDIF
330   WRITE ("Dear ", TITLE, " ", LAST.NAME, ";")
```

Statements 200 and 210 become PRINT and INPUT statements, respectively. It will also be necessary to attach a ' $ ' to the end of all the variable names in the INPUT statement to make them character string variables, since they all will be used to store characters:

```
200   PRINT "Enter last name, sex, and marital status:"
210   INPUT "", LAST.NAME$, SEX$, MARITAL.STATUS$
```

Statements 230, 250, 270, 290, 310, and 320 will need to have single quotation marks inserted in them following the line numbers and preceding the words THEN, ELSE, or ENDIF. The assignment statements at lines 240, 280, and 300 are translated by changing the pseudocode assignment operators (←) to BASIC language assignment operators (=). Making these changes, the program would appear like this:

```
200  PRINT "Enter last name, sex, and marital status:"
210  INPUT "", LAST.NAME$, SEX$, MARITAL.STATUS$
220  IF SEX$ = "MALE"
230  'THEN
240     TITLE$ = "Mr."
250  'ELSE
260       IF MARITAL.STATUS$ = "MARRIED"
270  '   THEN
280        TITLE$ = "Mrs."
290  '   ELSE
300        TITLE$ = "Miss"
310  '   ENDIF
320  'ENDIF
330  WRITE ("Dear ", TITLE, " ", LAST.NAME, ";")
```

Statement 330 needs to be translated into a PRINT statement, and the IF statements at lines 220 and 260 need to be translated. Statement 330 would become

```
330  PRINT "Dear ";TITLE$;" ";LAST.NAME$;";"
```

The IF statement at line 220 needs the phrase THEN 230 ELSE 250 appended to it, and the IF statement at line 260 needs THEN 270 ELSE 290 added to it. If these changes are made in the program, it would now look like this:

```
200  PRINT "Enter last name, sex and marital status:"
210  INPUT "", LAST.NAME$, SEX$, MARITAL.STATUS$
220  IF SEX$ = "MALE" THEN 230 ELSE 250
230  'THEN
240     TITLE$ = "Mr."
250  'ELSE
260     IF MARITAL.STATUS$ = "MARRIED" THEN 270 ELSE 290
270  '   THEN
280        TITLE$ = "Mrs."
290  '   ELSE
300        TITLE$ = "Miss"
310  '   ENDIF
320  'ENDIF
330  PRINT "Dear ";TITLE$;" ";LAST.NAME$;";"
```

Two GOTO statements need to be inserted in the program to complete the translation to BASIC. One GOTO statement is inserted before the 'ELSE statement at line 250 to transfer control to its matching 'ENDIF statement at line 320. A second GOTO statement is inserted before the 'ELSE statement at line 290 to transfer control to its matching 'ENDIF statement at line 310. Making these insertions, the final program would look like this:

```
200  PRINT "Enter last name, sex and marital status:"
210  INPUT "", LAST.NAME$, SEX$, MARITAL.STATUS$
220  IF SEX$ = "MALE" THEN 230 ELSE 250
230 'THEN
240      TITLE$ = "Mr."
245      GOTO 320
250 'ELSE
260      IF MARITAL.STATUS$ = "MARRIED" THEN 270 ELSE 290
270  '   THEN
280          TITLE$ = "Mrs."
285          GOTO 310
290  '   ELSE
300          TITLE$ = "Miss"
310  '   ENDIF
320 'ENDIF
330  PRINT "Dear ";TITLE$;" ";LAST.NAME$;";"
```

You may wish to perform a few hand traces of this program and enter various input values for SEX$ and MARITAL.STATUS$ to ensure that the program will produce the expected results.

Let's look at one more example of a problem that makes use of nested IF-THEN-ELSE statements just to make sure you are comfortable with their use and translation. Given the following formal problem definition:

☐ **Formal Problem Definition**

General Description

A program is to be written that will assign the appropriate letter grade to a student based upon his or her average score for five tests.

Input Specifications

Input will consist of five numeric values representing the student's scores on five examinations. Each value will be entered on a separate line, prompted by the message:

```
Enter score for test #<n>:
```

where <n> will be replaced by a test number 1 through 5.

Output Specifications

Output will consist of two lines. The first line will be:

```
Average score on the five tests is: <average>
```

where <average> will be replaced by the student's average score on the five tests, computed by dividing the sum of the five test scores by 5. The second line displayed will be:

```
Letter grade assigned is: <grade>
```

where <grade> will be replaced by a letter grade of A, B, C, D, or F. Letter grades will be determined as follows:

Test score average	Letter grade
Average >= 90	A
Average >= 80 and < 90	B
Average >= 70 and < 80	C
Average >= 60 and < 70	D
Average < 60	F

Normal Example

Input:

```
Enter score for test #1: 67
Enter score for test #2: 78
Enter score for test #3: 80
Enter score for test #4: 83
Enter score for test #5: 79
```

Output:

```
Average score on the five tests is: 77.4
Letter grade assigned is: C
```

Unusual or Error Conditions

1. If a negative test score is entered, it will be included in the student's average.
2. If fewer than five scores are entered for a student, no output will occur.
3. If more than one score is entered on a line, only the first score will be read—the rest will be ignored.

Let's see if we can develop a pseudocode solution to this problem. The first level of the top-down design for this problem might be:

Level I

{*enter five scores, each with its own prompt*}
{*compute the sum of the five scores*}
{*compute the average of the scores*}
{*display the average*}
{*determine the letter grade*}
{*display the letter grade*}

A refinement of these comments might result in the following:

Level II

WRITE (*"Enter a score for test #1:"*)
READ (SCORE1)
WRITE (*"Enter a score for test #2:"*)
READ (SCORE2)
WRITE (*"Enter a score for test #3:"*)
READ (SCORE3)
WRITE (*"Enter a score for test #4:"*)
READ (SCORE4)
WRITE (*"Enter a score for test #5:"*)
READ (SCORE5)
SUM ← SCORE1 + SCORE2 + SCORE3 + SCORE4 + SCORE5
AVERAGE ← SUM / 5
WRITE (*"Average score on the five tests is:"*, AVERAGE)
IF AVERAGE >= 90
THEN
    {*letter grade is an A*}
ELSE
    {*determine if letter grade is a B, C, D, or F*}
ENDIF
WRITE (*"Letter grade assigned is:"*, LETTER.GRADE)

This solution is not all in pseudocode, so another level will be needed. Notice that the determination of the letter grade starts out with an IF-THEN-ELSE statement. However, this statement has determined only the letter grade of "A". Much work remains to be done under the ELSE clause to assign the rest of the letter grades. If the program reaches the ELSE clause, the AVERAGE must be less than

90. This means that the only condition needed to be tested for a letter grade of "B" is if the AVERAGE >= 80. Another IF-THEN-ELSE structure will be needed, nested under the ELSE clause of the first IF-THEN-ELSE. Inserting this in the pseudocode solution to replace the comment, {*determine if letter grade is a B, C, D, or F*}, yields the next level:

Level III

WRITE (*"Enter a score for test #1:"*)
READ (SCORE1)
WRITE (*"Enter a score for test #2:"*)
READ (SCORE2)
WRITE (*"Enter a score for test #3:"*)
READ (SCORE3)
WRITE (*"Enter a score for test #4:"*)
READ (SCORE4)
WRITE (*"Enter a score for test #5:"*)
READ (SCORE5)
SUM ← SCORE1 + SCORE2 + SCORE3 + SCORE4 + SCORE5
AVERAGE ← SUM / 5
WRITE (*"Average score on the five tests is:"*, AVERAGE)
IF AVERAGE >= 90
THEN
    {*letter grade is an A*}
ELSE
    IF AVERAGE >= 80
    THEN
        {*letter grade is a B*}
    ELSE
        {*determine if letter grade is a C, D, or F*}
    ENDIF
ENDIF
WRITE (*"Letter grade assigned is:"*, LETTER.GRADE)

Progress is being made. A letter grade of an "A" or a "B" will now be assigned, if appropriate. All that remains are "C", "D", and "F". More IF-THEN-ELSE statements will be needed. One will be needed for a letter grade of "C", and another for a letter grade of "D". The letter grade of "F" will be assigned in the ELSE clause of the "D" letter grade (if the grade is not a "D", the only remaining possibility is a grade of "F"). Making these insertions, the next level would look like this:

Level IV

WRITE ("Enter a score for test #1:")
READ (SCORE1)
WRITE ("Enter a score for test #2:")
READ (SCORE2)
WRITE ("Enter a score for test #3:")
READ (SCORE3)
WRITE ("Enter a score for test #4:")
READ (SCORE4)
WRITE ("Enter a score for test #5:")
READ (SCORE5)
SUM ← SCORE1 + SCORE2 + SCORE3 + SCORE4 + SCORE5
AVERAGE ← SUM / 5
WRITE ("Average score on the five tests is:", AVERAGE)
IF AVERAGE >= 90
THEN
  {letter grade is an A}
ELSE
  IF AVERAGE >= 80
  THEN
    {letter grade is a B}
  ELSE
    IF AVERAGE >= 70
    THEN
      {letter grade is a C}
    ELSE
      IF AVERAGE >= 60
      THEN
        {letter grade is a D}
      ELSE
        {letter grade is an F}
      ENDIF
    ENDIF
  ENDIF
ENDIF
WRITE ("Letter grade assigned is:", LETTER.GRADE)

Several comments remain in the program—they will all need to be replaced with pseudocode assignment statements. Once this has been done, the final level becomes

Level V

WRITE *("Enter a score for test #1:")*
READ *(SCORE1)*
WRITE *("Enter a score for test #2:")*
READ *(SCORE2)*
WRITE *("Enter a score for test #3:")*
READ *(SCORE3)*
WRITE *("Enter a score for test #4:")*
READ *(SCORE4)*
WRITE *("Enter a score for test #5:")*
READ *(SCORE5)*
SUM ← SCORE1 + SCORE2 + SCORE3 + SCORE4 + SCORE5
AVERAGE ← SUM / 5
WRITE *("Average score on the five tests is:",AVERAGE)*
IF AVERAGE >= 90
THEN
    LETTER.GRADE ← "A"
ELSE
   IF AVERAGE >= 80
   THEN
      LETTER.GRADE ← "B"
   ELSE
      IF AVERAGE >= 70
      THEN
         LETTER.GRADE ← "C"
      ELSE
         IF AVERAGE >= 60
         THEN
            LETTER.GRADE ← "D"
         ELSE
            LETTER.GRADE ← "F"
         ENDIF
      ENDIF
   ENDIF
ENDIF
WRITE *("Letter grade assigned is:",LETTER.GRADE)*

Now that the solution is all in pseudocode, the translation to BASIC may begin. The first step is to place line numbers on all the lines:

```
100   WRITE ("Enter a score for test #1:")
110   READ (SCORE1)
120   WRITE ("Enter a score for test #2:")
130   READ (SCORE2)
140   WRITE ("Enter a score for test #3:")
150   READ (SCORE3)
160   WRITE ("Enter a score for test #4:")
170   READ (SCORE4)
180   WRITE ("Enter a score for test #5:")
190   READ (SCORE5)
200   SUM ← SCORE1 + SCORE2 + SCORE3 + SCORE4 +
      SCORE5
210   AVERAGE ← SUM / 5
220   WRITE ("Average score on the five tests is:", AVERAGE)
230   IF AVERAGE >= 90
240   THEN
250       LETTER.GRADE ← "A"
260   ELSE
270       IF AVERAGE >= 80
280       THEN
290           LETTER.GRADE ← "B"
300       ELSE
310           IF AVERAGE >= 70
320           THEN
330               LETTER.GRADE ← "C"
340           ELSE
350               IF AVERAGE >= 60
360               THEN
370                   LETTER.GRADE ← "D"
380               ELSE
390                   LETTER.GRADE ← "F"
400               ENDIF
410           ENDIF
420       ENDIF
430   ENDIF
440   WRITE ("Letter grade assigned is:", LETTER.GRADE)
```

Statements 100 through 220 are translated using the normal procedure—WRITE statements become PRINT statements, READ statements become INPUT statements, and assignment statements need to have the (←) symbol changed to an equal sign (=):

```
100  PRINT "Enter a score for test #1:";
110  INPUT "", SCORE1
120  PRINT "Enter a score for test #2:";
130  INPUT "", SCORE2
140  PRINT "Enter a score for test #3:";
150  INPUT "", SCORE3
160  PRINT "Enter a score for test #4:";
170  INPUT "", SCORE4
180  PRINT "Enter a score for test #5:";
190  INPUT "", SCORE5
200  SUM = SCORE1 + SCORE2 + SCORE3 + SCORE4 + SCORE5
210  AVERAGE = SUM / 5
220  PRINT "Average score on the five tests is:";AVERAGE"
```

The IF-THEN-ELSE statements in lines 230 through 430, however, involves a little more work. First, the IF statements are modified to include the line numbers of the corresponding THEN and ELSE statements in them:

```
230  IF AVERAGE >= 90 THEN 240 ELSE 260
240      THEN
250          LETTER.GRADE ← "A"
260      ELSE
270          IF AVERAGE >= 80 THEN 280 ELSE 300
280          THEN
290              LETTER.GRADE ← "B"
300          ELSE
310              IF AVERAGE >= 70 THEN 320 ELSE 340
320              THEN
330                  LETTER.GRADE ← "C"
340              ELSE
350                  IF AVERAGE >= 60 THEN 360 ELSE 380
360                  THEN
370                      LETTER.GRADE ← "D"
380                  ELSE
390                      LETTER.GRADE ← "F"
400                  ENDIF
410              ENDIF
```

```
420        ENDIF
430   ENDIF
```

The next step is to insert the single quotation marks (') in front of the THEN, ELSE, and ENDIF statements, convert the pseudocode assignment operators (←) to equal signs (=), and convert the variable name LETTER.GRADE to a BASIC language character string variable name, LETTER.GRADE$:

```
230   IF AVERAGE >= 90 THEN 240 ELSE 260
240  'THEN
250       LETTER.GRADE$ = "A"
260  'ELSE
270     IF AVERAGE >= 80 THEN 280 ELSE 300
280    'THEN
290        LETTER.GRADE$ = "B"
300    'ELSE
310       IF AVERAGE >= 70 THEN 320 ELSE 340
320      'THEN
330          LETTER.GRADE$ = "C"
340      'ELSE
350        IF AVERAGE >= 60 THEN 360 ELSE 380
360       'THEN
370          LETTER.GRADE$ = "D"
380       'ELSE
390          LETTER.GRADE$ = "F"
400        'ENDIF
410      'ENDIF
420    'ENDIF
430  'ENDIF
```

The last thing to be done to this section of code to complete its translation from pseudocode to BASIC is to insert GOTO statements immediately before each ELSE statement to pass program control to the proper ENDIF statement. The corresponding ENDIF statement for each ELSE statement is lined up under it. This will help determine which ENDIF goes with which ELSE. Another helpful hint is to remember that when a nested IF-THEN-ELSE structure is used, the ENDIF furthest indented goes with the last (highest-numbered) IF-THEN-ELSE, the next furthest indented ENDIF with the next to the last IF-THEN-ELSE, etc. Inserting the needed GOTO statements results in the following final version of the IF-THEN-ELSE structure:

```
230 ┌ IF AVERAGE >= 90 THEN 240 ELSE 260
240 │'THEN
250 │     LETTER.GRADE$ = "A"
255 │     GOTO 430
260 │'ELSE
270 │   ┌ IF AVERAGE >= 80 THEN 280 ELSE 300
280 │   │'THEN
290 │   │     LETTER.GRADE$ = "B"
295 │   │     GOTO 420
300 │   │'ELSE
310 │   │   ┌ IF AVERAGE >= 70 THEN 320 ELSE 340
320 │   │   │'THEN
330 │   │   │     LETTER.GRADE$ = "C"
335 │   │   │     GOTO 410
340 │   │   │'ELSE
350 │   │   │   ┌ IF AVERAGE >= 60 THEN 360 ELSE 380
360 │   │   │   │'THEN
370 │   │   │   │     LETTER.GRADE$ = "D"
375 │   │   │   │     GOTO 400
380 │   │   │   │'ELSE
390 │   │   │   │     LETTER.GRADE$ = "F"
400 │   │   │   └─'ENDIF
410 │   │   └─'ENDIF
420 │   └─'ENDIF
430 └─'ENDIF
```

Another method that may be used to ensure that each IF statement is matched correctly with its corresponding ENDIF statement is to draw a line from each IF to its corresponding ENDIF, as is shown above. If this cannot be done without the lines crossing one another, the matching is incorrect.

The last statement to be translated to BASIC is statement 440:

440   WRITE (“Letter grade assigned is:”, LETTER.GRADE)

Its BASIC language version would be:

```
440  PRINT "Letter grade assigned is: ";LETTER.GRADE$
```

The final version of the problem solution, all in BASIC, then, is:

```
100  PRINT "Enter a score for test #1:";
110  INPUT "", SCORE1
120  PRINT "Enter a score for test #2:";
130  INPUT "", SCORE2
```

```
140   PRINT "Enter a score for test #3:";
150   INPUT "", SCORE3
160   PRINT "Enter a score for test #4:";
170   INPUT "", SCORE4
180   PRINT "Enter a score for test #5:";
190   INPUT "", SCORE5
200   SUM = SCORE1 + SCORE2 + SCORE3 + SCORE4 + SCORE5
210   AVERAGE = SUM / 5
220   PRINT "Average score on the five tests is:";AVERAGE"
230   IF AVERAGE >= 90 THEN 240 ELSE 260
240   'THEN
250       LETTER.GRADE$ = "A"
255       GOTO 430
260   'ELSE
270       IF AVERAGE >= 80 THEN 280 ELSE 300
280       'THEN
290           LETTER.GRADE$ = "B"
295           GOTO 420
300       'ELSE
310           IF AVERAGE >= 70 THEN 320 ELSE 340
320           'THEN
330               LETTER.GRADE$ = "C"
335               GOTO 410
340           'ELSE
350               IF AVERAGE >= 60 THEN 360 ELSE 380
360               'THEN
370                   LETTER.GRADE$ = "D"
375                   GOTO 400
380               'ELSE
390                   LETTER.GRADE$ = "F"
400               'ENDIF
410           'ENDIF
420       'ENDIF
430   'ENDIF
440   PRINT "Letter grade assigned is: ";LETTER.GRADE$
```

You may wish to perform hand traces of several sample sets of scores to convince yourself that this is a correct solution to the problem and will assign and output the appropriate letter grade for each calculated average.

This completes the discussion of the use of selection statements in problem solutions. It cannot be stressed too strongly that the methods illustrated in this chapter for implementing IF-THEN and IF-THEN-ELSE control structures must be used if structured programming principles are to be followed and spaghetti code avoided. Selection statements written in the manner shown are easy to read, understand, and modify.

5.7 SUMMARY

Relational operators are used in both pseudocode and BASIC to form the simple conditional expressions used to describe the relationship between two constants, variables, and/or expressions. The logical operators AND, OR, and NOT may be used to combine these simple conditional expressions into more complex compound conditional expressions. When a conditional expression is evaluated during program execution, it is assigned a truth value of "TRUE" or "FALSE".

Conditional expressions are used in the selection statements IF-THEN and IF-THEN-ELSE to determine which of a pair of actions is to be performed depending upon the truth value of a given condition.

Both the IF-THEN and IF-THEN-ELSE pseudocode control structures are converted to equivalent BASIC language code segments through the use of the BASIC IF-THEN-ELSE statement. A GOTO statement must be inserted into the pseudocode IF-THEN-ELSE translation to implement this control structure correctly. This is the only situation where the GOTO statement will be used in the structured BASIC implementation taught in this text.

Nested IF-THEN and IF-THEN-ELSE statements are needed in some problem situations to implement multiple decision making. A primary concern in the use of a nested structure is that proper indenting and matching of IF and ENDIF statements is done.

Pseudocode Selection Statements and Their BASIC Language Equivalents

The IF-THEN statement

Pseudocode	BASIC
100 IF *<condition>*	100 IF <condition> THEN 110 ELSE 160
110 THEN	110 'THEN
120 *<statement>*	120 <statement>
130 .	130 .
140 .	140 .
150 .	150 .
160 ENDIF	160 'ENDIF

The IF-THEN-ELSE statement

Pseudocode	BASIC
100 IF *<condition>*	100 IF <condition> THEN 110 ELSE 160
110 THEN	110 'THEN
120 *<statement>*	120 <statement>
130 .	130 .
140 .	140 .
	150

Pseudocode Selection Statements and Their BASIC Language Equivalents
(*Continued*)

The IF-THEN-ELSE statement	
Pseudocode	BASIC

150 .	155	GOTO 210
160 *ELSE*	160	'ELSE
170 <statement>	170	<statement>
180 .	180	.
190 .	190	.
200 .	200	.
210 *ENDIF*	210	'ENDIF

EXERCISES

1. Write BASIC conditional expressions to describe the following relations. You will need to choose your own variable names for some of the problems.

   a. A variable TOTAL is equal to zero.
   b. The month is April.
   c. The winning team's score is greater than the losing team's score.
   d. The balance due is more than $100.00.
   e. The customer's name is not Robert Jones.
   f. The amount is more than 50 but less than 100.
   g. The test score must be between 0 and 100 inclusive.
   h. Today is not Friday.
   i. The color is red or blue.
   j. The girl is Jane or the boy may not be Tom or Joe.

2. Determine the truth value ("TRUE" or "FALSE") of each of the following conditional expressions:

   a. $A > B$, if $A = 5$ and $B = 7$
   b. $C <= D$, if $C = 3$ and $D = 3$
   c. E$ $<>$ F$, if E$ $=$ "aaa " and F$ $=$ "aaa"
   d. NOT ($G > H + 2$), if $G = 4$ and $H = 3$
   e. $J > K$ AND $K >= L$, if $J = 4$, $K = 3$, and $L = 5$
   f. $J > K$ OR $K > = L$, if $J = 4$, $K = 3$, and $L = 5$
   g. $M <= N$ OR $P <> Q$ AND $R < S$, if $M = 4$, $N = 3$, $P = 2$, $Q = 2$, $R = 5$, and $S = 7$
   h. ($M <= N$ OR $P <> Q$) AND $R < S$, if $M = 4$, $N = 3$, $P = 2$, $Q = 2$, $R = 5$, and $S = 7$

3. The following segment of BASIC code will, when executed:

```
10  INPUT NEST
20  INPUT TEST
30  IF TEST <> 35 THEN 40 ELSE 60
40  'THEN
50     PRINT TEST
60  'ELSE
70     PRINT NEST
80  'ENDIF
```

   a. Produce incorrect output because of a logic error.

   b. Create a syntax error message.

   c. Cause a compilation error message.

   d. Run correctly because it contains no error.

4. Which of the following pseudocode segments is a correct refinement of the comment:

{display number if number is greater than zero;
otherwise display only a zero}?

   a. WRITE (NUMBER)
      IF NUMBER < 0
      THEN
         WRITE ("0")
      ENDIF

   b. IF NUMBER > 0
      THEN
         WRITE (NUMBER − 0)
      ELSE
         WRITE (NUMBER)
      ENDIF

   c. IF NUMBER > 0
      THEN
         WRITE (NUMBER)
      ELSE
         IF NUMBER < 0
         THEN
            WRITE ("0")
         ENDIF
      ENDIF

   d. IF NUMBER > 0
      THEN
         WRITE (NUMBER)
      ELSE
         WRITE ("0")
      ENDIF

   e. Two of the above are correct.

5. Which of the following segments of BASIC is a correct (structured) translation of the following pseudocode segment?

```
100  IF TODAY$ = "MONDAY"
110  THEN
120     WRITE ("Today is the first day of the workweek")
130  ELSE
140     IF TODAY$ = "FRIDAY"
150     THEN
160        WRITE ("The week is all but over")
170     ENDIF
180  ENDIF
```

a.
```
100    IF TODAY$ = "MONDAY" THEN 110 ELSE 130
110    'THEN
120       PRINT "Today is the first day of the workweek"
130    'ELSE
140       IF TODAY$ = "FRIDAY" THEN 150
150    '   THEN
160          PRINT "The week is all but over"
170    '   ENDIF
180    'ENDIF
```

b.
```
100    IF TODAY$ = "MONDAY" THEN 110 ELSE 160
110    'THEN
120       PRINT "Today is the first day of the workweek"
125       GOTO 180
130    'ELSE
140       IF TODAY$ = "FRIDAY" THEN 150 ELSE 170
150    '   THEN
160          PRINT "The week is all but over"
165          GOTO 175
170    '   ELSE
175    '   ENDIF
180    'ENDIF
```

c.
```
100    IF TODAY$ = "MONDAY"
110    'THEN
120       PRINT "Today is the first day of the workweek"
125       GOTO 180
130    'ELSE
140       IF TODAY$ = "FRIDAY"
150    '   THEN
160          PRINT "The week is all but over"
170    '   ENDIF
180    'ENDIF
```

d. More than one of the above is correct.

e. None of the above are correct.

6. What would be printed if the following BASIC program were executed?

```
10    VALUE = 10
20    IF (VALUE < 0) OR (VALUE > 10) THEN 30 ELSE 50
30    'THEN
40       PRINT "#1"
45       GOTO 70
50    'ELSE
60       PRINT "#2"
70    'ENDIF
```

a. #1   b. #1   c. #2   d. "#1"   e. "#2"
   #2

7. What would be displayed by the following?

```
10    VALUE = -17
20    NUM = 0
30    IF (VALUE < 0) AND (NUM > 0) THEN 40  ELSE 60
40   'THEN
50       PRINT "#1"
60   'ENDIF
70    PRINT "#2"
```

a.#1   b.#1   c.#2   d."#1"   e."#2"
  #2

8. What would be displayed by the following BASIC program when it is executed?

```
100    INPUT SPEED
110    IF SPEED > 60  THEN 120 ELSE 140
120   'THEN
130       FINE = 50
140   'ENDIF
150    IF SPEED > 50 THEN 160 ELSE 180
160   'THEN
170       FINE = 35
180   'ENDIF
190    IF SPEED > 40 THEN 200 ELSE 220
200   'THEN
210       FINE = 20
215       GOTO 240
220   'ELSE
230       FINE = 0
2240  'ENDIF
2250   PRINT FINE
```

INPUT

65

a. 50
b. 35
c. 20
d. 0

Use the following segment of pseudocode to answer questions 9 and 10:

```
60    IF COMMISSION > 5000
70    THEN
80        BONUS ← 500
90    ELSE
100       BONUS ← 0
110   ENDIF
```

9. To convert line 60 to BASIC language (using the structured programming method as taught in this book), the best choice would be

a. IF COMMISSION > 5000 'THEN GOTO 70 'ELSE GOTO 90
b. IF COMMISSION > 5000 THEN BONUS = 0 ELSE BONUS = 500
c. IF COMMISSION > 5000 THEN GOTO 80 ELSE GOTO 100
d. IF COMMISSION > 5000 THEN GOTO 70 ELSE GOTO 90

10. To convert lines 70 through 90 from pseudocode to BASIC, the best choice would be

a.
```
70   THEN
80      BONUS = 500
90   ELSE
```

b.
```
70   'THEN
80      BONUS = 500
85      GOTO 110
90   'ELSE
```

c.
```
70   'THEN
80      BONUS = 500
90   'ELSE
```

d. None of the above

11. What is printed by the following BASIC program when it is executed?

```
10   INPUT X$
20   Y$ = "X$"
30   IF Y$ = "X$" THEN 40 ELSE 60
40   'THEN
50      X$ = "Y$"
55      GOTO 80
60   'ELSE
70      Y$ = X$
80   'ENDIF
90   PRINT X$;Y$
```

<u>INPUT DATA</u>

Y$

a. XY

b. XX

c. YX

d. YY

Use the following two segments of BASIC code to answer question 12:

```
#1:  10   INPUT X
     20   IF X < 5 THEN 30 ELSE 50
     30   'THEN
     40      PRINT X
     45      GOTO 70
     50   'ELSE
     60      PRINT X + 2
     70   'ENDIF
```

```
#2:  10   INPUT X
     20   IF X < 5 THEN 30 ELSE 50
     30   'THEN
     40      PRINT X
     50   'ENDIF
     60   IF X > 5 THEN 70 ELSE 90
     70   'THEN
     80      PRINT X + 2
     90   'ENDIF
```

12. Which of the following statements best describes the above two segments of BASIC code?

a. Segment #1 and segment #2 will produce identical results when executed.

b. Segment #1 is more efficient than segment #2.

c. Segment #2 is more efficient than segment #1.

d. Segments #1 and #2 do not produce the same results when executed.

Identify the best answers in questions 13 through 15 for changing the following segment of pseudocode into BASIC:

```
60    IF AMOUNT < QUOTA
70    THEN
80        BONUS ← 0
90    ELSE
100       BONUS ← 1000
110   ENDIF
```

13. For line 60 the best answer would be:

   a. 60 IF AMOUNT < QUOTA THEN GOTO 70 ELSE GOTO 90
   b. 60 IF AMOUNT > QUOTA THEN BONUS = 1000 ELSE BONUS = 0
   c. 60 IF AMOUNT < QUOTA THEN GOTO 80 ELSE GOTO 100
   d. None of the above.

14. For lines 70 through 90 the best answer would be

   a. 70 THEN   **b.** 70 'THEN
        80   BONUS = 0   80   BONUS = 0
        90 ELSE   90 'ELSE

   c. 70 'THEN
        80   BONUS = 0   **d.** None of these are correct
        85   GOTO 110
        90 'ELSE

15. For lines 90 through 110 the best answer would be:

   a. 90   'ELSE   **b.** 90   ELSE
        100   BONUS = 1000   100   BONUS = 1000
        110 'ENDIF   110 ENDIF

   c. 90   'ELSE   **d.** None of these are correct
        100   BONUS = 1000
        105   GOTO 110
        110 'ENDIF

16. What would be printed by the following program when it is executed?

```
100    BOTTOMS = 1
110    TOPS = 5
120    TOPS = TOPS + BOTTOMS
130    IF TOPS < 6 THEN 140 ELSE 160
140    'THEN
150        PRINT "EASY"
155        GOTO 230
160    'ELSE
170        IF TOPS > 6 THEN 180 ELSE 200
180    '   THEN
190            PRINT "CHALLENGING"
195            GOTO 220
200    '   ELSE
210            PRINT "DIFFICULT"
220    '   ENDIF
230    'ENDIF
240    PRINT TOPS
```

  a. EASY
        6
  b. CHALLENGING
        6
  c. DIFFICULT
        6
  d. None of the above

17. Design and write a program to carry on a conversation with the user. Input to the program should be answers to questions displayed on the screen. Output should make use of the user's responses to the questions to provide appropriate responses back to the user. A short example of such a dialogue might be (the user's responses to the computer's questions are underlined):

```
What is your name? Jack
Hi, Jack! What is your favorite hobby? fishing
That's interesting, my favorite hobby is fishing, too.
How old are you? 35
Over the hill, hunh?
        .
        .
        .
```

18. Design and write a BASIC program to find the smallest of four values input to the computer. The program should display an input prompt, get the four values, and print the smallest value, appropriately labeled.

CHAPTER 6

Repetition Statements

This chapter discusses the last control structure needed to design solutions to problems—the repetitive control structure. There are two different repetitive structures that may be used in programs—indeterminate loops and determinate loops. Microsoft BASIC contains two different pairs of repetition statements that may be used to form these looping structures—the WHILE-WEND statements and the FOR-NEXT statements. The operation of these statements, and when to use which pair of statements in designing a pseudolanguage solution to a problem, are explained.

6.0 OBJECTIVES

Upon completing this chapter, the student should be able to:

1. Define determinate and indeterminate looping structures and explain the differences between the two.
2. Determine which type of loop is appropriate for a given problem situation.

3. Use the FOR-NEXT statements correctly when they are appropriate in designing problem solutions.

4. Use the WHILE-WEND statements correctly in writing solutions to problems that require this type of loop.

5. Trace and construct nested loops.

6.1 DETERMINATE AND INDETERMINATE LOOPS

When designing the solution to a particular problem, it is often necessary to repeat a group of statements more than once. One way this may be handled is to include the group of statements in the program as many times as they need to be repeated. If the number of repetitions is large, however, this may result in a needlessly long program. A repetitive control structure allows a group of statements to be performed several times before execution of the remainder of the program occurs.

As mentioned in Chapter 2, there are two types of loops that may be encountered in program solutions. In the first situation it is known before execution of the loop begins just how many times it will be executed. This occurs in a problem such as "Compute the average of ten student scores . . ." or "Print a table of the squares and square roots of the whole numbers from 1 to 100 . . .". In both of these problem descriptions, it is known before the loop begins how many times it will need to be performed—in the first case 10 times, in the second 100 times. This type of loop is referred to as a *determinate,* or counted, *loop.*

Pseudocode solutions to problems of this type would most likely contain FOR-NEXT statements to control the number of times the loop is executed. The WHILE-ENDWHILE pseudocode statements can be used to form determinate loops, but the FOR-NEXT is simpler to use in this type of problem.

In the second type of looping situation that may occur in problem solutions it is not known when the loop is first entered just how many times it will be executed. This situation occurs in problems such as "Compute the average of a set of student scores. The last score will be followed by the value − 99 . . ." or "Determine the number of years that a sum of $1000 must be on deposit at an interest rate of 9 percent, compounded quarterly, until the amount doubles . . .". Both of these examples contain *indeterminate loops.*

The first example given above uses a "flag," a value of − 99, to indicate when the loop is to be terminated. The value − 99 may occur after 5 repetitions of the loop, or 20, or 500. The number of times the loop will be executed is dependent upon the input data. The second example uses a value calculated inside the loop, the amount of principal plus interest, to determine when the loop is to be terminated. In either case, it is not known when the loop is initially encountered how many times it will be executed.

Pseudocode solutions to problems of the above type most often use WHILE-ENDWHILE statements to control the loop. A WHILE loop indicates that a group of statements is to be repeated as long as a particular condition is true. The conditions in the above examples might be stated, "the student score is not -99", and, "the amount is less than $2000." As long as these conditions are true, the statements contained within the loops will continue executing.

Let's examine the exact form of the BASIC language statements used to translate these two pseudocode looping structures into BASIC.

6.2 THE FOR-NEXT STATEMENT

The FOR and NEXT statements in BASIC, which are used to implement determinate loops, have the following general form:

```
line#  FOR <variable> = <starting value> TO <ending value>
                                          [STEP <increment>]
```

and

```
line#  NEXT [<variable>]
```

The general forms of both of these statements are given above since they must always appear in matching pairs. Whenever a FOR statement is used in a program, there must be a corresponding NEXT statement later in the program.

The <variable> that occurs in both the FOR and NEXT statements has two purposes. The first function performed by this variable is a counting function. It is used to determine when the loop has been repeated the specified number of times, and should be exited. The second function of this variable is to indicate to the BASIC interpreter where the end of the loop occurs. Both the FOR and NEXT statements that delimit a loop must contain exactly the same variable name. As the square brackets ([ ]) indicate in the general form of the NEXT statement, the inclusion of this variable name in the NEXT statement is optional in certain situations. For now, we will always include the variable name in the NEXT statement.

The <starting value> that immediately follows the equal sign in the FOR statement is the initial value assigned to <variable> the first time the FOR statement is executed. This will be the value of <variable> during the first execution of the statements contained in the loop. In the case where the optional

STEP feature is not used, the value of <variable> will be automatically incremented by 1 when the NEXT statement is encountered, and program control will return to the FOR statement. The <ending value> that follows the word TO in the FOR statement indicates when the loop is to be terminated. Once the value of <variable> *exceeds* this <ending value>, program execution continues with the statement following the NEXT statement. Both <starting value> and <ending value> may be constants, variables, and/or expressions.

For example, if the following FOR-NEXT loop occurred in a problem solution:

```
100  FOR NUM = 1 TO 5
110     <statement>
120     <statement>
130  NEXT NUM
140  <statement>
       .
       .
       .
```

NUM would initially be assigned the value of 1. When statement 130 NEXT NUM is encountered, the value of NUM is incremented by 1, and program control returns to the FOR statement at line 100. Since the value of NUM, which is now 2, does not exceed the ending value, 5, the statements at lines 110 and 120 are executed again. When line 130 is reached, NUM is incremented again, so it is now 3, and control returns to line 100. Eventually, NUM attains the value of 6 upon an execution of line 130, and when program control is returned to line 100, the FOR statement, the computer determines that the ending value has been exceeded (6 is greater than 5). At this point, program execution continues with the statement at line 140.

The Step Feature

The optional STEP <increment> feature included in the general form permits the value of the counter variable in the FOR-NEXT loop to be incremented by some value other than one. If, for example, it was desired to have the counter variable assigned the values of the odd numbers from 1 to 11, the FOR statement

```
20  FOR COUNT = 1 TO 11 STEP 2
```

could be used. COUNT will initially be set to 1, and then rather than being automatically incremented by 1 by the NEXT COUNT statement, as normally occurs in a FOR-NEXT loop, STEP 2 would cause COUNT to be incremented by 2. The values 3, 5, 7, etc., would be successively assigned to COUNT.

This feature also permits the counter variable to be decremented by using a negative number for the value of STEP. In this situation, the <starting value> would be larger than the <ending value>. As an example,

```
100 FOR SIZE = 10 TO 1 STEP −1
```

SIZE would take on an initial value of 10, and then the succeeding values of 9, 8, 7, etc., down to a value of 1. In this example, termination of the loop occurs when the value of the counter variable (SIZE) is *less than* the ending value (1). The values of SIZE within the loop would be 10, 9, 8, . . . , 1. When the program exits the loop, however, SIZE would be equal to 0.

The value of the counter variable can be used inside a FOR-NEXT loop, either as a value to be displayed or in calculations. It is important, however, never to change the value of the counter variable with an assignment or input statement inside a loop. If this were done, it could no longer be easily determined how many times the loop would be executed, and logic errors could easily be introduced into the program. It is also a good idea never to use the value of the counter variable once the loop has been exited since the value of the counter variable cannot always be relied upon once the program has exited the loop.

Example Problems

Translation of pseudocode FOR-NEXT statements into BASIC language FOR-NEXT statements is quite simple. Placing line numbers in front of the FOR and NEXT statements is all that needs to be done. The following example is a problem whose solution requires a FOR-NEXT loop:

☐ **Formal Problem Definition**

General Description

A program is to be written to produce a three-column table listing the radii, circumferences, and areas of circles having radii of 1, 2, 3, . . . , 10. Appropriate headings are to be displayed above each column of output.

Input Specifications

There will be no input to the program. All needed values are contained within the program.

Output Specifications

Output will consist of a table with the following column headings:

```
Radius  Circumference  Area
```

Following this line of headings will be a blank line, followed by 10 rows of three columns of numbers. The first column will be the values 1, 2, 3, . . . , 10. The second column will be the circumferences of circles having these radii. The third column will be the areas of circles having these radii. The following formulas may be used to compute the circumference and area:

$$\text{Circumference} = 2 \times \pi \times \text{radius}$$
$$\text{Area} = \pi \times \text{radius} \times \text{radius}$$

Use the value 3.14159 for π.

Normal Example

Input:

    None

Output:

Radius	Circumference	Area
1	6.28318	3.14159
2	12.56636	12.56636
.	.	.
.	.	.
.	.	.
10	62.8318	314.159

Unusual or Error Conditions

There should be no unusual or error conditions since no input will be entered.

A top-down design of this problem might proceed as follows. A loop would be useful, as the same process of calculating circumferences and areas will need to be performed 10 times. The fact that the loop is to be performed a set number of times, 10, indicates that a determinate loop is needed. A FOR-NEXT loop would be the simplest way to implement the needed loop. Since headings are to be printed at the top of each of the columns, they will need to be output first, before the loop is entered. Level I of the top-down design, therefore, might be

Level I

{print column headings}
{print a blank line}
FOR RADIUS = 1 TO 10
    {compute circumference}
    {compute area}
    {display radius, circumference, and area}
NEXT RADIUS

The next level, Level II, would consist of the pseudocode refinements of the comment statements above:

Level II

```
WRITE ("Radius", "Circumference", "Area")
WRITE
FOR RADIUS = 1 TO 10
    CIRCUMFERENCE ← 2 * 3.14159 * RADIUS
    AREA ← 3.14159 * RADIUS * RADIUS
    WRITE (RADIUS, CIRCUMFERENCE, AREA)
NEXT RADIUS
```

Since Level II is all in pseudocode, the next step in the solution to the problem is to translate the pseudocode solution into BASIC. The first step in this process is to assign line numbers to the pseudocode statements:

```
10   WRITE ("Radius", "Circumference", "Area")
20   WRITE
30   FOR RADIUS = 1 TO 10
40       CIRCUMFERENCE ← 2 * 3.14159 * RADIUS
50       AREA ← 3.14159 * RADIUS * RADIUS
60       WRITE (RADIUS, CIRCUMFERENCE, AREA)
70   NEXT RADIUS
```

Next, each pseudocode statement is translated into an equivalent BASIC language statement:

```
10   PRINT "Radius","Circumference","Area"
20   PRINT
30   FOR RADIUS = 1 TO 10
40      CIRCUMFERENCE = 2 * 3.14159 * RADIUS
50      AREA = 3.14159 * RADIUS * RADIUS
60      PRINT RADIUS, CIRCUMFERENCE, AREA
70   NEXT RADIUS
```

If you were to enter this program and run it, you would see that it would produce the desired output. The radius, circumference, and area values would line up under the column headings since commas are used in the PRINT statements at lines 10 and 60, causing zone printing to be performed.

Let's look at another example. Suppose we were asked to write a program to solve the following problem:

☐ **Formal Problem Definition**

General Description

A program is to be prepared to compute the weekly gross pay for the five hourly employees of the ABC Computer Company. Input for each employee is to be the employee name, hours worked, and hourly pay rate. Output is to be the employee name and gross pay, arranged in tabular form, appropriately labeled. Employees are paid time and a half for any hours over 40.

Input Specifications

Input is to consist of three values for each employee, one value per line. The first input value, employee name, will be entered in response to the prompt:

```
Enter employee name: <employee name>
```

where <employee name> is to be replaced by the actual name of the employee. The second value entered, hours worked, will be prompted by the message:

```
Enter hours worked: <hours worked>
```

where <hours worked> is to be replaced by the number of hours the employee worked this week. The third line of input, hourly pay rate, will be entered in response to the message:

```
Enter hourly pay rate: <pay rate>
```

where <pay rate> is replaced by the employee's hourly rate of pay. The data entered for each employee will be separated from the next employee's data by a blank line.

Output Specifications

Output is to be sent directly to the printer. The first line of output is to be the name of the company, "ABC Computer Company." The second line of output is to be the name of the report, "Weekly Payroll Report." Two blank lines are to be printed next, followed on the next line by the column headings,

```
Employee            Gross Pay
```

This line of output is to be followed by one blank line, followed by the body of the table, single spaced.

Normal Example

Input: (all on screen)

```
Enter employee name: Mary White
Enter hours worked: 38
Enter hourly pay rate: 12.50
```

```
Enter employee name: Bill Brown
Enter hours worked: 37
Enter hourly pay rate: 11.00

Enter employee name: John Richards
Enter hours worked: 41
Enter hourly pay rate: 10.50

Enter employee name: Sue Smith
Enter hours worked: 42
Enter hourly pay rate: 15.00

Enter employee name: Jane Johnson
Enter hours worked: 40
Enter hourly pay rate: 13.50
```

Output: (all on the printer)

```
                ABC Computer Company
                Weekly Payroll Report


         Employee              Gross Pay

         Mary White            475.00
         Bill Brown            407.00
         John Richards         435.75
         Sue Smith             645.00
         Jane Johnson          540.00
```

Unusual or Error Conditions

1. If all three data values for an employee are entered on a single line, the error mesage, "?Redo from start," will be displayed and all data for that employee must be reentered.
2. If nonnumeric data is entered for either the second or third data item for an employee, the error message, "?Redo from start," will be displayed and the data must be reentered.
3. If a negative number of hours or rate of pay is entered, calculations will be made with this data and an incorrect amount of gross pay will be displayed.

This problem also involves a determinate loop. We are told that the firm has five hourly employees. Since we know, therefore, before the loop is entered, how many times it will need to be executed (5 times), a FOR-NEXT loop would be the appropriate repetitive control structure to use. Level I of the top-down design could be the following:

Level I

{*print the report headings*}
FOR EMPLOYEE = 1 TO 5
    {*enter the employee information*}
    {*compute gross pay*}
    {*display the employee information*}
NEXT EMPLOYEE

Notice that the report headings need to be printed before the loop is entered. Otherwise, headings would be printed before each line of employee information. Level II might look like this:

Level II

WRITE ("*ABC Computer Company*")
WRITE ("*Weekly Payroll Report*")
WRITE
WRITE
WRITE ("*Employee*", "*Gross Pay*")
WRITE
FOR EMPLOYEE = 1 TO 5
    WRITE ("*Enter employee name:*")
    READ (EMPLOYEE.NAME)
    WRITE ("*Enter hours worked:*")
    READ (HOURS.WORKED)
    WRITE ("*Enter rate of pay*")
    READ (PAY.RATE)
    WRITE
    {*compute gross pay*}
    WRITE (EMPLOYEE.NAME, GROSS.PAY)
NEXT EMPLOYEE

The only comment remaining to be refined is {*compute gross pay*}. The output specifications section of the formal problem definition states that overtime pay is paid if the employee works more than 40 hours. Otherwise, GROSS.PAY will be HOURS.WORKED times PAY.RATE. This implies that a selection statement is needed to examine the value of HOURS.WORKED to see if it exceeds 40. The first refinement of this comment, then, might be

IF HOURS.WORKED > 40
THEN
    {*compute regular pay plus overtime pay*}

ELSE
        GROSS. PAY ← HOURS. WORKED * PAY. RATE
ENDIF

Level III, then, would be

Level III

WRITE ("ABC Computer Company")
WRITE ("Weekly Payroll Report")
WRITE
WRITE
WRITE ("Employee", "Gross Pay")
WRITE
FOR EMPLOYEE = 1 TO 5
        WRITE ("Enter employee name:")
        READ (EMPLOYEE. NAME)
        WRITE ("Enter hours worked:")
        READ (HOURS. WORKED)
        WRITE ("Enter rate of pay")
        READ (PAY. RATE)
        WRITE
        IF HOURS. WORKED > 40
        THEN
                {compute regular pay plus overtime pay}
        ELSE
                GROSS. PAY ← HOURS. WORKED * PAY. RATE
        ENDIF
        WRITE (EMPLOYEE. NAME, GROSS. PAY)
NEXT EMPLOYEE

One comment remains to be refined, {compute regular pay plus overtime pay}. According to the output specifications, if an employee works more than 40 hours, the employee is still paid at the regular rate of pay for the first 40 hours worked that week:

40 * PAY. RATE

The quantity (HOURS. WORKED − 40) would be the number of overtime hours worked, and the output specifications indicate that these hours are to be paid at a rate of 1.5 times the regular pay rate. This means that the amount of overtime pay could be calculated by multiplying the overtime hours (HOURS. WORKED − 40) by 1.5 times the PAY.RATE:

$$(HOURS.WORKED - 40) * 1.5 * PAY.RATE$$

GROSS.PAY, then, for an employee working more than 40 hours in the week, would be the sum of the above two expressions:

$$GROSS.PAY \leftarrow 40 * PAY.RATE$$
$$+ (HOURS.WORKED - 40) * 1.5 * PAY.RATE$$

Replacing the comment, {*compute regular pay plus overtime pay*}, with the above refinement results in the following for Level IV, which is our final solution, all in pseudocode:

Level IV

```
WRITE ("ABC Computer Company")
WRITE ("Weekly Payroll Report")
WRITE
WRITE
WRITE ("Employee", "Gross Pay")
WRITE
FOR EMPLOYEE = 1 TO 5
    WRITE ("Enter employee name:")
    READ (EMPLOYEE.NAME)
    WRITE ("Enter hours worked:")
    READ (HOURS.WORKED)
    WRITE ("Enter rate of pay")
    READ (PAY.RATE)
    WRITE
    IF HOURS.WORKED > 40
    THEN
        GROSS.PAY ← 40 * PAY.RATE
                + (HOURS.WORKED - 40) * PAY.RATE * 1.5
    ELSE
        GROSS.PAY ← HOURS.WORKED * PAY.RATE
    ENDIF
    WRITE (EMPLOYEE.NAME, GROSS.PAY)
NEXT EMPLOYEE
```

All that remains to be done, then, is to translate this solution into BASIC. The first step is to assign line numbers to each pseudocode statement:

```
100   WRITE ("ABC Computer Company")
110   WRITE ("Weekly Payroll Report")
```

```
120   WRITE
130   WRITE
140   WRITE ("Employee", "Gross Pay")
150   WRITE
160   FOR EMPLOYEE = 1 TO 5
170       WRITE ("Enter employee name:")
180       READ (EMPLOYEE.NAME)
190       WRITE ("Enter hours worked:")
200       READ (HOURS.WORKED)
210       WRITE ("Enter rate of pay")
220       READ (PAY.RATE)
230       WRITE
240       IF HOURS.WORKED > 40
250       THEN
260           GROSS.PAY ← 40 * PAY.RATE
                     + (HOURS.WORKED − 40) * PAY.RATE * 1.5
270       ELSE
280           GROSS.PAY ← HOURS.WORKED * PAY.RATE
290       ENDIF
300       WRITE (EMPLOYEE.NAME, GROSS.PAY)
310   NEXT EMPLOYEE
```

Next, a line-by-line conversion of the pseudocode into BASIC is performed. The first six statements, lines 100 through 150, become LPRINT statements since we wish to have the headings appear on the report, which is being sent directly to the printer:

```
100   LPRINT TAB(20) "ABC Computer Company"
110   LPRINT TAB(20) "Weekly Payroll Report"
120   LPRINT
130   LPRINT
140   LPRINT , "Employee", "Gross Pay"
150   LPRINT
```

The LPRINT statement at line 140 has a comma preceding the first column heading. This causes the heading "Employee" to be printed starting at the beginning of the second print zone, column 15.

The FOR-NEXT statement at line 160 needs no changes made in it:

```
160   FOR EMPLOYEE = 1 TO 5
```

Statements 170 through 230, which perform the input of employee data on the screen, become PRINT and INPUT statements:

```
170      PRINT "Enter employee name:";
180      INPUT "", EMPLOYEE.NAME$
190      PRINT "Enter hours worked:";
200      INPUT "", HOURS.WORKED
210      PRINT "Enter rate of pay";
220      INPUT "", PAY.RATE
230      PRINT
```

PRINT statements are used in this section of the program rather than LPRINT statements since we wish to have the input prompts displayed on the screen rather than on the printer. Notice that the variable name EMPLOYEE.NAME used in the pseudocode statement needs a $ placed after it in the BASIC language translation to make it acceptable to the BASIC interpreter as a character string variable. The semicolons (;) at the ends of the three PRINT statement prompts are needed to permit entry of the data values on the same screen lines as the prompt messages: the comma following the INPUT "" in each INPUT statement suppresses the ? normally printed by the INPUT statement.

Statements 240 through 290 are an IF-THEN-ELSE control structure, and are translated into BASIC as was explained in the previous chapter. The THEN, ELSE, and ENDIF statements need single quotation marks inserted between their line numbers and the control words. A GOTO statement sending program control to the ENDIF statement at line 290 needs to be inserted before the ELSE statement at line 270; 265 GOTO 290. The IF statement at line 240 needs to have the line numbers of the THEN and ELSE statements added to it, and the assignment statements at lines 260 and 280 need the pseudocode assignment operators (←) replaced by their BASIC language equivalent (=). All these changes would result in the following translation of these statements:

```
240      IF HOURS.WORKED > 40 THEN 250 ELSE 270
250      'THEN
260          GROSS.PAY = 40 * PAY.RATE
                           + (HOURS.WORKED - 40) * PAY.RATE
265          GOTO 290      * 1.5
270      'ELSE
280          GROSS.PAY = HOURS.WORKED * PAY.RATE
290      'ENDIF
```

Statement 300 becomes an LPRINT statement, and line 310, the NEXT statement, needs to have no changes made in it:

```
300     LPRINT , EMPLOYEE.NAME$, GROSS.PAY
310  NEXT EMPLOYEE
```

If we now combine these sections of code, we have the following BASIC language equivalent of the pseudocode solution:

```
100  LPRINT TAB(20) "ABC Computer Company"
110  LPRINT TAB(20) "Weekly Payroll Report"
120  LPRINT
130  LPRINT
140  LPRINT , "Employee" , "Gross Pay"
150  LPRINT
160  FOR EMPLOYEE = 1 TO 5
170     PRINT "Enter employee name:";
180     INPUT "", EMPLOYEE.NAME$
190     PRINT "Enter hours worked:";
200     INPUT "", HOURS.WORKED
210     PRINT "Enter rate of pay";
220     INPUT "", PAY.RATE
230     PRINT
240     IF HOURS.WORKED > 40 THEN 250 ELSE 270
250     'THEN
260        GROSS.PAY = 40 * PAY.RATE
                     + (HOURS.WORKED - 40) * PAY.RATE * 1.5
265        GOTO 290
270     'ELSE
280        GROSS.PAY = HOURS.WORKED * PAY.RATE
290     'ENDIF
300     LPRINT , EMPLOYEE.NAME$, GROSS.PAY
310  NEXT EMPLOYEE
```

All the examples in this section have dealt with problems involving determinate loops in their solutions. Now let's take a look at the other type of looping situation—problem solutions that require indeterminate loops.

6.3 THE WHILE-WEND STATEMENTS

The WHILE and WEND statements are the other pair of BASIC statements that may be used to implement a repetitive control structure. These statements may be used to implement both determinate and indeterminate loops but are most often used when indeterminate loops are needed in problem solutions.

General Form

The general forms of these two statements are:

```
line#   WHILE <condition>
```

and

```
line#   WEND
```

The <condition> in the WHILE statement may be any conditional expression that states the relationship between two variables, constants, and/or expressions, and may be a simple or compound conditional expression. The statements in a program contained between the WHILE and WEND statements are performed repetitively as long as the <condition> in the WHILE statement is true. These statements may be performed once, many times, or not at all; it is entirely dependent upon the truth value of <condition>.

One word of caution when using WHILE-WEND statements. It is quite easy to inadvertently construct a WHILE loop that is an *infinite loop*. By this is meant that once the program enters the looping structure, it will never exit from this loop unless program execution is manually interrupted. This situation occurs when none of the statements inside the loop ever cause the <condition> in the WHILE statement to become false. Remember how the loop works; the statements inside the loop will be repeated as long as the <condition> in the WHILE statement is true. If the <condition> is always true, program control will never exit from the loop.

Suppose we have the following section of a BASIC program:

```
100   WHILE <condition>
110       <statement>
120       <statement>
130   WEND
140   <statement>
          .
          .
          .
```

Execution of this program segment would proceed as follows. When the WHILE statement at line 100 is encountered for the first time during program execution, the <condition> in the statement is evaluated as either "true" or "false." If the <condition> is "true," the two statements at lines 110 and 120 are then executed.

When the WEND statement at line 130 is executed, program control is returned to the WHILE statement at line 100. The <condition> is evaluated once again, and if it is still "true," statements 110 and 120 are executed again. This looping continues until the <condition> in the WHILE statement finally evaluates as "false." At this time, program control is sent to line 140, and program execution continues with this statement.

As can be seen from the discussion above, it is entirely possible that the statements contained in a WHILE loop may never be executed in a particular run of a program. If the <condition> in the WHILE statement evaluates as "false" the first time the WHILE statement is encountered in the program, program control passes over the entire loop to the statement following the WEND statement. The statements within the loop are not executed.

Translation of a pseudocode WHILE-ENDWHILE loop into equivalent BASIC language statements is quite straightforward. The pseudocode WHILE statement needs only a line number preceding it to convert it to BASIC, and the pseudocode ENDWHILE statement is replaced by the BASIC language WEND statement. Let's examine some example problems whose solutions require WHILE loops.

Example Problems

☐ Formal Problem Definition

General Description

A program is to be written to compute the average of a set of student scores. Input will be a number of scores, one score per line. End of input will be indicated by entry of a negative value. Output is to be the number of scores and the average of these scores.

Input Specifications

Input will be a set of student scores, one value per line. Each score is to be prompted by the message:

```
Enter score: <score>
```

where <score> is a student score. End of input will be indicated by entry of a negative value. This negative value is not to be counted or included in the average.

Output Specifications

Two lines of output will be produced by the program. The first line of output is to be

```
Number of scores: <number>
```

where <number> is replaced by the number of scores averaged. The second line of output is to be

```
Average is: <average>
```

where <average> is replaced by the sum of the scores divided by the number of scores.

Normal Example

Input:

```
Enter score: 68
Enter score: 80
Enter score: 78
Enter score: 85
Enter score: 65
Enter score: -9
```

Output:

```
Number of scores: 5
Average is: 75.2
```

Unusual or Error Conditions

1. If nonnumeric data is entered in response to the prompt, "Enter score:", the error message, "?Redo from start", will be displayed, and the score must be reentered.
2. If a negative value is not entered after the last student score is entered, no output will be produced.
3. If no values are entered prior to the negative value, the error message, "Division by zero", will be displayed by the system, and the average will be incorrect.

This problem is similar to an earlier problem we encountered in Chapter 2. The difference is that in this case we do not know before entering the loop how many student scores are to be averaged. In this situation we have an indeterminate loop, and a WHILE loop will be needed. The first level of the top-down design might be

Level I

{*display input prompt and input a student score*}
WHILE {*score is not negative*}
    {*add 1 to number of scores*}
    {*add score to total*}
    {*display input prompt and input a student score*}

ENDWHILE
{compute average}
{display number of scores}
{display average}

The first level of the design demonstrates a pattern that is frequently used with a WHILE loop. There are two points in the program where input occurs—just prior to the WHILE statement, and just prior to the ENDWHILE statement.

The first input is referred to as a "priming read." Its purpose is to provide an initial value to be used in the conditional expression in the WHILE statement. The WHILE condition is *{score is not negative}*. This condition can be evaluated only if a value has been entered for the student score prior to execution of the WHILE statement. This first input, then, is executed only once, and provides an initial value for the student score that is used in the evaluation of the conditional expression in the WHILE statement.

The second input statement, which occurs immediately before the END-WHILE statement, performs the rest of the inputs occurring in the program. It is inside the loop, so it will be executed each time the loop is executed. Its location at the end of the loop is also critical in this problem. As soon as a score has been entered, the ENDWHILE statement requires program control to the WHILE statement. The score that has just been entered is then checked to determine whether or not it is negative. If not, the score is counted by the statement, *{add 1 to number of scores}*, and added to the total by the statement, *{add score to total}*. If the score is negative, however, it will not be counted or added to the total, since program control will be sent to the statement following the ENDWHILE, *{compute average}*.

This pattern of two input statements in a WHILE loop, one just before the WHILE statement and the other immediately preceding the ENDWHILE statement, will be encountered again and again in program solutions. It is important that you become familiar with this pattern and understand its purpose.

Something we did not to do in Level I, which needs to be added to make Level I a complete and correct solution to the problem, is to initialize the variables that will be used to count the number of scores, and to accumulate the total of the scores. These two variables need to be set to zero before the assignment statements inside the loop that use them are encountered for the first time. This procedure could be indicated by the comment, *{initialize number of scores and total to zero}*. Placing this comment in Level I, we now have for a revised first level:

Level I (revised)

{initialize number of scores and total to zero}
{display input prompt and enter a student score}

> *WHILE {score is not negative}*
> *   {add 1 to number of scores}*
> *   {add score to total}*
> *   {display input prompt and enter a student score}*
> *ENDWHILE*
> *{compute average}*
> *{display number of scores}*
> *{display average}*

Level II is a refinement of the comment statements in Level I. The first two comment statements might be refined as follows:

Level II
> *NUMBER.OF.SCORES ← 0*
> *TOTAL ← 0*
> *WRITE ("Enter score:")*
> *READ (SCORE)*

The condition in the WHILE statement would become

> *SCORE >= 0*

so the WHILE statement would be

> *WHILE SCORE >= 0*

The next two comments would become assignment statements:

> *NUMBER.OF.SCORES ← NUMBER.OF.SCORES + 1*
> *TOTAL ← TOTAL + SCORE*

The next comment, *{display input prompt and enter a student score}*, would be refined into the same two statements as was the second comment statement in the program:

> *WRITE ("Enter score:")*
> *READ (SCORE)*

and the ENDWHILE statement would remain unchanged.

The next comment, *{compute average}*, becomes the assignment statement:

> *AVERAGE ← TOTAL / NUMBER.OF.SCORES*

and the last two coments become WRITE statements:

WRITE (*"Number of scores:"*, NUMBER.OF.SCORES)
WRITE (*"Average is:"*, AVERAGE)

A completed Level II, then, would be

Level II
NUMBER.OF.SCORES ← 0
TOTAL ← 0
WRITE (*"Enter score:"*)
READ (SCORE)
WHILE SCORE >= 0
    NUMBER.OF.SCORES ← NUMBER.OF.SCORES + 1
    TOTAL ← TOTAL + SCORE
    WRITE (*"Enter score:"*)
    READ (SCORE)
ENDWHILE
AVERAGE ← TOTAL / NUMBER.OF.SCORES
WRITE (*"Number of scores:"*, NUMBER.OF.SCORES)
WRITE (*"Average is:"*, AVERAGE)

Since Level II is all pseudocode, we may now begin translating it into BASIC. The first step is to assign line numbers to each statement:

```
100   NUMBER.OF.SCORES ← 0
110   TOTAL ← 0
120   WRITE ("Enter score:")
130   READ (SCORE)
140   WHILE SCORE >= 0
150       NUMBER.OF.SCORES ← NUMBER.OF.SCORES + 1
160       TOTAL ← TOTAL + SCORE
170       WRITE ("Enter score:")
180       READ (SCORE)
190   ENDWHILE
200   AVERAGE ← TOTAL / NUMBER.OF.SCORES
210   WRITE ("Number of scores:", NUMBER.OF.SCORES)
220   WRITE ("Average is:", AVERAGE)
```

The BASIC language translation of this would be

```
100  NUMBER.OF.SCORES = 0
110  TOTAL = 0
120  PRINT "Enter score:";
130  INPUT "", SCORE
140  WHILE SCORE >= 0
150     NUMBER.OF.SCORES = NUMBER.OF.SCORES + 1
160     TOTAL = TOTAL + SCORE
170     PRINT "Enter score:";
180     INPUT "", SCORE
190  WEND
200  AVERAGE = TOTAL / NUMBER.OF.SCORES
210  PRINT "Number of scores:"; NUMBER.OF.SCORES
220  PRINT "Average is:"; AVERAGE
```

The pseudocode assignment operator (←) has been replaced with its BASIC language equivalent (=) in all assignment statements, WRITE statements have been translated into PRINT statements, and READ statements have become INPUT statements. The WHILE statement has not been changed, but the pseudocode ENDWHILE statement has become a BASIC language WEND statement.

Let's try another example:

☐ Formal Problem Definition

General Description

Write a program to determine the number of months it would take for your salary to exceed $100,000 if you are paid 1 cent the first month, 2 cents the second month, 4 cents the third month, etc. In other words, your salary keeps doubling each month.

Input Specifications

There will be no input to the program. All values needed are internal to the program.

Output Specifications

There will be one line of output from the program:

```
It will be <months> months until your salary exceeds
$100,000.
```

where <months> is replaced by the number of months determined by the program for your salary to exceed $100,000.

Normal Example

Input:

   None

Output:

   `It will be 25 months until your salary exceeds $100,000.`

Unusual or Error Conditions

There are none that need to be considered since no entry of data will be performed in the program.

Two values need to be initialized in the solution to this problem, the number of months, and your initial salary. This could be performed by the following two statements:

Level I

$MONTHS \leftarrow 1$
$SALARY \leftarrow .01$

A WHILE loop would be the appropriate repetition structure to use since it is not known how many times the doubling of your salary must occur before it exceeds $100,000. The condition to be tested in the WHILE loop deals with your salary—keep looping until salary exceeds $100,000. This could be stated as follows:

$WHILE\ SALARY <=\ 100000$

Two computations need to be performed inside the loop. Your salary needs to be doubled, and the number of months must be incremented by 1. These calculations could be performed by the following two assignment statements:

$SALARY \leftarrow 2 * SALARY$
$MONTHS \leftarrow MONTHS + 1$

All that remains is to end the loop (ENDWHILE) and print the answer to the problem. A final Level I would be

Level I

$MONTHS \leftarrow 1$
$SALARY \leftarrow .01$

WHILE SALARY <= 100000
    *SALARY ← 2 * SALARY*
    MONTHS ← MONTHS + 1
ENDWHILE
WRITE ("It will be", MONTHS, "months until your salary
            exceeds $100,000")

Conversion of this to BASIC would result in

```
10  MONTHS = 1
20  SALARY = .01
30  WHILE SALARY <= 100000
40     SALARY = 2 * SALARY
50     MONTHS = MONTHS + 1
60  WEND
70  PRINT "It will be";MONTHS;"months until your salary
              exceeds $100,000"
```

6.4 NESTED LOOPS

Some problems may be encountered in which not only are more than one loop needed in a problem solution, but one or more loops may need to be contained within another loop. These situations are said to require *nested loops.*

Let's examine some sample problems that require nested loops:

☐ **Formal Problem Definition**

General Description

Triangular numbers are numbers that can be represented by a triangular pattern of dots arranged as follows:

```
1                3                6                10               etc.
.                .                .                .
                 . .              . .              . .
                                  . . .            . . .
                                                   . . . .
```

A program is to be written to display the first ten triangular numbers and their corresponding patterns on the printer.

Input Specifications

There will be no input to the program.

Output Specifications

Output is to consist of the first ten triangular numbers and their corresponding patterns printed on the printer. Output is to be in the following form:

```
1     .

3     .
      . .
etc.
```

Normal Example

Input:
     None
Output:

```
1     .

3     .
      . .

6     .
      . .
      . . .

  etc.
```

Unusual or Error Conditions

There are no unusual or error conditions listed since no data values will be entered into the program.

There are two separate problems to be solved in designing a solution to this problem. The first is the generation of the actual numeric values of the triangular numbers themselves, and the second is generating the corresponding pattern of dots for each number. Let's consider first the problem of calculating the values of the triangular numbers themselves.

The values of the first five triangular numbers are 1, 3, 6, 10, and 15. We need to discover a pattern that shows us how these values are obtained. We notice that the difference between the first and second numbers, 1 and 3, is 2. The difference between the second and third numbers, 3 and 6, is 3. The difference between the third and fourth numbers, 6 and 10, is 4. This difference keeps increasing by 1 as successive pairs of numbers are examined. An algorithm can be developed using this pattern that has been discovered. If the first number, 1, is stored in a variable called NUMBER, and the difference between the first pair of numbers, 2, is stored in a variable called DIFFERENCE, successive triangular numbers can be generated by repeating the following two statements:

$$NUMBER \leftarrow NUMBER + DIFFERENCE$$
$$DIFFERENCE \leftarrow DIFFERENCE + 1$$

We are now ready to attempt a first-level solution to the problem:

Level I

$$NUMBER \leftarrow 1$$
$$DIFFERENCE \leftarrow 2$$
FOR COUNT = 1 TO 10
    WRITE (NUMBER)
    {display the pattern of dots corresponding to
      this number}
    $NUMBER \leftarrow NUMBER + DIFFERENCE$
    $DIFFERENCE \leftarrow DIFFERENCE + 1$
NEXT COUNT

As was mentioned earlier, there are two distinct parts to the problem. We have solved the first—generating the actual numeric values of the first ten triangular numbers. Now comes the second part—generating the appropriate pattern of dots for each number.

Again, we need to look for a pattern. The first five sets of dots to be produced are:

```
 .           .           .           .           .
            ..          ..          ..          ..
                       ...         ...         ...
                                  ....        ....
                                             .....
```

If you notice, the pattern of dots for the first triangular number consists of one row. The pattern for the second number consists of two rows, and the pattern for the third, three rows. This tells us that the number of rows of dots for a given number is equal to which number in the series that it is—3 rows for the third number, 5 rows for the fifth number, and n rows for the nth number. The second pattern that can be observed above is that the number of dots in a row is equal to the row number: 2 dots in the second row, 4 dots in the fourth row, and n dots in the nth row. Again, observation of patterns leads us to an algorithm for the solution.

Refinement of the comment, *{display the pattern of dots corresponding to this number}*, then, might proceed as follows. The variable COUNT, which is the counter variable for the FOR-NEXT loop, tells us the number currently being generated—the first number, the fourth number, the seventh number, etc. The number of rows of dots needed for a given number, then, will be equal to the value of COUNT. The first refinement of the above comment, then, might be

{*print COUNT rows of dots*}

How do we print COUNT rows of dots? One way would be to use another FOR-NEXT loop:

FOR ROW = 1 TO COUNT
    {*print a row of dots*}
NEXT ROW

The next problem is to display the right number of dots in each row. If you recall our earlier discussion, we observed that the number of dots in each row is equal to the row number. One dot in the first row, two dots in the second row, etc. We might refine our loop above to be the following:

FOR ROW = 1 TO COUNT
    {*print ROW dots*}
NEXT ROW

This is more specific than previously, but it is still not in pseudocode. How do we output ROW dots? Another loop is needed:

FOR ROW = 1 TO COUNT
    FOR DOTS = 1 TO ROW
        WRITE (".")
    NEXT DOTS
NEXT ROW

This looks pretty good, but one problem remains. Remember that an automatic carriage return and line feed occur after a WRITE statement is executed. This means that the dots in a given row will be printed down the page rather than across the page. This can be corrected by placing a semicolon (;) after the WRITE (".") statement. This, however, creates another problem since we do want a carriage return and line feed generated at the end of a row, and the semicolon at the end of the WRITE statement has suppressed carriage return and line feed. This problem can be solved by inserting a WRITE statement after NEXT DOTS and before NEXT ROW to produce a carriage return and line feed before the next row of dots is printed. A WRITE statement is also needed after NEXT ROW to generate a blank line between the triangular pattern of dots and the next number in the series:

```
FOR ROW = 1 TO COUNT
    FOR DOTS = 1 TO ROW
        WRITE (".");
    NEXT DOTS
    WRITE
NEXT ROW
WRITE
```

Inserting the above pseudocode segment in place of the comment, {*display the pattern of dots corresponding to this number*}, we arrive at the following Level II solution:

Level II

```
NUMBER ← 1
DIFFERENCE ← 2
FOR COUNT = 1 TO 10
    WRITE (NUMBER)
    FOR ROW = 1 TO COUNT
        FOR DOTS = 1 TO ROW
            WRITE (".");
        NEXT DOTS
        WRITE
    NEXT ROW
    WRITE
    NUMBER ← NUMBER + DIFFERENCE
    DIFFERENCE ← DIFFERENCE + 1
NEXT COUNT
```

Now that we have a solution all in pseudocode, it can be converted to BASIC. The first step is to place line numbers on the pseudocode statements:

```
500   NUMBER ← 1
510   DIFFERENCE ← 2
520   FOR COUNT = 1 TO 10
530       WRITE (NUMBER)
540       FOR ROW = 1 TO COUNT
550           FOR DOTS = 1 TO ROW
560               WRITE (".");
570           NEXT DOTS
580           WRITE
590       NEXT ROW
600       WRITE
```

```
610        NUMBER ← NUMBER + DIFFERENCE
620        DIFFERENCE ← DIFFERENCE + 1
630   NEXT COUNT
```

Next, each pseudocode statement is converted to BASIC:

```
500  NUMBER = 1
510  DIFFERENCE = 2
520  FOR COUNT = 1 TO 10
530      PRINT NUMBER,
540      FOR ROW = 1 TO COUNT
550         FOR DOTS = 1 TO ROW
560            PRINT ".";
570         NEXT DOTS
580         PRINT
585         PRINT TAB(15);
590      NEXT ROW
600      PRINT
610      NUMBER = NUMBER + DIFFERENCE
620      DIFFERENCE = DIFFERENCE + 1
630  NEXT COUNT
```

An additional PRINT statement is inserted at line 585 to line up the rows of dots after the first row with the first row.

This solution incorporates three loops. The loop:

```
550  FOR DOTS = 1 TO ROW

570  NEXT DOTS
```

is nested inside the loop:

```
540  FOR ROW = 1 TO COUNT

590  NEXT ROW
```

and both of these loops are nested within the loop:

```
520  FOR COUNT = 1 TO 10

630  NEXT COUNT
```

Notice that the DOTS loop is completely contained within the ROW loop, as is the ROW loop completely contained within the COUNT loop. This must always be the situation when loops are nested—they may not overlap. The following diagram indicates this:

Nested Loops

Valid nesting	Invalid nesting
FOR I = 1 TO 5	FOR I = 1 TO 5
FOR J = 1 TO 3	FOR J = 1 TO 3
M ← I + J	M ← I + J
NEXT J	NEXT I
NEXT I	NEXT J

In the valid example on the left, the span of control of the J loop is completely contained within the span of control of the I loop. In the invalid example on the right, the span of the I loop overlaps the span of the J loop. This is not permitted.

WHILE loops may also be nested. The following problem requires nested WHILE loops in its solution:

☐ Formal Problem Definition

General Description

A program is to be written to keep track of monthly expenses. A report giving monthly totals, as well as a year-to-date total, needs to be produced. Input will be the name of a month, followed on the next several lines by the expenses for that month. The end of the expenses for a given month will be indicated by a value of 0. The entry of "DONE" for the name of a month will indicate the end of the report. Output is to be a total of the expenses for each month, followed by a year-to-date total. All output is to be appropriately labeled.

Input Specifications

Input will consist of several sets of data, each set representing the expenses for a single month. Each set of data will have the following form: The first line of input for a data set will be the name of a month. It will be prompted by

```
Enter the month: <month>
```

where <month> is replaced by the name of the month whose expenses are to be entered. The next several lines of input will be prompted by the message

```
Enter amount: <amount>
```

where <amount> is the amount of an expense for that month. The last entry for the month will be followed by the entry of a 0 in response to the "Enter amount:"

prompt. This will complete the data entry for a data set. Entry of the word "DONE" in response to the prompt, "Enter the month:", will indicate no more months are to be processed.

Output Specifications

Output from the program is to be sent directly to the printer. The first line of output will be the title of the report:

```
Monthly Expense Report - Year-to-Date
```

Next will be two blank lines, followed by the column headings,

```
 "Month"       "Amount"
```

Following this line will be another blank line, followed by the body of the report, which will be single spaced. Each line of the body of the report will consist of the name of the month and the total of the expenses for the month:

```
<month>        <total>
```

When a month name of "DONE" is encountered, a blank line is to be printed, followed by the following line:

```
Total expenses YTD: $ <YTD expenses>
```

where <YTD expenses> is replaced by the sum of the totals of the monthly expenses.

Normal Example

Input:

```
Enter the month: January
Enter amount: 130.20
Enter amount: 83.45
Enter amount: 45.57
Enter amount: 0
Enter the month: February
Enter amount: 0
Enter the month: March
Enter amount: 56.70
Enter amount: 43.95
Enter amount: 89.65
Enter amount: 73.20
Enter amount: 0
Enter the month: "DONE"
```

Output

```
              Monthly Expense Report - Year-to-Date


              Month                        Amount

              January                      259.22
              February                     0
              March                        263.50

              Total expenses YTD:      $   522.72
```

Unusual or Error Conditions

1. If an invalid month name is entered, the program will accept it as valid and print it on the report.
2. If a negative expense amount is entered, it will be accepted and added into the total of the expenses for the month.
3. If a 0 is not entered for the expense amount after the last expenses for the month, the program will not request another month name to be entered.
4. If DONE is not entered in reponse to the "Enter the month:" prompt, the final total of expenses will not be printed.

The first task that might be performed in solving the above problem is to print the report headings. This could be expressed in the form of the comment, {*print report headings*}. Since an overall expense total for all expenses year-to-date (YTD) needs to be computed, a variable for this total needs to be initialized to zero, {*set total YTD expenses to zero*}. This gives us the first two steps in the first level of the top-down design:

Level I

{*print report headings*}
{*set total YTD expenses to zero*}

Since we do not know how many month's expenses are to be processed, a WHILE loop will be needed to repeat the process of summing each month's expenses. The flag that indicates the end of processing is the word "DONE" entered in response to the input prompt requesting entry of the name of a month. In order that there be an initial value for the name of the month for the condition in the WHILE statement to evaluate, input of a month name would be the next step in the pseudocode solution:

{*prompt and enter the name of a month*}

Next would come the WHILE statement to determine if the last month has yet been processed:

WHILE {*month name is not "DONE"*}

The statements inside this WHILE loop would need to process the data for a single month, and then add the expense total for the month to the total YTD expenses. At this point we would be ready to request the entry of the name of another month. These steps could be stated, in comment form, as:

{*process and display the month's expenses*}
{*add the month's expense total to total YTD expenses*}
{*prompt and enter the name of a month*}

This would be the end of the loop, so next would come an ENDWHILE statement. Combining what we have so far, Level I would be

Level I

{*print report headings*}
{*set total YTD expenses to zero*}
{*prompt and enter the name of a month*}
WHILE {*month name is not "DONE"*}
        {*process and display the month's expenses*}
        {*add the month's expense total to total YTD expenses*}
        {*prompt and enter the name of a month*}
ENDWHILE

Examining the normal example in the formal problem definition, it can be seen that once the word "DONE" has been entered for the name of a month, all that remains to be done is to print the final YTD expense total. Placing a comment indicating this step after the ENDWHILE statement results in this final form of Level I:

Level I

{*print report headings*}
{*set total YTD expenses to zero*}
{*prompt and enter the name of a month*}

```
WHILE {month name is not "DONE"}
    {process and display the month's expenses}
    {add the month's expense total to total YTD expenses}
    {prompt and enter the name of a month}
ENDWHILE
{print total YTD expenses}
```

In the next level of the design we need to refine the above comments into more specific steps. The comment, {print report headings}, becomes a series of WRITE statements to produce the headings described in the Output Specifications section of the formal problem definition:

```
WRITE ("   Monthly Expense Report — Year-to-Date")
WRITE
WRITE
WRITE ("        Month              Amount")
WRITE
```

The next comment, {set total YTD expenses to zero}, results in an assignment statement,

```
TOTAL.YTD.EXPENSES ← 0
```

The comment, {prompt and enter the name of a month}, translates into the two pseudocode statements:

```
WRITE ("Enter the month:")
READ (MONTH)
```

Combining the above refinements, Level II would look like this at this point in its development:

Level II

```
WRITE ("   Monthly Expense Report — Year-to-Date")
WRITE
WRITE
WRITE ("        Month              Amount")
WRITE
TOTAL.YTD.EXPENSES ← 0
WRITE ("Enter the month:")
READ (MONTH)
```

The next step in our refinement of Level I is to specify the condition in the WHILE statement, {*month name is not "DONE"*}, in the form of a conditional relation. The WHILE statement with this refinement would be

WHILE MONTH <> "DONE"

The first comment inside the loop, {*process and display the month's expenses*}, describes a rather major operation. Since we do not know how many expenses there will be in a given month, another WHILE loop will be needed. This loop is to be repeated as long as the amount entered in response to the prompt, "Enter amount", is not zero. Since the amount will need to be tested in a conditional expression in the WHILE statement, the amount needs to be entered prior to the WHILE statement.

Since it will also be necessary in the processing of the month's expenses to sum the expense amounts entered, a variable to accumulate these amounts will need to be initialized to zero before the loop is entered. So far our refinement of the comment, {*process and display the month's expenses*}, would result in the following steps:

{*set month's expense total to zero*}
{*prompt and enter an expense amount*}
WHILE {*expense amount is not equal to zero*}

We are still not finished with the refinement of the comment, {*process and display the month's expenses*}. What needs to be done inside the WHILE loop? One thing is to add the expense amount to the month's expense total. Once this has been done, another expense amount must be requested and entered. Finally, the loop needs to be ended with an ENDWHILE statement. These steps could be stated as follows:

{*add the expense amount to the month's expense total*}
{*prompt and enter an expense amount*}
ENDWHILE

Let's collect these refinements together and see where we are with Level II so far:

Level II
WRITE ("   Monthly Expense Report—Year-to-Date")
WRITE
WRITE

```
WRITE ("        Month                Amount")
WRITE
TOTAL.YTD.EXPENSES ← 0
WRITE ("Enter the month:")
READ (MONTH)
WHILE  MONTH <> "DONE"
      {set month's expense total to zero}
      {prompt and enter an expense amount}
      WHILE {expense amount is not equal to zero}
            {add the expense amount to the month's expense total}
            {prompt and enter an expense amount}
      ENDWHILE
```

We have still not finished with the comment, {process and display the month's expenses}. When we exit this second WHILE loop we have processed the month's expenses, but we still need to print them. This could be indicated by the comment

{print the name of the month and the month's expense total}

We have finally finished refining the comment, {process and display the month's expenses}. It has resulted in seven more specifically stated steps in our solution.

The next comment from Level I to be refined is {add the month's expense total to total YTD expenses}. Since we have not yet selected a variable name to store the value of the month's expense total, we might wish to leave this comment as

{add the month's expense total to TOTAL.YTD.EXPENSES}

The next comment, {prompt and enter the name of a month}, is the same as a comment that has already been refined. As you may recall, it translated into the two statements,

```
WRITE ("Enter the month:")
READ (MONTH)
```

Next comes the ENDWHILE statement, which terminates the outer WHILE loop, so it needs no changes. The last comment in Level I is {print total YTD expenses}. Referring to the output specifications once more for the exact form of this output, this comment results in the following two WRITE statements:

```
WRITE
WRITE ("  Total expenses YTD: $", TOTAL.YTD.EXPENSES)
```

A completed Level II then, would be:

Level II

WRITE (``   Monthly Expense Report — Year-to-Date'')
WRITE
WRITE
WRITE (``   Month   Amount'')
WRITE
TOTAL.YTD.EXPENSES ← 0
WRITE (``Enter the month:'')
READ (MONTH)
WHILE MONTH <> ``DONE''
    {set month's expense total to zero}
    {prompt and enter an expense amount}
    WHILE {expense amount is not equal to zero}
        {add the expense amount to the month's expense total}
        {prompt and enter an expense amount}
    ENDWHILE
    {print the name of the month and the month's expense total}
    {add the month's expense total to TOTAL.YTD.EXPENSES}
    WRITE (``Enter the month:'')
    READ (MONTH)
ENDWHILE
WRITE
WRITE (``   Total expenses YTD: $'', TOTAL.YTD.EXPENSES)

Since there are still comment statements remaining in Level II, another level is needed. The first comment could be replaced by the assignment statement

MONTH.TOTAL ← 0

The refinement of the comment, {prompt and enter an expense amount}, results in two statements:

WRITE (``Enter amount:'')
READ (AMOUNT)

The condition in the WHILE statement, {expense amount is not equal to zero}, could be expressed as AMOUNT <> 0, resulting in the following WHILE statement.

WHILE AMOUNT <> 0

The first comment inside the inner WHILE loop, {*add the expense amount to the month's expense total*}, would be translated into an assignment statement,

MONTH.TOTAL ← MONTH.TOTAL + AMOUNT

The comment, {*prompt and enter an expense amount*}, results in two statements, just as it did when refined previously:

WRITE ("Enter amount:")
READ (AMOUNT)

The translation of the comment immediately following the ENDWHILE statement, {*print the name of the month and the month's expense total*}, into pseudocode would result in a WRITE statement:

WRITE (MONTH, MONTH.TOTAL)

The calculation indicated by the comment, {*add the month's expense total to TOTAL.YTD.EXPENSES*}, would be performed by the assignment statement:

TOTAL.YTD.EXPENSES ← TOTAL.YTD.EXPENSES +
MONTH.TOTAL

If the refinements indicated above are inserted into Level II, a final level of the solution to the problem, all expressed in pseudocode, would be

Level III

WRITE (" Monthly Expense Report — Year-to-Date")
WRITE
WRITE
WRITE (" Month Amount")
WRITE
TOTAL.YTD.EXPENSES ← 0
WRITE ("Enter the month:")
READ (MONTH)
WHILE MONTH <> "DONE"
   MONTH.TOTAL ← 0
   WRITE ("Enter amount:")

```
READ (AMOUNT)
WHILE  AMOUNT <> 0
    MONTH.TOTAL ← MONTH.TOTAL + AMOUNT
    WRITE ("Enter amount:")
    READ (AMOUNT)
ENDWHILE
WRITE (MONTH, MONTH.TOTAL)
TOTAL.YTD.EXPENSES ← TOTAL.YTD.EXPENSES +
                                          MONTH.TOTAL

    WRITE ("Enter the month:")
    READ (MONTH)
ENDWHILE
WRITE
WRITE ("  Total expenses YTD: $", TOTAL.YTD.EXPENSES)
```

Notice that the inner WHILE loop, WHILE AMOUNT <> 0, is completely contained within the outer loop, WHILE MONTH <> "DONE". Just as is the case with nested FOR-NEXT loops, nested WHILE loops must also not overlap in their spans of control.

To convert the above pseudocode solution to BASIC, the first step is, of course, to assign line numbers to each pseudocode statement:

```
100   WRITE ("   Monthly Expense Report — Year-to-Date")
110   WRITE
120   WRITE
130   WRITE ("        Month              Amount")
140   WRITE
150   TOTAL.YTD.EXPENSES ← 0
160   WRITE ("Enter the month:")
170   READ (MONTH)
180   WHILE  MONTH <> "DONE"
190       MONTH.TOTAL ← 0
200       WRITE ("Enter amount:")
210       READ (AMOUNT)
220       WHILE  AMOUNT <> 0
230           MONTH.TOTAL ← MONTH.TOTAL + AMOUNT
240           WRITE ("Enter amount:")
250           READ (AMOUNT)
260       ENDWHILE
270       WRITE (MONTH, MONTH.TOTAL)
```

280   TOTAL.YTD.EXPENSES ← TOTAL.YTD.EXPENSES +
MONTH.TOTAL
290   WRITE ("Enter the month:")
300   READ (MONTH)
310 ENDWHILE
320 WRITE
330 WRITE (" Total expenses YTD: $", TOTAL.YTD.EXPENSES)

The next step is to convert each pseudocode statement to an equivalent BASIC language statement. Since the report produced by the above program is to be sent directly to the printer, it will be necessary to convert some WRITE statements to LPRINT statements whereas others that provide screen prompts for data entry will be converted to PRINT statement.

```
100  LPRINT "   Monthly Expense Report - Year-to-Date"
110  LPRINT
120  LPRINT
130  LPRINT "      Month                    Amount"
140  LPRINT
150  TOTAL.YTD.EXPENSES = 0
160  PRINT "Enter the month:";
170  INPUT "", MONTH$
180  WHILE  MONTH$ <> "DONE"
190     MONTH.TOTAL = 0
200     PRINT "Enter amount:";
210     INPUT "", AMOUNT
220     WHILE  AMOUNT <> 0
230        MONTH.TOTAL = MONTH.TOTAL + AMOUNT
240        PRINT "Enter amount:";
250        INPUT "", AMOUNT
260     WEND
270     LPRINT TAB(8) MONTH$ TAB(32) MONTH.TOTAL
280     TOTAL.YTD.EXPENSES = TOTAL.YTD.EXPENSES +
                                          MONTH.TOTAL
290     PRINT "Enter the month:";
300     INPUT "", MONTH$
310  WEND
320  LPRINT
330  LPRINT "  Total expenses YTD: $" TAB(32)
                                    TOTAL.YTD.EXPENSES
```

As is no doubt obvious, nesting of FOR-NEXT loops inside WHILE loops, and vice versa, is certainly permitted. The only caution that should be mentioned is that when the two types of loops are combined in a program, it is just as essential that there is no overlapping of spans of control between the two types of loops as it is within the same loop types.

6.5 Summary

The last control structure needed to design solutions to problems, the repetition structure, has been discussed in this chapter. Two major repetitive structures are used in problem solutions—determinate and indeterminate loops.

The FOR and NEXT statements are most often used to construct determinate loops. In this type of loop, the number of times the loop is to be repeated is known before the loop is entered. The STEP option of the FOR statement allows the incrementing of the counter variable by some value other than one.

The WHILE and WEND statements are used primarily to form indeterminate looping structures. As long as the conditional expression in the WHILE statement is true, the group of statements contained in the WHILE loop will be repeated. It is not necessary to know before the loop is entered how many times it is to be executed. A major concern with using WHILE loops in a program is not to inadvertently construct an infinite loop.

More than one loop may be needed in the solution to any given problem. When a program contains a loop inside another loop, the inner loop is said to be "nested" within the outer loop. It is important when a program contains several loops to ensure that the loops do not overlap in their spans of control.

The conversion process for translating pseudocode repetition statements into their BASIC language equivalent statements is summarized in the following table:

Translation of Pseudocode FOR-NEXT and WHILE-ENDWHILE Loops to Their BASIC Language Equivalents

Pseudocode

FOR $<variable>$ = $<starting\ value>$ TO $<ending\ value>$
$[STEP\ <increment>]$

   $<statement>$
   .
   .
   .

NEXT $<variable>$

Translation of Pseudocode FOR-NEXT and WHILE-ENDWHILE Loops to Their BASIC Language Equivalents (*Continued*)

BASIC

```
line#   FOR <variable> = <starting value> TO <ending value>
                                        [STEP <increment>]
           <statement>
                 .
                 .
                 .
line#   NEXT <variable>
```

Pseudocode

WHILE <conditional expression>
     <statement>
        .
        .
        .

ENDWHILE

BASIC

```
line#   WHILE <conditional expression>
           <statement>
                 .
                 .
line#   WEND
```

EXERCISES

1. Indicate which looping structure, a FOR-NEXT or a WHILE loop, would be more appropriate to use in designing a solution to each of the following problems:

   a. Compute the amount to be deducted monthly for life insurance for each of a company's 25 employees.

   b. Determine the average monthly electricity bill for a home given the 12 monthly bills from last year.

   c. Calculate the amount of interest earned in one year on an amount of $5000, compounded daily at an interest rate of 8 percent per year.

d. Compute the total dollar amount of ticket sales for the next home football game.

e. Calculate the average amount spent on groceries by all customers at the local grocery store in one day.

f. Count the number of times the letter "e" appears in one hundred words selected at random from the dictionary.

g. Count the number of A grades, B grades, C grades, etc., that were given as final course grades by the English department last semester.

h. Determine the number of miles per gallon your car averaged on the last 5 tankfuls of gasoline.

Use the following program to answer the next three questions:

```
100  COUNTER = 125
110  WHILE  COUNTER >= 100
120     PRINT COUNTER
130     COUNTER = COUNTER + 25
140     IF COUNTER > 110 THEN 150 ELSE 180
150     'THEN
160        PRINT COUNTER
170        COUNTER = COUNTER - 50
175        GOTO 210
180     'ELSE
190           COUNTER = 100
200           PRINT COUNTER
210     'ENDIF
220  WEND
230  PRINT COUNTER
240  COUNTER = COUNTER + 20
250  PRINT COUNTER
260  END
```

2. The third number printed by the above program is:

   a. 100

   b. 110

   c. 125

   d. 150

3. The last number printed by the above program is:

   a. 75

   b. 95

   c. 100

   d. 125

4. The total number of values printed by the above program is:

   a. 2

   b. 5

c. 6

d. An infinite number

5. If the values 35, 25, and 30 are entered as input to the following program, what is the output produced by the program?

```
20   INPUT A, B, C
30   FOR COUNT = 1 TO 3
40      IF A < B THEN 50 ELSE 120
50      'THEN
60         IF B > C THEN 70 ELSE 110
70         'THEN
80            M = B
90            B = C
100           C = M
110        'ENDIF
115        GOTO 160
120     'ELSE
130        M = A
140        A = B
150        B = M
160     'ENDIF
170  NEXT COUNT
180  PRINT A, B, C
190  END
```

Use the following program to answer the next six questions:

```
10   COUNT1 = 1
20   COUNT2 = 0
30   WHILE  COUNT1 <= 3
40      COUNT1 = COUNT1 + COUNT2
50      IF COUNT2 < COUNT1 THEN 60 ELSE 90
60      'THEN
70         COUNT2 = COUNT2 + 1
80         PRINT COUNT2
85         GOTO 120
90      'ELSE
100        COUNT2 = COUNT1 + COUNT2
110        PRINT COUNT1
120     'ENDIF
130  WEND
140  PRINT COUNT1, COUNT2
150  END
```

6. What is the first line printed by the above program?

    a. 0

    b. 1

    c. 2

    d. 3

7. How many lines of output are produced by the above program?

 a. None
 b. 1 only
 c. 2 only
 d. 3 only

8. What is the last value displayed within the loop by the above program?

 a. 0
 b. 1
 c. 2
 d. 3

9. How many times is the loop executed in the above program?

 a. None
 b. 1 time only
 c. 2 times only
 d. 3 times only
 e. More than three times

10. What is the value printed for COUNT1 when the loop is exited?

 a. 1
 b. 2
 c. 3
 d. 4

11. What is printed for COUNT2 when the loop is exited?

 a. 1
 b. 2
 c. 3
 d. 4

Use the following program to answer the next two questions:

```
110  TOTAL1 = 0
120  TOTAL2 = 0
130  READ VALUE
140  WHILE  VALUE <> 0
150     IF VALUE > 0 THEN 160 ELSE 180
160    'THEN
170        TOTAL1 = TOTAL1 + 1
175        GOTO 200
180    'ELSE
190        TOTAL2 = TOTAL2 + 1
200    'ENDIF
210     READ VALUE
220  WEND
230  PRINT TOTAL1
240  PRINT TOTAL2
250  DATA 3,-7,2,4,-3,1,0
```

12. What is the value of TOTAL1 printed when the above program is executed with the data shown?

   a. 0
   b. 4
   c. 10
   d. None of the above

13. What is the value of the TOTAL2 printed when the above program is executed with the data shown?

   a. 0
   b. 2
   c. 3
   d. − 10

14. What will the following BASIC program print when it is executed?

```
10  FOR I = 1 TO 3
20     READ NUM1
30  NEXT I
40  SUM = NUM1 + NUM1 + NUM1
50  PRINT SUM
60  DATA 1,3,5
70  END
```

   a. 3
   b. 6
   c. 9
   d. 15

15. What would be displayed for the value of TOTAL when the following BASIC program is executed?

```
10  TOTAL = 0
20  SUM = 3
30  WHILE SUM < 2
40     TOTAL = TOTAL + SUM
50     SUM = SUM + 3
60  WEND
70  PRINT TOTAL
80  END
```

   a. 2
   b. 3
   c. 0
   d. 6

16. When the following program is executed, it will:

```
10  FOR I = 1 TO 5
20     READ X
30  NEXT I
40  PRINT "X"
50  DATA 1,5,10,15
60  END
```

    a. Print "Out of data in line 20"
    b. Print a question mark
    c. Print the letter 'X'
    d. Print 15
    e. Halt without displaying any output

17. Which of the following program segments would *NOT* be an infinite loop when executed?

I.
```
10  INDEX = 1
20  WHILE INDEX < 5
30     PRINT "Hi there"
40        COUNT = COUNT + 1
50  WEND
```

II.
```
10  INDEX = 10
20  WHILE INDEX > 5
30     PRINT "Hi there"
40        INDEX = INDEX + 1
50  WEND
```

III.
```
10  INDEX = 1
20  WHILE INDEX > 5
30     PRINT "Hi there"
40  WEND
```

    a. I
    b. II
    c. III
    d. They all contain infinite loops.

Use the following BASIC program to answer questions 18 through 21. (*Note:* Not all input data given may be used.)

```
10   INPUT START, STOP, INCREMENT          INPUT DATA
20   WHILE  START <> 0
30      COUNT = 0                           2,    10,    2
40      SUM = START                         1,    10,    1
50      WHILE  SUM <= STOP                  10,    2,    2
60         COUNT = COUNT + 1               101,   200,   1
70         SUM = SUM + INCREMENT             0,    10,    1
80      WEND                              -10,   -10,   -1
90      PRINT COUNT                          0,     0,    0
100     INPUT START, STOP, INCREMENT
110  WEND
120  END
```

18. What is the value of COUNT when the PRINT statement at line 90 is executed for the first time?

    a. 0
    b. 2
    c. 5
    d. 10

19. What is the value of COUNT when the PRINT statement at line 90 is executed for the second time?

    a. 0
    b. 2
    c. 5
    d. 10

20. What is the value of COUNT when the PRINT statement at line 90 is executed for the third time?

    a. 0
    b. 2
    c. 5
    d. 10

21. How many times does the PRINT statement at line 90 execute in this program with the above data?

    a. 4
    b. 5
    c. 6
    d. 7

22. Perform a complete top-down design and then write a BASIC program to solve the following problem:

    General Description

    Mr. Smith is a stockbroker for the ABC Company and he has three clients. Write a program to tell Mr. Smith the total dollar amount of transactions for each client, and which of his clients did the most business with him for the month in terms of the largest dollar amount of transactions.

    Input Specifications

    Input to the program will consist of several lines of data, each of which represents a transaction made by one of Mr. Smith's clients. Each line contains two values: the first an integer value representing client 1, 2, or 3 and the second value representing the dollar value of the transaction. The last line entered will be a 0 followed by any other number. Each line of input is to be prompted by the message:

    ```
    Enter client number and amount: <client #, amount>
    ```
    Output Specifications

    Output is to consist of the following:

a. `Client #1's transactions totaled $ <xxxxx>`
`Client #2's transactions totaled $ <xxxxx>`
`Client #3's transactions totaled $ <xxxxx>`

where $<xxxxx>$ represents the total dollar transactions of each client.

b. Two blank lines
c. A message indentifying the client with the largest total dollar transactions

Normal Example

Input:

```
Enter client number and amount: 1,5000
Enter client number and amount: 2,3000
Enter client number and amount: 2,3000
Enter client number and amount: 1,500
Enter client number and amount: 4,600
Enter client number and amount: 3,5000
Enter client number and amount: 2,7000
Enter client number and amount: 3,10000
Enter client number and amount: 0,0
```

Output:

```
Client #1's transactions totaled $ 5500
Client #2's transactions totaled $ 13000
Client #3's transactions totaled $ 15000

Client #3 was your best customer
```

Unusual or Error Conditions

1. If a client number of 0 is not encountered as an input value, no output will be printed.
2. Any lines of input entered after a line having a client number of 0 will be ignored.
3. If more than two values are entered per line, the error message, "?Redo from start", will be displayed by the system.
4. If only one value is entered on a line, the error message, "?Redo from start", will be displayed on the system.
5. If a client number other than 0, 1, 2, or 3 is entered, the program will ignore that line of input and read the next line. The dollar value of the transaction line containing a client number of 0 will not be added to any of the totals.

CHAPTER 7

Data Types

The different data types available in Microsoft BASIC are examined in this chapter. Character string variables, and the operations that may be performed on them, are discussed. Numeric data types—their uses, declaration, and storage requirements—are explained. The last section of the chapter describes the use of formatted output in BASIC to control the form in which output will be displayed.

7.0 OBJECTIVES

Once the material in this chapter has been studied, the student should be able to:

1. Write program statements that use and manipulate data stored in character string variables.
2. Select the appropriate numeric data type for a particular application.
3. Write numeric expressions that make use of any of the numeric data types permitted in Microsoft BASIC.

4. Determine the amount of storage needed to store data of different variable types.

5. Use formatted output in programs to display output in desired forms.

7.1 CHARACTER STRING VARIABLES AND CONSTANTS

We have made frequent use of character string variables in several of the programs we have designed and written thus far. Primarily, these programs have dealt with the input and output of the values of character string variables, or the comparison of two character strings to see whether or not they were equal. There are other operations that may be performed on variables of this type, and it is these operations that will be discussed in this section of the chapter.

To review briefly, a character string constant is a group of one or more characters delimited by double quotation marks. The maximum length of a character string constant is 255 characters. These characters may be letters of the alphabet, the digits 0 through 9, punctuation marks, and other special characters. Numeric digits contained in a character string constant may not be used in arithmetic calculations.

A character string variable name must include a $ as the last character of its name. This is necessary if the BASIC interpreter is to recognize that the variable is a character string variable and not a numeric variable. A character string constant may be assigned to a particular character string variable by an INPUT statement, a READ statement, or an assignment statement.

Concatenation of Character Strings

One operation that may be performed on character strings is *concatenation*. To concatenate two character strings means to combine them into a single string. This operation is performed using an assignment statement and the concatenation operator, '+'. This is the same operator used with numeric data to indicate addition. For example, if the character string variable A$ contained the value "any" and the character string variable B$ contained the value "body", the assignment statement:

```
50   C$ = A$ + B$
```

would assign the character string "anybody" to C$.

One way in which the concatenation operation with character string values differs from the addition operation performed upon numeric values is that A\$ + B\$ is not equal to B\$ + A\$. If the statement above had been:

```
50  C$ = B$ + A$
```

the resulting value of C\$ would have been "bodyany." The fact that the order in which the variable names are listed in the concatenation operation is important means that this operation is not *commutative*. In the arithmetic operation of addition, however, A + B is equal to B + A, so addition of numbers is a commutative operation.

An example of the use of the concatenation operation is when an individual's full name is needed in a program, as well as their first and last names, separately. The person could be asked to enter their first name, then their last name, and the program could then construct their full name, that is:

```
10  PRINT "What is your first name";
20  INPUT FIRST.NAME$
30  PRINT "What is your last name";
40  INPUT LAST.NAME$
50  FULL.NAME$ = FIRST.NAME$ + " " + LAST.NAME$
     .
     .
     .
```

Notice that it was necessary to insert a space between the first and last names of the individual when constructing the full name.

Comparing Character Strings

Relational comparisons are another type of operation frequently performed on character strings. Thus far in our discussion of BASIC programming, we have been primarily concerned with the equality or inequality of character strings. In order for two strings to be equal, they must be of the same length and contain exactly the same characters in the exact same order.

It is also possible to determine if one string is less than or greater than another string. If only character strings consisting of alphabetic characters are considered, one string may be thought of as being less than another string if the first string would come before the second string in an alphabetical listing of the strings. This relation holds true only if the corresponding characters in both strings are of the same case (both upper- or both lowercase). Otherwise, this alphabetic ordering breaks down, since uppercase letters are always considered to be less than their lowercase counterparts. Some examples of this ordering scheme follow:

"apple" < "orange"
"CAT" < "DOG"
"the" < "then"
"XYZ" < "abc"

The first example is straightforward. The word "apple" would appear earlier in a dictionary than would "orange," so "apple" is less than "orange." The reason that this ordering would occur is not that "apple" consists of five characters while "orange" consists of six, but rather than "a" comes before "o" in the alphabet. The second example, "CAT" < "DOG", is true for the same reason; "C" comes before "D" in the alphabet. The third example also follows the alphabetic rule, or can also be explained by the rule that if two character strings are of unequal length, but are identical in the characters they contain up through the length of the shorter string, the longer string is considered to be greater than (>) the shorter. The last example above, "XYZ" < "abc", illustrates the fact that uppercase letters are always considered to be less than lowercase letters.

If strings containing characters other than the alphabetic characters are considered, however, the idea of alphabetic order is no longer meaningful. The actual method by which relational comparisons are made is by comparing the strings, one character at a time from left to right, until a difference is found. If the two strings are equal in length, and no difference is found before the end of the strings is reached, the strings are determined to be equal. If a difference is found, however, the ordering of the strings will be determined by the ASCII (American Standard Code for Information Interchange) values of the two characters. The ASCII encoding scheme assigns numeric values from 0 to 255 to each character that may be represented on the computer. A complete listing of the characters and their corresponding ASCII values may be found in Appendix B.

Let's examine how a comparison is made using the process described above. Suppose the character string constants "bat" and "bad" are to be compared. The first character of each string is the same. So is the second character. The first difference in the two strings is found in the third character position. The letter "d" must be compared with the letter "t." Referring to the ASCII values in Appendix B, the letter "d" is found to have the ASCII value of 100 and the letter "t" the value 116. Since the ASCII value of "d" is less than the ASCII value of "t", the entire string "bad" is considered to be less than the string "bat."

When comparing two strings, remember that they must be identical with regard to length, characters that they contain, and the order in which the characters appear, if they are to compare as equal. As was mentioned in a previous chapter, the blank space in a character string constant is a character. It therefore has an ASCII value, and a character string constant containing such a character is not equal to a character string constant that does not contain a space. For example, "the" is not equal to "the "; in fact, "the" is less than "the ".

7.2 NUMERIC DATA TYPES

Up to this point in the programs we have written, we have considered data to be of one of two types—character or numeric. Numeric values, however, may be represented in several different ways in Microsoft BASIC. Very large or very small numbers may be stored and displayed in exponential format. Integer values are stored differently than values containing decimal fractions. Decimal values may also be stored in one of two ways. In order to take full advantage of the computational and storage capabilities of the computer and the Microsoft BASIC language, it is necessary to spend some time discussing numeric values and the different ways in which they may be represented in the computer.

Integers

Integers are defined in BASIC as whole numbers between -32768 and $+32767$, inclusive. The reason that integers are limited in magnitude to the above range is that this is the range of values that can be represented by a 16-digit binary number. Since integers are whole numbers, they do not contain a decimal point. Examples of integer constants would be

```
3     456     -7189     0     -13862     31780
```

If we wish to have a value stored in a variable as an integer value, the computer must be specifically instructed to do so. One way in which this may be done is to include the character "%" as the last character of the variable name. For example, the variable NUM% would be understood by the BASIC interpreter to be a numeric variable that is to store an integer value. Whenever the variable NUM% is used in the program, it is necessary to include the percent sign as the last character of the variable name. The variable NUM is not the same as the variable NUM%.

There are several reasons to specifically instruct the computer to store numbers as integers when appropriate. One reason is that less computer memory is needed to store integer values than is needed to store values as other numeric data types. Two bytes of storage are required to store an integer constant. If a program being written is very large, and there is a concern that there may not be sufficient internal memory for the program, the use of integer values when possible will conserve memory.

The other major reason for using integer values is that numeric calculations are performed faster with integer values than with numbers stored in other forms. A program that contains FOR-NEXT loops that need to be executed a large number of times, for example, will execute notably faster if the counter variables for the FOR-NEXT loops are defined as integer values.

Exponential Notation

When very large or very small numbers are stored or displayed by the computer, these numbers are often represented in what is known as exponential form. This form of representing a number uses an integer or a decimal number multiplied by a power of 10. You may have already worked with a form similar to this known as scientific notation.

When a number is expressed in exponential form, it is composed of two parts. The first part is an integer or decimal value. The second part is a power of 10 by which the first part of the number is to be multiplied. This second part is written in BASIC as the letter 'E', followed by a positive or negative integer. The 'E', indicates exponential notation, and the integer value following it specifies the power to which 10 must be raised before being multiplied by the first part of the number.

Examples of numbers written using exponential notation are:

$$4E+03 \quad -1.234E+01 \quad 5.432E-03 \quad -1.123E-5$$

The equivalent forms of these values, written without using exponential notation, would be, respectively:

$$4000 \qquad -12.34 \qquad .005432 \qquad -.00001123$$

As can be seen in the above examples, the integer value following the letter 'E' may be thought of as the number of places to the right or left the decimal point must be moved in the first part of the exponential notation form if the number is to be written in standard form without the use of an exponent. If the first part of the exponential form is an integer, the decimal point is assumed to be immediately to the right of the rightmost digit in the integer.

In the first example above, the first part of the number 4E+03 is an integer. The exponent part of the number, +03, indicates that the decimal point in 4 is to be moved three places to the right. The sign (+ or −) preceding the power of 10 specifies the direction the decimal point must be moved—to the right if the sign is positive, to the left if the sign is negative. Since 4 is an integer, the decimal point is assumed to be just to the right of the digit 4. In order for the decimal point to be moved three places to the right, three zeroes must be added to the right of 4. Once this has been done, the number can be rewritten as 4000.

If the value 5.432E−03 is to be rewritten in a form without an exponent, the −03 says to move the decimal point in 5.432 three places to the left. Two zeros must be inserted to the left of the digit 5 in this case in order for the decimal point to be moved three places to the left, resulting in the answer, .005432.

In Microsoft BASIC, constants will be displayed and stored in exponential form if they contain more than seven digits. If the constants are stored in double-precision format, they will be stored and displayed in exponential form if they contain more than 17 digits. Double-precision format will be explained more fully later in the chapter.

Single-Precision Numbers

If the data type of a numeric variable is not specifically declared, the variable will normally default to single-precision. Single-precision constants are constants that are outside the range of allowed integer values and may be written with seven or fewer digits, contain a decimal point, or are expressed in exponential notation by use of the letter 'E'. Examples of single-precision constants are:

    34.7   123456   3.456E+ 12   − 7654321   1.0

The first value above is a single-precision constant since it contains a decimal point. The second value, although it does not contain a decimal point, is outside the allowed range of integers so it is stored in single-precision form. The third value, which is written in exponential form using the 'E' notation, would also be stored as a single-precision constant. The last two values displayed are also single-precision constants since they fit the definition of a single-precision constant given above.

Twice as much internal storage is required to store a single-precision constant as is needed to store an integer. Four bytes of storage are required for each single-precision constant, whereas integer storage requires only two bytes per constant. As previously mentioned, up to seven digits of a single-precision value will be stored and displayed. Only the first six digits, however, are assured to be accurate.

Even though numeric variables normally default to single-precision variables if they are not specifically declared to be of some other type, you may wish to explicitly declare certain numeric variables in a program to be of type single-precision. This may be done by using an exclamation mark (!) as the last character of the variable name, for example, X!. This will ensure that the values stored in this variable are stored in single-precision form.

Double-Precision Numbers

There are problem situations where the six-digit accuracy provided by single-precision values is not precise enough for the calculations that need to be performed. Microsoft BASIC provides for these situations through the use of double-precision variables and constants. Double-precision constants are constants that contain eight or more digits, or are expressed in exponential notation using the letter 'D'. Examples of double-precision constants are

$$1234567890 \qquad -3.4567D-06 \qquad 87654321.12345678$$

The first value, 1234567890, although it is a whole number, could not be stored as an integer constant since it is obviously outside the range of -32768 to $+32767$, the permitted range of integer constants. It also could not be stored as a single-precision constant if all the digits were to be retained, as single-precision constants can only store a maximum of seven digits. The second value above is considered to be a double-precision constant because the letter "D" is used to indicate exponential notation rather than the letter "E" used with single-precision numbers written in exponential notation form. The last value would also need to be stored as a double-precision constant if we wished to retain all the digits listed in the number.

Storage of a double-precision constant requires eight bytes of internal memory, twice the amount of memory needed to store a single-precision constant. Up to 17 digits of a number will be stored in the double-precision format; however, only the first 16 digits will always be accurate.

There are many situations in which double-precision values are extremely useful. If a program is written to perform typical business procedures such as accounts receivable or general ledger, it is important that answers are correct to the nearest penny. If rather large amounts of money are involved, the accuracy of the cents or even dollars portion may be lost if double-precision values are not used. Another situation in which a high degree of accuracy is important is if complex scientific calculations are to be performed. If these calculations result in very large or very small numbers, double-precision values may be needed to reduce the amount of rounding error that may occur when the calculations are performed.

Variables can be specified to be of type double-precision by including a pound sign or number sign (#) as the last character of the variable name. For example, the variable TOTAL# would be recognized by the BASIC interpreter as a double-precision variable.

Mixed-Mode Expressions

A numeric expression consisting of variables and/or constants having differing degrees of precision is referred to as a *mixed-mode expression*. When the BASIC interpreter encounters variables and/or constants of differing precisions in the same statement, it proceeds in the following manner:

1. If a numeric value having one precision is assigned to a variable of a different precision, the value will be stored with the precision of the

receiving variable. For example, if the following assignment statement were executed:

```
10   A% = 42.31
```

the integer variable A% would be assigned the value 42. The statement

```
20   X! = 23
```

stores the value 23 in the single-precision variable X! as 23.00000.

2. When a higher-precision value is assigned to a variable having a lower precision, the higher-precision value is rounded to the precision of the lower-precision variable when the assignment is performed. An example of this would be if the following assignment statement were executed:

```
30   B% = 52.765
```

the integer variable B% would be assigned the value 53. If the statement

```
40   Y = 12345.6789
```

were executed, the value 12345.6789 would be rounded correct to seven digits and stored in the single-precision variable Y.

3. If a lower-precision value is stored in a higher-precision variable, the resulting value of the higher-precision variable cannot be more accurate than was the original lower-precision value. If, for example, the following assignment statement were executed:

```
50   C = 457
```

C would be assigned a seven-digit value (three digits to the left, four digits to the right of the decimal point). The value of C, however, would be accurate only to the nearest whole number, since that is the accuracy of the integer value 457 assigned to it.

4. When a numeric expression containing variables and/or constants with differing degrees of precision is evaluated, all variables and/or constants are first converted to the highest degree of precision present in the variables and/or constants contained in the expression.

   The expression is then evaluated and this value is assigned to the variable that appears to the left of the assignment operator. If necessary, conversion of the value of the expression to the precision of the receiving variable will be performed before this assignment is made. For example, if the following assignment statement were performed:

```
60   D% = 32.7 * 4
```

the calculations would be performed in single-precision arithmetic, since 32.7 is a single-precision value. This would result in the value of 130.8

being calculated as the value of the expression. This result, however, is to be stored in an integer variable, D%. The result of the calculation, then, will be rounded to 131 and this will be the value stored in D%.

Even though the BASIC interpreter is able to perform mixed-mode calculations, as has been shown above, it is a good idea to avoid them when possible. As the example above illustrates, extra calculations must be performed when mixed-mode expressions are evaluated, which slows down program execution speed. A large number of mixed-mode expressions in a program may also indicate that insufficient time was spent designing the solution to a problem, since mixed-mode expressions are infrequently required in problem solutions.

7.3 DECLARING VARIABLE TYPES

In the material discussed in the last several sections, it was indicated that the last character of a variable name may be used to indicate the data type of the variable. For example, if the last character of a variable name is a dollar sign ($), BASIC interprets the variable as a character string variable. Another way in which variables may be declared to be of a particular data type is by use of a DEFtype statement. The general form of this statement is:

```
line# DEF<type> <letter>[-<letter>] [,<letter>[-letter>]]...
```

where <type> is INT, SNG, DBL, or STR, and <letter> is a letter of the alphabet.

The DEFtype statement declares all variables beginning with a particular letter or letters to be of a particular data type. INT means integer, SNG is single-precision, DBL refers to double-precision, and STR is character string. For example, the DEFtype statement

```
10  DEFINT I,J
```

states that all variables starting with the letters I and J are to be of type integer. Variables such as INTEREST, INVESTOR, and JUMP would automatically be integer variables if used in a program containing statement 10 above. A type declaration character ($, %, !, or #) used in a variable name, however, could be used to override the declaration made in the DEFtype statement. For example, the variable name INVENTOR$ would still refer to a character string variable, even though it starts with the letter I.

The general form of the DEFtype statement also indicates that a range of letters may be listed in the statement. For example, the DEFtype statement:

```
20  DEFDBL A-D,X
```

declares that all variables starting with the letters A, B, C, D, and X are to be of type double-precision.

If the DEFtype statement is used in a program, it must appear in the program before any variables it declares to be of a particular type are used. For this reason, the DEFtype statement is usually one of the first statements in a program.

7.4 FORMATTED OUTPUT—THE PRINT USING STATEMENT

There is another form of the PRINT statement that provides maximum control over the appearance of an output line. This is the PRINT USING statement, which has the following general form:

```
line# PRINT USING <v$>; <list of expressions> [;]
```

The format string <v$> is a string constant or variable consisting of special formatting characters that define the field width and format of the strings and/or numbers to be printed. This format string is followed by a semicolon to separate it from <list of expressions> that follows. The <list of expressions> is a list of the string and/or numeric variable names whose values are to be printed. The names of these variables are separated by commas or semicolons. An optional semicolon is permitted at the end of the list to suppress carriage return and line feed if so desired.

An LPRINT USING statement, which functions just as does the PRINT USING statement except that output is sent to the printer rather than the screen, is also available in Microsoft BASIC. The following discussion of the use of the PRINT USING statement also applies to the LPRINT USING statement.

Probably the easiest way to understand the function of the format string <v$> in a PRINT USING statement is to think of it as a picture of how an output line is to look. This format string describes the output line in terms of how many spaces are to be reserved for outputting strings, how many blank spaces are to be left between values, how many digits of a numeric value are to appear to the left and right of a decimal point, etc. As was mentioned above, special formatting characters are used in a format string to describe an output line. Let's first consider the description of string output.

Displaying Character String Data

There are three special formatting characters that may be used in a format string to describe how a character string is to be printed in an output line:

Formatting Characters used in String Output

Character	Purpose
!	Specifies that only the first character of the string is to be output.
\<n spaces>\	Specifies that the first 2 + n characters of the string are to be printed. For example, if three spaces are typed between the backslashes(\ ), the first five characters of the string are output.
&	Specifies that all characters in the string are to be output.

Suppose we had the following segment of BASIC code:

```
10  A$ = "BASIC"
20  PRINT USING "!"; A$
30  PRINT USING "\  \"; A$
40  PRINT USING "&"; A$
```

If this code segment were to be executed, the following output would be displayed on the screen:

```
B
BASI
BASIC
```

Statement 20, which produced the first line of output, uses the formatting character '!' in the format string. This causes only the first character of A$ to be displayed. The second line of output, BASI, is produced by statement 30. The two spaces between the backslashes in the format string contained in this statement cause the first four (2 + 2 spaces = 4) characters of A$ to be output. The last PRINT USING statement, at line 40, uses the format character '&', which causes the entire string constant contained in A$ to be displayed.

When the backslash formatting characters are used to indicate field width for a string, and the width of the field exceeds the length of the string constant, the string will be left-justified in the field and the remainder of the field to the right of the string will be filled with spaces. For example:

```
10  A$ = "BASIC"
20  PRINT "*";
30  PRINT USING "\ \"; A$;
40  PRINT "*"
```

If this segment of code were to be executed, the following output would be displayed:

```
*BASIC  *
```

The PRINT statements at lines 20 and 40 display an asterisk (*) on either side of the character string field declared in the PRINT USING statement at line 30 so that the field width can be easily observed. The format string in line 30 reserves seven character positions for A$, since there are five spaces between the backslashes. A$ contains only a five-character string, so two spaces are output to the right of the word BASIC to fill the declared field width.

Two further points should be mentioned with regard to format strings. Blank spaces may be used within a format string to separate output fields. The second point is that the number of fields specified in a format string need not be the same as the number of variables listed in the <list of variables>. If more fields are specified than there are variables, only the fields needed, starting from the left, will be used. If there are more variables than there are fields specified in the format string, the format string will simply be used repeatedly until all variables listed in <list of expressions> have been displayed. For example:

```
10  A$ = "red"
20  B$ = "green"
30  C$ = "brown"
40  D$ = "yellow"
50  PRINT USING "\    \   ";A$, B$, C$, D$
```

When this segment of BASIC code is executed, the following output will be displayed:

```
red     green   brown   yello
```

The format string in statement 50 specifies that a string five characters in length is to be output, followed by three blank spaces. This format is used repeatedly to display the values of each of the four variables listed in the statement.

Displaying Numeric Data

When the <list of expressions> in a PRINT USING statement contains numeric variables, constants, or expressions, a different set of formatting characters is used in the format string to describe the form in which these numeric values are to be displayed. The following table briefly describes these characters.

Formatting Characters used in Numeric Output

Character	Purpose
#	Specifies that a numeric digit is to be output. If the number to be printed has fewer digits than the format string indicates, the number is right-justified in the field.
.	A single decimal point may be included within any set of digit positions in the format string. Numbers will be rounded as necessary to fit the field specification.
+	This character at the beginning or end of a numeric format field indicates that the sign of the number ($+$ or $-$) is to be printed before or after the number.
−	A negative sign at the end of a numeric format field causes negative numbers to be printed with a trailing negative sign.
**	Two asterisks at the beginning of a numeric field cause unused digit positions preceding the number to be filled with asterisks.
$$	Two dollar signs at the beginning of a numeric field print a $ to the immediate left of the first digit of the number. Exponential format may not be used with $$, nor may negative values, unless a trailing minus sign has been specified.
**$	Specifies asterisk fill followed by a dollar sign to the immediate left of the first digit of a number.
,	A comma to the left of the decimal point in a format string causes a comma to be printed to the left of every third digit to the left of the decimal point.
^ ^ ^ ^	Used after digit position characters to specify exponential notation. The four carets reserve space for $E\pm nn$ or $D\pm nn$ to be printed.

As the table illustrates, numeric output has a wide range of formatting styles available. The following example shows several of these features:

```
10  A = 45.678
20  B = − 47.2
30  C = 14678
40  PRINT USING "+###.##  ######,.##  ###.##−"; A, C, B
```

When executed, the above statements would produce the following output:

```
+  45.68   14,678.00    47.2-
```

The sign of the first number is printed since the '+' character precedes the digit characters in the first numeric field description in the format string. The value of A is also rounded to two decimal places since only two digits are indicated to the right of the decimal point. A space appears between the '+' sign and the first digit of the number since the field specification reserves space for three digits to the left of the decimal point, and the value of A has only two.

The second value, the value of C, has a comma inserted between the 4 and 6 by the comma appearing just to the left of the decimal point in the field specification. Two zeros are printed to the right of the decimal point since the field specification reserved room for two digits to the right of the decimal point.

The last value printed, the value of B, was negative, and the field specification indicated that if the value was negative, the negative sign was to be printed following the number.

Let's look at another example. If we were to enter the following segment of BASIC code:

```
10  D = 3.57
20  E = 78.953
30  F = .00003574
40  G$ = "**####.##    $$####.##    **$####.##"
50  PRINT USING G$; D, D, E
60  PRINT USING "#.###^^^^"; F
```

it would produce the following output when executed:

```
*****3.57      $3.57   ***$78.95
3.574E-05
```

The format string used by the PRINT USING statement at line 50 is contained in the character string variable G$. This is an optional way in which a format string may be defined.

The first value printed, *****3.57, uses the field specification for asterisk fill of any unused digit positions to the left of the number. The two asterisks in the field specification that specify this output format also reserve two additional digit positions. Since only one position to the left of the decimal point is needed for a digit, and six positions have been reserved, five asterisks fill the unneeded position. This particular formatting style might be used if a check-writing program was being written, and we wanted to ensure that the amount written on a check could not be altered.

The second value printed, $3.57, uses a field specification for what is known as a floating dollar sign. The dollar sign is printed to the immediate left of the first digit of the number. As with the asterisk fill used by the previous value, the two dollar signs that specify this output format also specify two additional digit positions, for a total of six positions to the left of the decimal point. Since only two positions are needed—one for the dollar sign and one for the digit 3, four additional blank spaces are printed to the left of the number.

The third value printed, ***$78.95, makes use of the combined asterisk fill–floating dollar sign field specification. Two asterisks followed by a $ specify this output format in the format string, and also reserve three additional digit positions. Since only three digit positions are needed for the $ and the two digits of the number that are to the left of the decimal point, three asterisks are printed to fill the unused positions.

The next line of output is produced by the PRINT USING statement at line 60. The value of the variable F is displayed in exponential form. The field specification for this value consists of two parts—the specification of the digits and decimal point to the left of the letter 'E' in the exponential form, and second, the four carats (^ ^ ^ ^) reserve room in the output line for the letter 'E', a '+' or '−' sign, and the power of 10 by which the decimal portion of the expression is to be multiplied.

One disadvantage of using formatted output for displaying numeric values is that the programmer is responsible for ensuring that there will be a sufficient number of digit positions to the left of the decimal point in numeric field specifications. If too few digit positions are reserved for the size of the number to be printed, a percent sign (%) is printed in front of the number. For example, if the following segment of code were executed:

```
10  H =  12345.6
20  PRINT USING "####.##"; H
```

the following would be displayed on the screen:

```
%12345.6
```

This output occurred since only four digit positions to the left of the decimal point were specified by the format string in the PRINT USING statement at line 20, and the constant stored in H contained five digits to the left of the decimal point.

There is also a limit to the maximum number of digit positions permitted in a numeric field specification. If more than 24 digit positions are specified for a single numeric field, the error message, "Illegal function call", will be displayed when the PRINT USING statement containing this field specification is executed.

When both numeric and character data are output by a single PRINT USING statement, it is important that the field specifications in the format string correspond as to data type with the respective variable names in the <list of expressions>. That is, a numeric variable must correspond to a numeric field specification, and a character string variable must correspond to a string field specification. For example, if the following BASIC code segment were to be typed in:

```
10  I = 34.75
20  J$ = "Hello!"
30  PRINT USING "& ##.##"; I, J$
```

When executed, this program would result in a data type mismatch. The error message, "Type mismatch", would be displayed.

Displaying Literal Data

Literal characters and string constants may also be printed with PRINT USING statements. If an underscore (_) appears in a format string, the next character in the format string will be output just as it appears. For example:

```
10  I = 3
20  PRINT USING "_##"; I
```

When executed, the above segment of BASIC code would display:

```
#3
```

The underscore before the first number sign (#) causes this character to be output as a literal character, rather than to be treated as a format character reserving a print position for a numeric digit. The second number sign in the format string reserves room for the single numeric digit, 3, which is printed immediately following the literal, '#'.

String constants may be output with PRINT USING statement by including the string constant in the format string. As an example, the two lines of BASIC code:

```
10  J = 47.92
20  PRINT USING "The answer is ##.##"; J
```

would produce, when executed:

```
The answer is 47.92
```

The only restriction on the inclusion of string constants in a format string occurs when the string constant contains a special formatting character as one of the characters in the string. In this case, the underscore would need to be used to cause this special character to be displayed rather than interpreted as a formatting character. An example of this would be

```
10  K = 4
20  PRINT USING "Problem _##"; K
```

When executed, the above code would produce the following display:

```
Problem #4
```

7.5 SUMMARY

This chapter has discussed the various data types provided in Microsoft BASIC. The two basic data types are character and numeric. Numeric data types can be more specifically declared as integer, single-precision, or double-precision values.

Exponential notation is a method of writing a number as an integer or decimal value multiplied by a power of 10. BASIC uses this notation for single-precision values when there are more than seven decimal places to the left or right of the decimal point, and for double-precision values when there are more than 17 decimal places to the left or right of the decimal point.

Mixed-mode expressions occur when variables and/or constants of more than one numeric data type are used in a single numeric expression. BASIC follows a particular set of rules when evaluating mixed-mode expressions.

The DEFtype statement may be used to declare all variables starting with a particular letter or letters to be of a certain data type. The declaration characters used as the last character of a variable name may be used to override the data type declared by the DEFtype statement.

Formatted output is used in BASIC to control the form and appearance of output. The PRINT USING and LPRINT USING statements are used to perform formatted output. Special formatting characters are used in the format string portion of these statements to describe the exact form of the output line.

The following table summarizes the general forms of the BASIC statements discussed in this chapter:

BASIC Statements Introduced in Chapter 7

The DEF type statement:

```
line# DEF<type> <letter>[-<letter>] [,<letter> [-<letter>]]...
```

where <type> is INT, SNG, DBL, or STR, and <letter> is a letter of the alphabet.

The PRINT USING statement:

```
line# PRINT USING <v$>; <list of expressions> [;]
```

where <v$> is a format string composed of special formatting characters, and <list of expressions> is the names of string and/or numeric variables whose values are to be printed.

EXERCISES

1. Given the following pairs of character string constants, indicate which member of the pair is *less than* the other member.
   a. "pear" "peach"
   b. "table" "tables"
   c. "boys" "boy"
   d. "happy" "Happy"
   e. "girl" "GIRL"
   f. "$800.00" "500.00"
   g. "85%" "85#"
   h. "everyone" "every one"

2. If A$ = "Aunt Sally", B$ = "bit," and C$ = "the dog", what would be the value of D$ when each of the following assignment statements is performed:
   a. 10   D$ = C$ + B$ + A$
   b. 20   D$ = A$ + ", " + C$ + " " + B$
   c. 30   D$ = C$ + " " + B$ + " " + A$
   d. 40   D$ = A$ + " " + B$ + " " + C$

3. Indicate if each of the following relational expressions is "true" or "false":
   a. "yes" <= "YES"
   b. "no" <> "NO"
   c. "late " >= "late"
   d. "YES " = "YES"
   e. "any" + "body" = "any body"
   f. "!" > "&"

4. Given the following BASIC program:

```
10   INPUT A$
20   B$ = "YES"
30   IF A$ = B$ THEN 40 ELSE 60
40   'THEN
50      PRINT "Strings are compared as equal"
55      GOTO 80
60   'ELSE
70      PRINT "Strings are compared as unequal"
80   'ENDIF
90   END
```

indicate which message would be printed for each of the following entries for A$:

a. ?YES
b. ? YES
c. ?" YES"
d. ?   YES
e. ? YES I WANT TO QUIT

5. State the data type of each of the following constants. If more than one data type would be correct, list all that are. Possible data types are: character string, integer, single-precision, or double-precision.

a. -874
c. 579.86
e. "sad"
g. 234.567

b. 9.876E-03
d. -123456.4321
f. "16"
h. 7.53186D+08

6. Write the following values which are expressed in exponential notation in standard form (no exponents):

a. 3.4567E+04
c. 6.39867E−02
e. $-2.5E+00$
g. 4.6785E+10

b. $-2.4518924D+09$
d. 6.90784523D−04
f. 3.628E+03
h. $-9.47285E−06$

7. Write the following values which are expressed in standard form in BASIC language exponential notation form:

a. 367.9
c. -47.8954829
e. .00789
g. 8974635241.85

b. 8.6753
d. $-.0523$
f. 5478
h. .0000000000000001

8. Indicate what value would be stored in the variable on the left side of the equal sign when each of the following assignment statements is executed:

a. J% = 789.6
c. X! = 80 * 150
e. Y# = 357986.42
g. Z! = 357986.42

b. K% = 3.6 * 2 / 4.0
d. W! = 3 + 1.4 * 2.5
f. L% = 3 / 2 * 3.0
h. M% = 3 / 2 * 3

9. Write DEFtype statements to perform each of the following data declarations:

   a. Declare all variables starting with the letters I, J, K, and L to be of type integer.

   b. Declare all variables starting with the letters X and Z to be of type character.

   c. Declare all variables starting with the letters D, E, F, and H to be of type double-precision.

   d. Declare all variables starting with the letter S to be of type single-precision.

10. Write a single PRINT USING statement for each of the following output operations:

    a. Display on a single line on the screen the first character of A$, three spaces, and the first six characters of B$.

    b. Display on the screen all the characters contained in C$, four spaces, and the first character of D$, all on the same line.

    c. Print on a single line on the printer the integer value contained in A, which will not be larger than 999, followed by four spaces, followed by the value of B, which is a single-precision value, less than 9999. The value of B is to be printed correct to hundredths.

    d. Display on the screen the value of C, three spaces, and the value of D#, all on one line. C is a single-precision value expressed in exponential notation, with one digit to the left of the decimal point and four digits to the right. D# is a double-precision value expressed in exponential notation, with one digit to the left of the decimal and eight digits to the right.

    e. Display on a single line on the screen the values of E, F, and G, separated by three spaces. All three values, E, F, and G, are single-precision values less than 9999.99. The first digit in E is to be preceded by a $. Any unused digit positions to the left of the decimal point in F are to be filled with asterisks. If F is a negative value, it is to be followed by a trailing minus sign. The first digit in G is to be preceded by a $, and any unused digit positions to the left of the $ are to be filled with asterisks.

    f. Display on the screen on a single line the message, "Account #", followed by a single space, followed by the customer's account number, which is an integer value greater than or equal to 1000 and less than or equal to 9999 stored in the variable ACCOUNT.NUM.

    g. Display on a single line on the screen the name, department, and hourly rate of pay of an employee of the ABC Company. The name is contained in a character string variable, EMPLOYEE.NAME$, of which a maximum of 25 characters are to be printed. The employee name is to be printed four spaces to the right of the left margin. The department name is contained in a character string variable, DEPARTMENT$, which is a maximum of 10 characters in length. There are to be four spaces after the employee name and before the name of the department. The hourly rate of pay is less than 99.99, and is contained in the variable PAY.RATE. The hourly pay rate is to appear eight spaces to the right of the department name.

h. Print a single line on the printer containing the values of H# and I#, separated by six spaces. H# and I# are double-precision variables. H# contains a 12-digit number, with two digits to the right of the decimal point. It is to be printed with commas inserted between each set of three digits to the left of the decimal point. I# contains a 15-digit number with no digits to the left of the decimal point. The sign of I# is to be printed preceding it, whether the value of I# is positive or negative.

11. What will be printed by the following program when it is executed?

```
10  FIRST$ = "BASIC"
20  SECOND$ = " is a "
30  THIRD$ = "piece of cake"
40  ANSWER$ = FIRST$ + SECOND$
50  PRINT "ANSWER$"
60  PRINT ANSWER$
70  PRINT THIRD$
80  END
```

a. BASIC is a
   BASIC is a
   piece of cake

b. "ANSWER$"
   ANSWER$
   THIRD$

c. ANSWER$
   BASIC is a
   piece of cake

d. None of the above

12. What is printed by the following BASIC code segment?

```
10  INPUT X$ , Y$
20  PRINT Y$ ; X$
30  END
```

```
INPUT DATA
───────────

A B,CD
```

a. B,CDA
b.   B,CDA
c. CDAB
d. CDA B

13. What is printed by the following BASIC program?

```
10    INPUT X$
20    Y$ = "X$"
30    IF Y$ = "X$" THEN GOTO 40 ELSE GOTO 60
40    'THEN
50       X$ = "Y$"
55       GOTO 80
60    'ELSE
70       Y$ = X$
80    'ENDIF
90    PRINT X$;Y$
100   END
```

```
INPUT DATA
───────────

Y$
```

a. XY
b. XX
c. YX
d. YY

Use the following BASIC program to answer questions 14 and 15:

```
10    A$ = "dasher"
20    B$ = "dancer"
30    C$ = "vixen"
40    D$ = "rudolph"
50    E$ = "lead deer"
60    REINDEER = 0
70    INPUT SANTA
80    WHILE E$ <> "rudolph"
90       SANTA = SANTA + 1
100      IF SANTA < 110  THEN GOTO 110 ELSE GOTO 200
110      'THEN
120         A$ = C$
130         C$ = D$
140         D$ = E$
150         WHILE REINDEER <= 20
160            REINDEER = REINDEER + 5
170            SANTA = SANTA + REINDEER
180         WEND
190         GOTO 250
200      'ELSE
210         C$ = D$
220         E$ = A$
230         A$ = C$
240         SANTA = SANTA + 5
250      'ENDIF
260   WEND
270   PRINT SANTA
280   END
```

14. What is printed by the above program if the value of 32 is entered for SANTA?

   a. 109
   b. 110
   c. 115
   d. Cannot be determined

15. What is the value of the variable REINDEER at the end of the program if the value of 32 is entered for SANTA?

   a. 20
   b. 25
   c. 32
   d. Program contains an infinite loop—it never ends

16. Modify the solution to question 24 in the set of exercises for Chapter 6 to make use of formatted output in printing the dates, charges, and totals. In what way does this change the output to produce a better-looking report?

17. Write a formal problem definition, perform a complete top-down design, and write a BASIC program to solve the following problem:

    For large positive integers n, $(1 + (1/n))\hat{\ }n$ is a good approximation of the number e, which is the base of the natural logarithms. Write a program that computes the value of e using the formula $(1 + (1/n))\hat{\ }n$ for consecutive values of n starting with n = 10. Continue computing the approximation for e until two successive approximations differ by less than $1.0D-12$. At this point, print out the last value computed for e.

18. Write a formal problem definition, perform a complete top-down design, and write a BASIC program to solve the following problem:

    If n is a nonnegative whole number, the value n! is called "n factorial" and is defined to be the value $n(n - 1)(n - 2) \ldots (2)(1)$. 0! is defined to be equal to 1. Even for relatively small values of n, n! is a large value, for example, 10! = 3628800. Write a program to print a two-column table, with appropriate headings, which displays the values of n and n! for n = 0 to 20.

19. Write a formal problem definition, perform a complete top-down design, and write a BASIC program to solve the following problem:

    The Fibonacci sequence is the series of numbers 1, 1, 2, 3, 5, 8, . . . This sequence starts with the values 1 and 1, and each succeeding term in the sequence is the sum of the previous two terms. The ratio of two successive terms approaches a value known as the "golden ratio." That is, 1/1 = 1, 2/1 = 2, 3/2 = 1.5, 5/3 = 1.66, . . . , etc. Write a program to print a two-column table listing the first 30 terms of the sequence, and the value of the ratio of each term after the first to its predecessor.

20. Write a formal problem definition, perform a complete top-down design, and write a BASIC program to solve the following problem:

    A series of data statements each contains the following information concerning items manufactured at the ABC Company: a department number, an item number, a quantity, and a cost per item. The data statements are arranged in ascending order by department number. The last data statement contains the values 0,0,0,0. Write a program to produce a summary report as follows:

ABC Company
Production Report

Department	Item number	Quantity	Cost/ item	Value	Totals
33	1368	14	3.20	44.80	
33	2357	12	7.00	84.00	
					128.80
37	1426	7	2.50	17.50	
					17.50
41	2344	110	.13	14.30	
41	2345	22	4.80	105.60	
41	2569	4	86.00	344.00	
					463.90
				Grand Total	610.20